LITERATURE AND SOCIETY

LITERATURE AND SOCIETY

by

DAVID DAICHES

Lecturer in English at the University of Chicago
Formerly Fellow of Balliol College, Oxford

HASKELL HOUSE PUBLISHERS Ltd.
Publishers of Scarce Scholarly Books
NEW YORK. N. Y. 10012
1970

First Published 1938

HASKELL HOUSE PUBLISHERS Ltd.
Publishers of Scarce Scholarly Books
280 LAFAYETTE STREET
NEW YORK, N. Y. 10012

Library of Congress Catalog Card Number: 74-95422

Standard Book Number 8383-0970-4

Printed in the United States of America

FOREWORD

In trying to trace the relation between literature and society in England from the early Middle Ages to the present day in the brief compass of such a book as this, compression, omission, and simplification are inevitable. I am very conscious of the gaps in the following survey, especially of the omission of many Victorian and modern writers whom I should have liked to discuss. The temptation, in a sketch of this kind, is to employ the method of the gentleman in *Pickwick* who, in order to write on Chinese metaphysics, looked up the articles on "China" and on "metaphysics" in the encyclopædia and "combined the information." I hope, however, that I have succeeded in bringing the two aspects of my subject into a clear relation, and that the excursions into social and economic history that I have found necessary will be seen as attempts to provide a background that I was warned not to take for granted. I should like to emphasise that this is not in any sense a history of English literature: my aim has been to provide data for a consideration of that vital question, the place of literature in human activity and the extent to which the nature and function of literature is determined by the social conditions under which the writer lives. This book is meant to be suggestive rather than final, and its end will be achieved if it stimulates thought and further reading on this all-important subject.

D. D.

Balliol College, Oxford. 1937.

INTRODUCTION

THE PRODUCTION OF LITERATURE of one kind or another has been a normal activity among men for so long that it rarely occurs to us to pause and consider the nature and value of this activity. Yet it is our view on this question that determines not only our estimate of the *use* of poetry and drama, of fiction and romance, but also our attitude to the professional writer and his place in society. Bard, minstrel, story-teller, writer—whatever form the profession of letters takes in any given age, it is our opinion of the function and importance of its products taken generally that decides the place we assign to the " dealer in words " (to use the Anglo-Saxon idiom) among the numerous other kinds of dealers of that age. What place has the literary artist had in societies of the past, what place has he in society to-day, and what place would we give him in the ideal society? Or, looking at things from a different point of view, we might ask three different questions: what has been the function of literature in the past, what is its function to-day, and what would we consider its function to be in the ideal society? The two sets of questions cannot be separated: to seek the answer to the first set is to seek the answer to the second. The problems raised are not entirely sociological, not entirely æsthetic. Indeed, the more we consider the nature and function of any product of the human mind, the more we are led to the belief that categories denoted by such terms as " æsthetic " or " ethical " cannot be dealt with in isolation; at some point they overlap with other categories, and ultimately the complete study of any one human activity necessitates the study of all other human activities.

Such an ideally complete study is probably impossible under any circumstances, and certainly will not be attempted here. What will be attempted is a sketch of literature in its social implications over an arbitrarily chosen period, followed by some general conclusions suggested by this sketch and a discussion of what is to be desired in an ideal state of affairs. The period discussed will have to be limited for reasons of space, and for the same reason the consideration of representative cases will have to take the place of a full and continuous history. But the aim of this book is rather to suggest the nature of the problem of the relation of literature to society than to make any final pronouncement either about the past or the future. For the whole question of literature and the social forces which produce it, of the writer and his public, of the attitude of different strata of society to different kinds of writing, of the nature of literary objectivity and the extent to which it is possible—these and many other related questions are aspects of a problem which *is* a problem, not a mere academic argument to which there is a stereotyped conclusion. It is to help towards a realisation of the nature of this problem, and of the practical issues involved, that this essay is intended.

It is, of course, usual for " practical " men and women to dismiss any question concerned with literature or the other arts as " theoretical." In fact to-day, more, perhaps, than at any other time in history, the arts are regarded as the province of the specialist into which the ordinary man has neither the wish nor the ability to intrude. We read novels in the train in order to pass the time, and go to cinemas in order to " relax," and if these purposes are achieved we are satisfied and make no attempt to probe into questions of literary or artistic value. That we do so is an important aspect of the very problem we are about to discuss, but apart from this let us consider if the dismissal of any serious study of literary value is really justified on the grounds that it has no " practical " purpose.

What, after all, are " practical " issues? Here we are, men and women, born into a world in the making of which we had no say, endowed with various mental and physical faculties and appetites, among other men and women similarly endowed—what are the issues which face us that we must deem to be practical? It is clear that such issues must be divided into two classes, viz. social and personal. The practical social issues are concerned with the definition of our relations with our neighbours, with the working out of a process of give-and-take which will enable the maximum of benefit and the minimum of interference to go to either side, with the co-operation with others in order to try to remould the world we found awaiting us nearer to our ideal, with the carrying on of activities prompted by our more insistent humanitarian impulses, with the utilising of any scientific ability we have to help in the progress of invention and discovery which will lighten physical toil and contribute to human health and happiness, and with playing our part in the development of social organisation without which none of these activities could be carried on. No one, surely, will deny that these are all intensely practical matters. But comparatively few will at once realise that, for example, the study of history will enable us to understand and so to control the world into which we are born (and a proper study of history necessitates the study of past literature); that the reading, with understanding, of poetry and imaginative writing generally will give us an insight into the mind of man—his impulses and passions, his dreams and longings—without which we can have no real knowledge of the motives that impel him to act, the ideals for which he can be induced to strive, or any of the numberless half-consciously realised forces that are so important in determining his moods and attitudes; that the communal enjoyment of music or painting or drama can produce a sense of fellowship that will enable the most diverse types of people to understand and co-operate with each other to a degree and in a manner otherwise hardly possible. This is not to say that the justification and ideal function of scholarship and art lie in their contributions to the solving of practical social questions, but that these seemingly non-practical activities serve a practical purpose even when judged from the point of view of social utility, the sphere in which they would seem least valuable. And if we consider the personal issues that can be deemed to be practical we find these " theoretical " interests to be practical in a much more direct way. The practical personal issues which face us are simply those connected with the maximum development of the physical and mental attributes with which we are endowed. We have certain faculties, which we have pleasure and satisfaction in using, and therefore the full utilisation of these faculties is the chief—indeed the only—personal matter that really concerns us. (Of course there is a point where personal appetites involve social questions, but for reasons of simplicity we are separating the personal and the social into two rigid categories.) We work to earn our living, because without bread we would starve and would be unable to use any of our physical or mental faculties. And " working to earn a living " includes all those numerous activities associated with the provision of economic security. This, undoubtedly, is the basic practical activity, because without it we should not be able to do anything else at all. But having got our bread to eat we are only a mass of unfulfilled potentialities unless we take steps to develop and use those faculties in the utilisation of which human activity becomes most full, most satisfying, most " normal " in the psychological sense. Thus, as it is a practical matter that we should eat and take exercise so that our physical potentialities may be realised, so it is an equally practical matter that we should think, read, and enjoy works of art in order that our mental potentialities should be realised. Those who indulge only in the former types of activity are only half-men; their distinctive characteristics as human beings are undeveloped; their capacity for happiness is appallingly limited. It is ridiculous to call activities of the former type " practical " and refuse that name to those of the latter type. If practical issues be taken to mean those connected with the attainment of a full and happy life, with the building up of a rounded personality, with the utilising, to the full extent that is compatible with equilibrium, of the faculties with which man is endowed, with the development of the potentialities which exist in him—if these be practical personal issues, then the appreciation of literature is an intensely practical matter. For man is endowed with an ability to enjoy and derive benefit from the use of those faculties which we call " æsthetic " or " artistic " in the same way as from the use of his other faculties. For those who have not developed their non-physical faculties to assert that such faculties are of little importance is as though a blind man were to assert that sight is of no practical value and is a faculty that can add nothing to human happiness.

Literature *is* a practical activity in any adequate sense of the phrase. Far from being a concern only of the specialist and the academician, it has been, in all healthy societies, a real part of the life of the people. Literature originates socially, in the folk-song, the folk-ballad, the folk-dance, as a result of an urge to expression (" self-expression " is a tired and overworked term) that is characteristic of human personality. Its subsequent developments give it a richer and more profound function until, at its highest, literary activity becomes at once comment on and epitome of all that is of value in human life. To study the relations of literature and society is to see how one of the most important products of the human mind has been moulded by social conditions and has itself helped to mould those conditions; how men have interpreted the life of their age; how they have criticised it and commented on it and how at times they have been at its mercy; how the state of society can sometimes compel the literary artist to be false to his mission and how sometimes it can give to his work a richness and universality and cogency that springs from contact with the most elemental facts of life—and death; finally, such a study can help us to come to some conclusion regarding the true function of literature, to see it as one human activity among many others and discover standards of value by which it is to be judged. It is not claimed that the following sketch will serve all these purposes, but it is hoped that as an introduction to the problem it will enable the reader to come to the study of literature and the history of literature with some idea of the nature of the problems to be discussed and an impulse to formulate his own attitude towards them.

It may be argued that the function of literature is something which is constant throughout history, and that it is ridiculous to talk of the functions of literature in different ages. It is true that the greatest works of literature of all times do in fact have the same function, in the sense that their greatness lies in their presenting to the reader organic pictures of certain universal and ever-present aspects of human experience. But this does not mean that the conscious purpose with which they are written is in every case identical. Indeed, it is one of the most interesting tasks of the literary historian to note the number of times that diversity of object results in similarity of achievement. The value of *Hamlet* may be the same kind of value as that of a Greek tragedy or of a novel by George Moore, but it is indisputable that Shakespeare's work was the product of quite different forces than those which produced the

Antigone or *The Brook Kerith*. Of course ultimately all literary work may be described as the product of a certain single human faculty, and the satisfaction of a certain single human appetite, which are permanent parts of men's make-up, but the problem we are to consider concerns the conditions under which that faculty operates and that appetite seeks satisfaction. Further, not only do the social and other conditions under which literary men work differ in different ages; the professed object of writers also differs at different times. Thus Spenser's *Faerie Queene* was written " to fashion a gentleman or noble person in virtuous and gentle discipline," as the author himself expressed it, and to know what this implies we must realise what was understood in Elizabethan times by a " gentleman or noble person " and why it was thought necessary for a poet to write his chief work with the education of such a person in view. The actual value of the *Faerie Queene* as literature may owe nothing to the author's conscious design in writing it, but it is important to consider that conscious design and its relation to the achievement. Similarly *Hamlet* was written, as far as we know, to present to the theatre-going public of the time an interesting and pleasing drama written in a well-tried popular convention; Dr. Johnson's *Rasselas* was written to convey to the public the author's sombre philosophy of life as well as to pay for his mother's funeral; Shelley's *Prometheus Unbound* had for its aim the preaching of a philosophy of social revolt; and the work of many European poets at the end of the last century had no aim other than " art for art's sake," the pure indulgence in æsthetic sensation. In all these cases the purely literary value may be, in a general sense, a constant, but the fact that the works were produced with such different objects in view is surely worth careful consideration. We have also to consider the reasons for these changes in literary purpose, to see how far they can be explained by the social conditions under which the writer worked and how far literary integrity (once we have defined that term) is achieved in each case. So while it may be true that the nature of literary value is constant, and can be discovered by the understanding critic of any given body of literary work, this does not absolve us from trying to discover the different causes which at different times impelled men to produce works having this value, the extent to which these causes determined the nature of the product, and the general relation between literature and the authors of it to the conditions of the age in which they lived.

We cannot presume to set up an ideal for the future unless we first have some knowledge of what has happened, in that particular activity that concerns us, in the past. If we are planning an ideal society and wish to know where in that society to place literature and the literary artist, we must be guided by principles discovered by a method which is at least in part historical. Some may exclaim that it is impossible or at any rate undesirable for us to attempt to fix in advance the place of an art among the other activities of a civilisation. Every art, they may argue, finds its own place by a natural law, and any kind of conscious direction can only have a stultifying effect. This attitude of artistic *laissez faire* is hardly justifiable in the light of historical facts, but even to those who hold this point of view we can say that a study of the relations between literature and society is at least able to give us an understanding of processes that have gone on in the past and which have conditioned the present. We may reject any *normative* purpose in such a study and still attempt it in an endeavour to increase our insight into the nature of what has happened and is happening in this particular sphere of activity.

With this brief account of the nature of our subject and the reasons why we deem it worth treating, we may proceed to an historical sketch of the relations between literature and the social forces existing at the time of its production. We shall begin with the period of the flourishing of mediæval literature, and proceed—necessarily in a rather jerky fashion—through the " renaissance " period, the seventeenth century, the " Augustan " age, and the " Romantic " and later developments until we come to our own day, when we shall pause to consider what the past has to tell us about the present and the future. We may emphasise that this is not meant to be a history of English literature in the conventional sense, but a consideration of one particular problem (and the issues bound up with it) which the conscientious literary critic—and indeed all interested in literature—must face. It may be that we shall find ourselves touching on many other aspects of literary theory and history: the inquirer in such a field as this does well not to predict too definitely the way he may have to go or the goal at which he will eventually find himself.

CHAPTER I

THE RESULTS of the Norman Conquest of Britain were not merely political. The imposing on the country of a highly developed feudal system (already growing up in Anglo-Saxon times) was the most immediate economic effect, and this produced a set of social conditions which had its influence on every kind of activity. Conceptions of lord and vassal, of knighthood and chivalry, of feudal justice and feudal society in general, become a part of English thought, and though for a long time it is not the English language but Norman-French that is used by those capable of giving permanent form to their ideas, these conceptions were working a change that was eventually to manifest itself with a revived English language and literature. Anglo-Saxon England and its literature were now gone for good, swept away by the Norman conquerors with their French language and modes of thought. England became linked with the Continent. French was the language of the upper classes, and English was degraded to a dialect of " low men " as Robert of Gloucester's Chronicle puts it. For between two and three hundred years the language of cultured Englishmen was French, and only literature written in French was read. The old Anglo-Saxon heroic poetry was gone for ever, and the old language, driven underground and rapidly disintegrating and developing to become " Middle

English " some centuries later, was not to be used as a literary medium again.

When the transformed English language finally emerged after its victorious fight with Norman-French the state of society was very different from what it had been in the Anglo-Saxon days. The distinction between Norman and English had been blurred after centuries of inter-marriage and assimilation, and there was no simple division of society into conqueror and conquered. Social distinctions lay between different types of tenants, for it was on the holding of land that the feudal system was based. The tenants-in-chief held from the King, sub-tenants held from the tenants-in-chief and so on right down to the villeins who, though not slaves, were bound to the land and could not leave it to work elsewhere. Rents took the form of the obligation to perform service to the overlord, whether military service or, as we get lower down the scale, manual labour. The unit of social organisation was the manor, occupied by the lord of the manor, who held the surrounding land. Part of the fields round the manor were part of the lord's " demesne," the rest was divided in strips among his tenants, who were either " free tenants " or villeins. The lord kept his own court, in which justice was administered to his tenants (a profitable business for the lord, for the fines went to him). The manor was almost self-sufficient as an economic unit, the labour of the inhabitants providing for all, or nearly all, the requirements of themselves and the lord of the manor. Many had several manors, and moved round, consuming the produce of each in turn. It was not long before money-payments began to replace the different types of service due as rent, and this fact, together with the growth of towns with their trading communities and the increasing trade between town and country, produced a transition from a natural economy to a money economy (that is from a state of society where people produced what they wanted for themselves to one where they produced in order to sell the product—or some of it—to the community and lived on what they purchased with the money thus obtained). It is in the midst of such a transitional society, based partly on a natural and partly on a money economy, that we find ourselves when we come to examine the first important works of English literature produced after the " sleep " of the language since the Conquest. We have to ask ourselves to what extent the state of society and the social position of writer and reader affected the nature of literature at this time.

For some hundreds of years after the Conquest the literary influences that made themselves felt in England were almost exclusively French. If we take a look at English literature at about 1300—when the English language had not long emerged, changed and refreshed, from its " sleep "[1]—we find the most characteristic form of literature to be the metrical romance. The English language which had formed itself between 1066 and the end of the thirteenth century produced in these romances its first important literary expression. And even yet there was no emancipation from French

[1] Of course the " awakening " of the developed language was not a sudden one, nor was there any real " sleep." The French language was only superficially imposed upon the English, and gradually the popular speech of the people reasserted itself as the only national language, after itself undergoing change and grammatical simplification and assimilating a certain amount from French.

literature, as they were almost all translated and adapted from the French. What was the nature of these romances, what forces produced them, and what part did they play in the life of the people? To answer these questions we must first say a word or two about their French originals.

The beginnings of " modern " European literature—that is the literature of the new Europe that arose after the fall of the Western Roman Empire and the confusion of the "dark ages"—came from France. Quite suddenly we find a full-grown literature coming into existence in Provence, where the " troubadours," or professional minstrels who went round entertaining in the halls of the great houses, evolved a type of poetry—of lyric love poetry especially—which was distinguished from all previous literature in that (1) the language used was French, in its southern form known as the *langue d'oc*; (2) the metre was regular and syllabic; (3) rhyme was used (where we see the influence of late Latin hymns). The " heroic age,"[1] to the end of which the barbarian invaders and their literature had mostly belonged and whose literature was represented in England by the Anglo-Saxon epic *Beowulf*, was now definitely succeeded by a new civilisation, whose literature was highly sophisticated and " polite." It is this literature that begins the tradition of courtly love whose influence on mediæval and later literature was to be so profound. But for the moment we are concerned with seeking the origin of the narrative romances, which also come from France but not from Provence. While the beginnings

[1] For a full discussion of the heroic age, its society and its literature, which is outside the scope of this book, the reader is referred to H. M. Chadwick's classic study, *The Heroic Age* (Cambridge, 1912).

of French and of the new European literature are to be found in the south, there is another interesting literary movement which arose in the north of France a little later than the Provençal troubadour poetry, and which gave rise to an equally important kind of literature. This is the narrative poetry of the trouvères (the northern equivalent of the troubadours) which was written in the northern dialect of French, or *langue d'oïl*.[1] This poetry began in the eleventh century and flourished for over two hundred years.

This new narrative poetry still had something of the nature of the old heroic poetry, though as time went on it came to acquire many of the characteristics of the romantic poetry which came from the south. We may note that the chief difference between heroic and romantic poetry can be put simply thus: 1. Heroic poetry deals with persons and facts which have a real historical basis, however remote; it celebrates the exploits of heroes that have lived in the memory of the race, though the originals may have had only the remotest resemblance (if any at all) to the figures as they emerge in literature. 2. Romantic poetry is more purely imaginative, and has rarely any connection with historical fact, its affinities being, if anywhere, rather with mythology, though even this affinity is slight. The poetry of the *langue d'oïl*, though it had, in its earlier stages, some connections with the old heroic poetry, was from the beginning distinguished from the older literature by its interest in the marvellous for its own sake. It was probably from the meeting of east and

[1] The terms *langue d'oc* and *langue d'oïl* come from the words for " yes " (" oc " and " oïl," modern " oui ") in the different dialects.

west that resulted from the first Crusade (begun in 1095) that this impetus to the telling of adventure stories arose. The narrative romance (to which, the reader must note, we are *not* applying the adjective romantic, reserving that to designate the type of literature that arose in Provence, and its descendants) drew its material from many different sources, and it was to a large extent the activity of the Normans, in spreading over Europe from Sicily to Britain, that brought poets into contact with all the different sources simultaneously. In Normandy itself, the Normans had on their borders the Bretons, with their Celtic traditions; in England they were in contact with the traditions of Anglo-Saxon England and of Celtic Wales; while their settling in Apulia and Sicily brought them into touch with Greek and Arab ideas. Thus the Normans might well be regarded as the fertilisers of early mediæval literature.

Looking back on the French narrative romances, later historians have divided them into the three categories first suggested by the twelfth-century trouvère, Jean Bodel—the " Matter of France," the " Matter of Britain," and the " Matter of Rome the Great." The first group deals with the activities of Charlemagne and his knights, and finds its greatest expression in the *Chanson de Roland*. This group was the earliest to take shape, beginning with rough songs dealing with the exploits of Charlemagne and his twelve paladins and developing into the more elaborate *chansons de geste*, where we have a more artistic treatment of the same themes. The figures of Roland and his friend Oliver stand out in the literature of the " Matter of France," and the heroic nature of these poems, together with the historical background which lies, however remotely, behind them, show them to be the earliest of the three groups, with its roots in an earlier form of society. With the systematisation of feudalism—so far as such an institution could be systematised—there came an organisation and sophistication of social habits and ideas, a separating out of the ruling class and a theoretical codification of its manners and ways of thought. The influence of this process is manifest when we come to consider the "Matter of Britain" and the "Matter of Rome." Romances of the first of these groups deal with the stories which derive mainly from the Celtic traditions of Britain and Brittany, notably with the story of Arthur and his knights: those in the second group deal, not only with classical legend as interpreted by the Middle Ages, but with stories derived from classical antiquity in general, and the most notable theme of these is the story of Troy in one or other of its aspects. There are other subjects which cannot conveniently be fitted into this threefold grouping, many of these being non-Celtic stories from England.

In the romances dealing with the "Matter of Britain" and the "Matter of Rome" we find everywhere the sophistication and "politeness" of feudal ideas. There is, in fact, to some extent a linking up of the Provençal tradition with that of the trouvères, and we get stories of adventure, which arose in the north, informed with all the ideas of chivalry and courtly love which were first developed in the south. This was obviously the literature of a leisured class, and its function was quite simply to entertain. The older *chansons de geste*, with their crusading spirit and realistic narrative, had still a real link with contemporary life and work: however remote the incidents they narrated there was a certain vigour and force about their style and method of treatment which showed this literature to be not totally removed from that of *recording* and *celebrating* which is the original type of heroic poetry. With the entry of the new romantic spirit into narrative poetry literature acquired a new nature which was in intimate causal relation with its new function. In fact, social conditions had produced what we to-day would call a purely " escapist " literature.

There is a difference in kind between songs which are sung because the singer must sing, and those which he sings to keep his audience from boredom, and, without insisting on any hard and fast categories or definitions, we can say that there was some such difference between the older, more heroic narrative verse and the new more sentimental variety. With the feudalisation of society after the confusion of the dark ages, there emerged a system which guaranteed the differentiation in function between different classes. To take the case at its simplest: The lord of the manor lived with his lady in a little nucleus of civilisation of which he was the guardian. The work required to provide them with the necessities of life was done by his tenants, free or unfree, among whom he lived. The lord of the manor's job was to fight for his feudal superior—the King, if he was a tenant-in-chief—but apart from this he had no other occupation whatever: he was, apart from his military obligations, a man of leisure. Of course he presided over the manor court and looked after the affairs of his estate, but all the real work here was done by the numerous officials in his employ. His social function consisted of his being lord of land, land which he let out to tenants on condition that they worked it to provide him and themselves with food and which he himself held from his superior for whom in return he was bound to fight. On his continuing to be lord of the land, on his protection of those who lived on (and lived off) his land on condition of working for him, depended the stability of society. He might repudiate his obligations to those above him without any important practical result following, but he could not repudiate his obligations to those under him—his obligations to hold the land and protect those who worked on it—without the risk of shattering the nucleus of civilisation which had arisen out of chaos. Thus the lord of the manor served his function in society quite adequately by just staying put, as it were. Not that he did stay put as a rule: as likely as not he would go off to the Crusades or engage in some other profitable adventure. But he was not always engaged in the performance of knightly deeds, and as long as he resided at home (which he would have to do fairly regularly if he wished to be sure of keeping his estate[1]), the performance of his duty to society left him with plenty of leisure. He would not be literate, as a rule: reading and writing were left to " clerks," that is churchmen

[1] Readers of the Paston Letters will remember what happened when Sir John Paston was away from his manor of Drayton. The Duke of Suffolk set up a claim to it, and it was only by the energetic action of Margaret, Sir John's wife, that the Duke was foiled in his attempt to annex the manor.

of one kind or another. It would be the function of the professional trouvère or troubadour to entertain him in his hall by reciting poetry.[1] The object of such poetry would be to entertain simply. Even when the ability to read became more general and the services of the " wandering minstrel " were not indispensable, literature would have the same simple function of entertainment so long as society retained that kind of structure.

It is not any condemnation of literature to say that its function is to entertain: indeed it is frequently claimed that such is its sole function. But there are different ways of entertaining and different kinds of entertainment. There is the ploughman who sings at his work to entertain himself, and the leading lady in the musical comedy who sings and dances in order to entertain tired business men. There is the villager who plays the concertina to entertain himself and his fellow villagers in the crowded tap-room of the village inn, and the street-singer who hopes to earn a few pence by entertaining a theatre queue. The difference between these two kinds of entertainment will be obvious to the reader. It would be an unwarrantable simplification to suggest that the difference between the older *chansons de geste* and the later types of narrative poetry corresponded to this distinction, but at least we can say that something of this distinction existed. The *chansons de geste*, with their affinities with heroic poetry, were still in some small degree communal in tone, still partook to some extent of the nature of poetry

---

[1] George Moore's *Héloïse and Abelard* gives a good picture of the troubadour in the society of the time.

written by a man for the entertainment of himself and his fellows of his own class. The later poetry was more the work of professional craftsmen produced to satisfy a need that existed in a class not his own. This is not altogether true, because the writer of the sophisticated type of romance had to be so familiar with the conventions and manners of the society for which he wrote that he might be regarded as really part of it. In some cases the poet was quite certainly a feudal lord, belonging to the class for which he wrote. But the points to be stressed are that this literature was literature produced for the entertainment of a leisured class; that it did not spring out of the realities of life and work; that it dealt almost entirely with the wonderful and the extraordinary; that it was not in any real sense a communal literature, nor on the other hand was it in any sense personal; and that it was produced to amuse those who sought their amusement in escaping from the realities of existence into an adventurous make-believe. Its readers and hearers were not in the modern sense of the word " educated ": they were men whose minds were at bottom simple and practical, who nevertheless found a pleasure in retiring from the hard world in which they lived to the sophisticated and sentimental world provided by literature.

The nature of this sophisticated and sentimental world, with all its doctrines of romantic love and chivalry, its codes of honour and idealisation of knighthood and conception of service—all this we shall consider, and we shall try to discover its origins in the social organisation of the time, when we come to discuss romantic allegory, that influential descendant of the love poetry of the troubadours. At present we are dealing with the later narrative romances which arose in northern France but which were greatly influenced by the sentimental ideas which arose with the troubadours in the south. We have seen what function in society this literature had. It was a "polite" escapist literature, written for those who had leisure to interest themselves in tales of adventure served up with the particular kind of conventional sentimental sauce which was popular at the time.

There are two separable aspects of these narrative romances—the pure narrative, and what we have called the "sauce," that is the refined and sophisticated way in which the subject was treated, the long digressions debating fine points of the theory of love or honour. It is when we consider the translation of these French poems into English that the importance of the dual aspect of the former is brought out. Because in these English translations—in which English narrative poetry begins again, in that form of the language which had developed between the Conquest and the end of the thirteenth century—we find that the poems have undergone another process besides mere translation: they have been shorn of their trimmings, vulgarised, simplified. They are served without the sauce.

To consider why the English romances were cruder and simpler than the French from which they were translated and adapted is to consider the two different audiences contemplated by the English and the French writers respectively. The fact is that in England the telling of these stories was largely a popular art, having much more in common with the art of our tap-room concertina player than with that of the professional musical-comedy singer. The English language had not yet ousted French in high places: " courtly " readers would prefer to have their literature in French; it was for those a little lower down in the social scale that the English romances were intended. " The successful French novelists of the twelfth century ... dealt equally in sensation and sentiment; they did not often limit themselves to what was always their chief interest, the moods of lovers. They worked these into plots of adventure, mystery, fairy magic; the adventures were too good to be lost; so the less refined English readers, who were puzzled or wearied by sentimental conversations, were not able to do without elegant romances. They read them; and they skipped. The skipping was done for them, generally, when the romances were translated into English; the English versions are shorter than the French in most cases where comparison is possible. As a general rule, the English took the adventurous sensational part of the French romances and let the language of the heart alone."[1] This was not entirely because the average Englishman was a coarser person than the average Frenchman: it was because the production of the English romances sprang from a different motive and had a different social function.

Entertainment was the sole function of both kinds of literature, and both could be described as " escapist." But escape for the sophisticated French knight was a different thing from escape for the English freeman or citizen, naïve in literary matters to the point of stupidity. It is probably true, too, that even the upper stratum

[1] W. P. Ker, *English Literature: Mediæval*, p. 72.

of English society was never so "civilised," in the artificial sense, as the corresponding class of Frenchmen. And we find—what we would expect from the popular function of the English romances—that though they are popularised and simplified in the translating they show little trace of what we should call democratic feeling. Children still like to hear of kings and princesses, of fairies and goblins, of characters whom they would never expect to meet in everyday life; and so the simple-minded English preferred as a rule tales dealing with lords and ladies of high degree to stories about people like themselves. But the tales were crudely told, in rhymed accentual verse (it was some time before syllabic regularity appeared) that often degenerated into the merest doggerel.

There are other features of the English romances that indicate their more popular nature. The narrative of events is often direct and rapid, with swift and easy transitions, reminding us sometimes in movement and method of the ballads (that prototype of popular literature). Many, however, become tedious through the agglomeration of small and similar incidents. Another interesting feature of the English adaptations is their occasional inset pictures of natural scenery, and this shows that, for all their dealing with the marvellous adventures of lords and ladies, the stories were not wholly removed from the everyday lives and interests of the people. And this again is what we should expect of a popular literature: while it deals in general with experience beyond the ken of the people, when it comes to localising a scene with a description or going into some matter of detail we are liable to find the author going back to the real life with which he was familiar. Complete unreality together with touches of homely realism; simplicity, even crudity, combined with an attempt to capture the atmosphere of " high life"; rudimentary versification touched here and there with real poetic quality—such are the mixed characteristics of the English narrative romances, adapted from a polite French literature to become in England to some extent the literature of the people.

It is difficult to tell just how far down the social scale knowledge of this literature penetrated. Ability to read was as a rule confined to " clerks "—the numerous class of men connected in one way or another with the Church, many of whom were engaged in the purely secular work of government offices—to those of the ruling class who had leisure and inclination for such a luxury, and in increasing numbers to merchants and traders of every kind who were springing up rapidly with the growth of towns and of commercial activity. But among the different strata of workers in town and country there was room for many exceptions to this generalisation. Those who did the real work of production for society—villeins and agricultural workers of a slightly higher or slightly lower degree—were of course quite illiterate, as was the great majority of the more well-to-do peasantry[1] and town-dwellers. But we must remember that literature was read out, not merely read silently, in earlier times, and this would enable it to reach those who were unable to read for themselves.

[1] The commutation of service for money-payments, which went on steadily in all kinds of feudal contracts, helped to produce a class of fairly well-to-do peasants and of professional wage-earning labourers.

We often forget how recent is the habit of silent reading to oneself.

As English gradually replaced French in " polite " life it became more and more used for " polite " literature, and we find throughout the fourteenth century the style of the English romances approximating more closely to that of the French from which they were taken. Though the court was still largely under French influence, English became in this century the language used in the pleadings of courts of law and the medium of cultured people generally. The beginning of the Hundred Years' War provoked a certain self-consciousness among people of all classes, and most of all among the ruling class. The semi-international character of the old feudal order was giving way before national feeling. Men began to realise that the French were different from the English: they were different people, with different traditions and different tongues— they were, in fact, national enemies. The new concept of nationhood and national enmity never had the effect on intellectual that it had on political life: we find frequent literary intercourse between nations at war with one another right through this period and through succeeding ages. Yet the new national consciousness had this effect on literature: it changed the nature of literary influence, so that writers sought to copy accurately in their own tongue the foreign works they admired rather than to read those works in the original and be content with vulgarised rehashes for their own literature. That is how, paradoxically enough, the new sense of difference between French and English helped to make English literature more like French.

It was, then, the final victory of the English language, the completion of the welding of Norman and English into one people, and the rising sense of nationhood, that were the principal causes of the " refining " of English literature that went on in the fourteenth century. The ideas of chivalry and of courtly love that arose with the troubadours in Provence and had been incorporated into the French romances in the twelfth and thirteenth centuries now came into the vernacular literature of England. The English language rose in the social ladder, and its literature went with it. While the more homely and popular romances were still produced for those whose station in life did not permit them to appreciate the subtleties and refinements of the courtly writers, the better instructed and more sophisticated readers were provided with stories in their own tongue which possessed all the qualities they had so admired in the poetry of France. The change was more than an increase in artificiality, which in itself would have been a doubtful blessing. There came also an improvement in the technique of versification, a greater ease and fluency in handling the language, and a new beauty of style. It was in the poetry of Chaucer that these qualities were fully developed.

It must not be thought that the romances which we have been discussing were the only works produced in English during these centuries. Religious and didactic works of all kinds were produced in great numbers, some in the direct form of sermons, some in the form of pious histories, some in allegorical shape, and some in the shape of manuals of devotion. This was an activity which went on right through the Middle Ages,

Cs

and may even be regarded as its most characteristic product. Most of this literature is written in the plain style of the early romances, but it is in prose as well as in verse. Its object is generally to instruct the ordinary man in the teachings of the Church, especially in their practical implications, or to teach him the main points of Bible story and of the accepted history of the world. Quite often there is a considerable amount of sheer entertainment, to encourage the reader and, presumably, to keep him from boredom. This moral literature, with its simple didactic function, lies rather outside the scope of the present study: a complete survey of the mediæval Church and its position in the social life of the time would be necessary if we were to consider religious literature in an essay on " Literature and Society "; so we must pass on without further discussion, confining ourselves to those aspects of literature that throw the most direct light on the theme we wish to treat.

There is a great amount of lyric poetry in the Middle Ages, both secular and religious. Some is political, called forth spontaneously by a contemporary event such as the victory of Simon de Montfort at Lewes or the execution of the " rebel " Sir William Wallace, or by anti-French feeling as many of the poems of Lawrence Minot. But most of the mediæval lyric poetry which is not religious is concerned with love and with nature. It is perhaps in the history of the lyric that we can trace most distinctly the development from folk-song to successively more sophisticated kinds of writing. In the English lyric, there is not extant sufficient material for this development to be clear, but the development is well marked in French poetry, which, in this field as in others, is to a large extent the model for the rest of Europe. There are, of course, English ballads and folk-songs which owe nothing to foreign influence, but English literature is well past the folk-stage when we get our first glimpse of it, and apart from ballads and a few poems commemorating contemporary events there is little pure folk-poetry left to us. The ballad, however, is really a species apart, and we should distinguish these narrative poems (which are often quite genuine folk-literature) from the folk-*lyric* of which much fewer traces exist.

A glance at the development of the French lyric will show the changing social function of lyric poetry from its beginnings until the fourteenth century. Primitive folk-song was probably communal improvisation to the rhythm of work (for example, spinning, threshing, rowing) or of play (in the dance). Gradually it loses its communal authorship, and the words are supplied by one more skilled in versification, until we get the professional minstrel, who composes the songs for the people, though often retaining the popular refrain which may be little more than a conventionally onomatopœic imitation of the sound of the work or (probably a later development) of the twanging of the minstrel's lute. As the professional minstrel, developing into the troubadour or trouvère, comes into his own, folk-poetry develops into art-poetry, retaining many features which characterised the communally produced improvisations in which it originated. For the first time poetry expresses an emotion that may be purely personal, yet for long it tends to do so through the forms and conventions which grew up in the communal stage. " The forms of art are conservative; and, with whatever change of temper and intention, the trouvère is apt to continue the themes and conventions which were first shaped by the folk and still, through all modifications, carry their birth-marks upon them. One other feature of the transition is notable. Art-poetry, whether of the minstrel or trouvère variety, is mainly, if not wholly, masculine poetry. The relation of the minstrel to the *comitatus*, the literary advantage of the clerk, are perhaps sufficient between them to account for this. But it involved a distinct breach with the traditions of the folk, for whom woman, not man, is the characteristic singer. This also is intelligible, since woman's are the greater number of the more leisured and rhythmical of the folk-occupations, and to her, the primitive sower of seed and planter of herbs, has always been assigned the chief part in that persistent ritual of agriculture, at whose high seasons the festival excitement finds its ready outlet in the dance."[1] Thus with the development of folk-poetry into art-poetry the whole nature and function of poetic activity undergoes a change. What begins as a spontaneous accompaniment to work or play, largely feminine in inspiration, develops into the deliberate product of a conscious art, predominantly masculine in origin.

We get our first glimpse of written French poetry when this process had just been completed. The new development is recent enough for it still to bear marks of its origin, yet the process of sophistication is sufficiently far gone for the new ideas of courtly love to

[1] E. K. Chambers, " Some Aspects of Mediæval Lyric," in *Early English Lyrics*, ed. Chambers and Sidgwick, pp. 260–1.

have become the very basis of this poetry. The poet has become the type of the lover, loving and singing in accordance with the numerous conventions into whose nature and social origins we shall shortly be inquiring. This is that Provençal poetry with which, as we have noted at the beginning of this chapter, European literature as we have it begins again after the dark ages. From the point of view of the literary historian it marks the beginning of an epoch; on a wider view it is seen to be the end of a long development.

Coexisting with this highly conventional and sophisticated poetry there is a more popular type of song which seems to represent a development half-way between the folk-song and the written Provençal poetry just discussed. These are all of definite types, such as the *chanson d'aventure* where the poet tells of what happened to him when he went abroad one morning—he generally meets a maid in the wood, makes love to her, and then rides off. Or there is the *aube*, song of lovers parting at dawn, the *chanson de carole*, lyrical dance-song, the " mal mariée " type, where the woman complains of her husband, and others. This more popular type of poetry cannot always be sharply distinguished from the courtly love type, but we can say of it in general that it is closer to the original folk-art than is the latter. Gaston Paris has noted the significant fact that while the poems of courtly love invariably treat of love from the man's point of view, this more popular type of song often gives the woman's approach, and we have seen that the true folk-song is feminine rather than masculine in origin. But the fact that the courtly writers drew on these traditional themes in their own work makes it difficult to separate out the two stages with complete certainty.

While we have French lyrics from the twelfth century, we have no secular English lyrics earlier than the late thirteenth, and by this time they have already many of the characteristics of the French courtly poetry. Yet, for all the influence of French conventions, these early English lyrics have a freshness and vividness all their own. There is the note of welcome to spring— so genuine in the Middle Ages when winter was a time of real hardship, of darkness, cold, and salt meat—the note of passionate love, the note of joy that has no cause other than a sudden sense of well-being, and of melancholy which is perhaps an inheritance from the Anglo-Saxons, the note of sheer playfulness, the drinking song, the anecdote of personal experience. Though most of these songs are the product of deliberate and conscious art, they have nevertheless an air of spontaneity and sincerity that is most attractive to the modern reader. They are less the poetry of knights and courtiers than the French lyrics: often they seem to suit more the yeoman type, the independent peasant, with his frank passions and accurate knowledge of the countryside. But others are more similar to the French courtly type. If there were English lyrics extant from the twelfth and earlier centuries we might be better able to trace the development in the social function of English lyric poetry and to assess the effect of the Conquest on this branch of literature. With narrative poetry the process is fairly obvious: Anglo-Saxon poetry is aristocratic and courtly, the earliest English narrative poetry after the Conquest is rude and popular, while with the ousting of French by English as the language of the upper classes we find literature in English again taking on a courtly tone and function. No such simple tripartite development is visible in the lyric, but by analogy with French and our knowledge of the nature of early folk-literature, we can have some idea of the development of the English lyric from a communal folk-art to a more personal and more sophisticated type of poetry. The full development of the English lyric in this direction had yet a good way to go: it was some centuries before the purely personal and artificial lyric appeared in any numbers in England. That was one of the early products of the Renaissance in this country.

It is time we paused to say a word about the tradition of courtly love which arose in Provence and spread over Europe in the course of the Middle Ages, penetrating both lyrical and narrative literature from the Mediterranean to the North Sea, wherever the "Latin spirit" travelled. Not only did this tradition have a profound effect on mediæval literature, but it also had important effects on western thought which are still with us. With it, " romantic " love first comes on the scene. Hitherto love between the sexes had been regarded either as a purely physical matter, or as the normal affection of well-suited partners, or as a madness which every sensible man would do his best to shun. In the poetry of the troubadours a completely new conception appears. Love is service, as that of a slave to his master except that it is not based on outside compulsion. The knight serves the lady of his choice, suffers any and every kind of indignity for her sake, thinks only of her, commends himself to her when he goes into battle, and in referring to her uses language that is scarcely if at all distinguishable from that used in religious poems with reference to the Virgin Mary. The slightest favour she chooses to bestow upon him is sufficient reward for the greatest hardship he may undergo for her sake. He is her humble vassal, and she is his liege lady. He must be loyal to her for life, however she may treat him. However desperate he is, however hopeless of winning his lady's favour, however he may sigh and moan because of unrequited love, he must never think of ceasing to be the servant of her whom he has originally chosen, for it is better to be in love than to have no liege lady to serve. Love is, as it were, its own reward, and though a more concrete reward is desired and sometimes obtained the lover must not swerve in his allegiance if it does not come. This is not a relation between husband and wife: indeed, throughout most of this literature it is taken as a matter of course that a husband cannot be the lover of his own wife. That is a task for someone else. The courtly love tradition implies, in fact, an idealisation of adultery. When a poet offers love to a lady he does not bother himself about her husband at all: his real rival is anyone who seeks to be a lover of the lady in the same way as himself. The lover's conduct must conform at all points to a strict code of honour: in addition to the service of his lady he must dedicate himself to the cause of women in a general sense, always ready to defend them, always prepared to succour damsels in distress. The rules of knightly behaviour were carefully defined, and involved many subtle points of conduct: by these rules every lover was bound. There were even, in theory if not in practice, " Courts of Love," which adjudicated on subtle points of honour and knightly conduct.

No previous civilisation had known such an attitude to the relations between the sexes. The courtly love tradition is an absolutely new development. Originating with the troubadours in Provence it spread first over France, where it affected not only lyric poetry but the verse romances too, though not the very earliest of these. And it comes into English literature in the fourteenth century, with the " refining " of the English romance. The tradition is strong in Chaucer, and lasts as a dominant *motif* up to Spenser, while, altered but still recognisable, it continued in European literature and thought through the following three centuries and is the basis of the modern conception of romantic love which is still the view of the relation between the sexes most widely held. Can we find any features in the organisation of society at the time when this tradition arose that might help to explain its origin and its influence?

Mr. C. S. Lewis, whose admirable study of *The Allegory of Love* is far and away the best discussion of the subject we have in English, in seeking for the origins of courtly love says, " Something can be extracted from a study of the social conditions in which the new poetry arose, but not so much as we might hope,"[1] and, giving up the attempt really to explain this new attitude, tries only to account for " the peculiar form which it first took; the four marks of Humility, Courtesy, Adultery, and the Religion of Love."[2] Well,

[1] *The Allegory of Love* (Oxford, 1936), p. 11.   [2] Ibid., p. 12.

no explanation of the rise of an important new idea can be entirely adequate, and no one would maintain that social origins will completely account for any phenomenon. But at any rate we can recognise some causal connection between the state of society and the phenomena that arise in that society, and while admitting that this does not afford a complete explanation we can hope for a better understanding of the nature of the product by noting those factors which have had, at the least, considerable influence in its formation.

We have already seen how feudal society tended to resolve itself into separate islands of civilisation. The castle or manor was a more or less isolated home of leisure and even luxury round which all the life of that area was grouped. " There are many men in it, and very few women—the lady and her damsels. Around these throng the whole male *meiny*, the inferior nobles, the landless knights, the squires, and the pages— haughty creatures enough in relation to the peasantry beyond the walls, but feudally inferior to the lady as to her lord—her ' men ' as feudal language had it. Whatever ' courtesy ' is in the place flows from her: all female charm from her and her damsels. There is no question of marriage for most of the court."[1] As for the four marks of the new feeling, Mr. Lewis proceeds to sum up the conditions that produced them: " Before the coming of courtly love the relation of vassal and lord, in all its intensity and warmth, already existed; its was a mould into which romantic passion would almost certainly be poured. And if the beloved were also the feudal superior the thing becomes entirely

[1] *The Allegory of Love*, p. 12.

natural and inevitable. The emphasis on courtesy results from the same conditions. It is in courts that the new feeling arises: the lady, by her social and feudal position, is already the arbitress of manners and the scourge of ' villany ' even before she is loved."[1]

The genealogy of the courtly poet also throws some light on the ideals of humility and service so bound up with the new romantic attitude. Before the real troubadour poetry began, it was a common practice for the lord to have about him for his personal entertainment minstrels, " jongleurs," at first merely primitive mummers or acrobats. When the new Provençal poetry began to develop these humble entertainers—who were socially among the lowest of the castle servants—often took on the function of court poet, ceasing to be mere " jongleurs " and becoming troubadours. And though the troubadours rapidly rose in the social scale until they included in their number many of the lords themselves, it is not fantastic to see in the servile strain that characterised courtly love-poetry some trace of the humble position of the original troubadours, who were merely glorified clowns. That would help to explain why the language of these poems is not only that of a vassal to his feudal superior, but often that of the humblest of vassals to a superior infinitely removed in rank and station.

The reason why the ideal of courtly love was sought outside marriage is largely the simple one that in feudal times marriage was so bound up with the inheritance and transmission of property that questions of love could not even be considered. Lordship of land

[1] *The Allegory of Love*, p. 13.

being the very basis of the system, anything connected with the disposal or acquisition of estates was purely a business matter into which sentiment was not allowed to intervene. " All matches were matches of interest, and, worse still, of an interest that was continually changing. When the alliance which had answered would answer no longer, the husband's object was to get rid of the lady as quickly as possible. Marriages were frequently dissolved. The same woman who was the lady and ' the dearest dread ' of her vassals was often little better than a piece of property to her husband. He was master in his own house. So far from being a natural channel for the new kind of love, marriage was rather the drab background against which that love stood out in all the contrast of its new tenderness and delicacy."[1]

The teaching of mediæval religion was not calculated to drive the new conception of love into legal channels. Romantic passion in the relation between the sexes was not regarded as a religious virtue—or even something that religion might condone—under any circumstances, and there was no encouragement from the Church to graft the new feeling on to any conventional view of domestic happiness. From every point of view the difference between courtly love and the relations between man and wife was emphasised. The courtly lover did not even *wish* to marry his lady, though he sought a consummation of his love outside marriage. Marriage, it was thought, would spoil everything. It was only later that the romantic ideal of love was linked with marriage and the passion was regarded as virtuous provided that it had marriage in view; and

[1] *The Allegory of Love*, p. 13.

it is this modified form of the Provençal tradition that has been the general European view of love between man and woman for over three centuries. We shall see later how the change came about.

So we see that this conception of courtly love that swept over Europe and penetrated its literature was one that originated among the aristocracy and had little relation to the everyday loves of humbler men and women. It was, at its simplest, a conventionalisation of the attitude of the high-placed feudal servant to his lord's wife. And if, as so often happened during this period, the lord himself was away at the Crusades, there was all the more scope for the courtly lover. How far this attitude was a mere convention and how far it had a realistic basis is very difficult to say. Sometimes the whole business was nothing but a polite game, but there can be no doubt that on many occasions there was real intrigue behind it all. To some, the convention was just an opportunity to discourse subtly on the psychology of love, and it is to be noted that the psychological treatment of romantic love, so common in European literature, begins with the mediæval allegories of courtly love.

The sophistication which courtly love brought with it was not satisfied with the lyric and the narrative romance in which to manifest itself. We have seen how the spirit infected first French lyric, then French narrative romance, and finally the later narrative romances in English. Especially in the " Matter of Britain," in the stories of Arthur and his knights of the round table (the knights being much more prominent than Arthur) do we find the refinements of courtly love. But the most characteristic expression of the tradition of courtly love is the allegorical romance, where the desires and passions, the virtues and vices, of mortal men are personified, thus enabling the subtle psychological questions that arise in treating of courtly love to be discussed with a concreteness and reality otherwise unobtainable. The finer points of the code of love and honour had to be thus objectified before the mediæval writer could deal with them to his satisfaction.

We have no space to deal at any length with the origin of this new allegorical literature. It arose in France soon after the narrative romance had come into the field, and appealed only to the educated and sophisticated classes, with whom it became extraordinarily popular. Thus this was a courtly literature from the beginning, and did not develop from a more popular type. Its ancestry is to be found if anywhere in late Latin poetry and the learned and didactic literature of the very early Middle Ages. Allegory takes its place gradually as a literary mode, partly as a result of the allegorisation of the old Roman gods, partly as a result of a new introspective tendency that arose with the development of Christianity and induced men to objectify their mental and spiritual struggles by personifying the desires and aims, the appetites and qualities that produced them. By the time courtly love appears on the scene the allegorical mode is ready to be its medium, and so at length we have the allegorical romance, the most artificial and in many respects the most influential and tenacious of the different kinds of literature produced in the Middle Ages. Of the three kinds we have been considering—

the lyric, the narrative romance and now the allegory—this was the last to appear[1] and the only one which underwent no development from popular to courtly. This was essentially a " polite " literature from the beginning: or if it was not very " polite " in its earliest, germinal stages, it was at least learned.

The most noteworthy allegorical romance of the Middle Ages, the most elaborate specimen of its kind and the most influential on subsequent literature, for which it proved an inexhaustible quarry, is the *Roman de la Rose* of Guillaume de Lorris and Jean de Meun. Guillaume de Lorris's share in the poem was written in the latter half of the thirteenth century. It is the true allegory of courtly love, where the whole new psychology of love-making is treated with great subtlety and effectiveness. Qualities of the heroine, such as shame, fear, kindliness, courtesy, etc., are personified, and the hero's encounter with the lady in her different moods—in some of which she encourages and in others of which she repels his suit—is described as an attempt to obtain the " rose " (standing for the lady's love) which is enclosed within a hedge in a garden which is the scene of the action. In his attempt the hero is aided by such personified qualities as the heroine's natural kindliness and courtesy (*bialacoil*, " fair welcome ") and hindered by, for example, fear and shame. The whole background of the story is courtly life, a life of leisure and good breeding, where there is nothing to do but dance and sing and make love.

[1] The last to appear, that is, in the form of *allegorical romance*, where we have the allegorisation of the conceptions embodied in the idea of courtly love. Of course, allegory in the more general sense goes back through the dark ages and beyond.

The story as Guillaume de Lorris planned it is unfinished, and the conclusion by Jean de Meun about forty years later is quite different in aim and nature. Jean's work—which is many times as long as that of Guillaume—is quite formless beside the well-constructed earlier portion, and it shows no ability to handle the allegorical method with effectiveness. The allegory in the first part of the *Roman de la Rose* is done with real skill and finesse; but Jean is a clumsier and more realistic writer, and the fine allegorical fabric of Guillaume comes to pieces in his hands. His purpose is not to tell a subtle love story so much as to produce a piece of work which is at once didactic, philosophic, satiric, scientific, religious, and lots of other things besides. There is a strong satiric strain in his writing which is quite absent from the earlier part of the poem: he sometimes gives the impression that he is utterly contemptuous of the courtly love tradition and takes every opportunity to leave the story and digress at inordinate length on philosophic, satiric, or mythological subjects. We see in Jean's attitude something of the temper of the rising class of realistic writers which the new bourgeois element was producing at this time. Polite, courtly literature is no longer sufficient to satisfy the reading public even with the alternative of simple narrative romances of wonder and marvellous action. There is growing up a taste for something different both from the sentimental, sophisticated love story and the simple tale of derring-do. Jean de Meun is still working within the courtly tradition, but he is out of sympathy with it. He has more learning and philosophy, more of a serious didactic purpose, than the new class of realistic writing showed, yet in many ways he illustrates the transition from the courtly to the bourgeois tradition.

But before we proceed to discuss this new type of literature we must say something of the influence of the *Roman de la Rose*, which was enormous. The poem was translated all over Europe, and its characters and conventions are to be met with again and again throughout later literature. In England it was translated, at least in part, by Chaucer. The scene at the beginning of the *Roman de la Rose* is a river-bank outside a walled garden, and the hero enters into the garden through a wicket gate. This scene becomes a stock property in mediæval literature. The story is told by the narrator in the form of a dream, from which he awakes at the conclusion. Similarly, the dream form is copied by the later writers. And then there is the May morning, with the birds singing and nature looking her best. The May morning, the wandering into the country, the dream, the garden—these are the characteristic features of this type of literature, known as the dream allegory.

That this latest and most sophisticated type of mediæval courtly literature should take the form of dream allegory is significant. It is an artificial literature, produced for a leisured audience that was quite cut off from the realities of the life of the peasant and the worker; a literature for the introvert, whose life was mostly empty of active labour and who therefore had time and inclination to introspect and refine on his own emotions; a literature of self-conscious sensibility. The gulf between courtly and popular literature

Ds

is now complete. Only in one respect do we find the objective realism that comes from keeping one's eye on the object: this is in the descriptions of natural scenery outside and inside the garden. But even this often becomes stylised to a high degree.

It is only the leisured and cultured reader that feels the urge to analyse emotions rather than to hear a sequence of exciting incidents. We must not assume however that because this was to a large extent the literature of the idle, the amusement of courts and castles, it necessarily represents an inferior kind of art. When society is so clearly split up into sections as it was under the feudal system, and the specialisation of labour is such a simple and necessary fact, any profounder aspects of thought must be left to those who have the time for it. And those who have the time for it are those who belong to the class which is least productive economically. There is no question of the peasant coming home from his labour to spend the evening reading his favourite poet. If literature depended on the encouragement of that kind of audience it would not have been produced at all. The nature of the social system left all except the crudest literary and artistic activity to a small and privileged class, and the more the system becomes stabilised the more clearly the literature it produces bears the mark of the class that fosters it. The popular elements in mediæval literature are driven lower and lower down, to become ever cruder romance and ballad, as society becomes more rigid in its organisation. At the beginning of the Middle Ages popular and courtly elements exist side by side, but as the social and political system becomes more clearly defined these elements become separated and the professional writers produce a purely " polite " literature. This polite literature naturally reflects the habits and ways of thought of the class for which it is written, and we can explain most of the conventions of the dream allegory in this way. But psychological interest in character is not any the less valuable an activity because it first appears in this form, and, while recognising the limited functions of this kind of writing in contemporary society, we can at the same time see in it an important new step in literary art which ultimately gives us the modern psychological novel.

The feudal system, however, bore the seeds of its own destruction within itself, and it advanced only to decay. The development of a money economy out of a natural economy, hastened both by the commutation of different kinds of feudal service to money-payments and the growth of towns with their trading communities, gradually took away the very basis of the system by encouraging the growth of a class which had no place in it. This was the middle class, the bourgeoisie, who dwelt in towns and carried on commercial activity of one kind or another: they were traders and artisans, no longer living on the land, getting their food and their raw materials by selling to the peasants the goods they manufactured. It was this class that was to rise to a position of domination in society.

It is with this new middle class that is associated the realistic, often satiric, literature that developed parallel with but quite distinct from the courtly literature we have been discussing. This kind of writing has its origins in popular comic poetry and, like the other kinds, develops first in France. The type of the earliest French literature of this sort is the twelfth-century *Roman de Renart*, which is found in different forms in different European languages. This work is " generally, and justly, taken as the ironical counterpart of mediæval epic and romance; an irreverent criticism of dignitaries, spiritual and temporal, the great narrative comedy of the Ages of Faith and of Chivalry."[1] These characteristics remain those of the numerous realistic stories of town life which are found in France in the twelfth and thirteenth centuries, though not in England until the fourteenth. They are called *fabliaux*. Many types of *fabliau* exist: some are indecent stories of town life whose only point is their indecency; others are humorous, satiric tales of intrigue; others again, like the *Roman de Renart* cycle, are animal stories, also generally humorous and satiric in tone. In these tales we see for the first time something of the seamy side of mediæval urban life. They have a homely, realistic flavour, with, at times, something of the atmosphere of a Flemish *genre* painting. The town-dweller who makes his living by trade has no romantic illusions about life; he has no use for the refinements of courtly love or the subtleties of the chivalric code. His attitude of mind is something like that of the modern commercial traveller, whose chief relaxation is telling dirty stories in the bar. There seems to be some inherent connection between commerce and obscenity, not, perhaps, altogether difficult to account for.

Romance and *fabliau*, idealism and realism, these

[1] W. P. Ker, op. cit., p. 171.

are the two poles of mediæval literature as they are of subsequent writing. It is a distinction that runs right through succeeding ages because it corresponds to a dualism in the human mind. The romantic tradition, widening out under Petrarcan and neo-Platonic influences, gives us the courtly poetry of the sixteenth century, Spenser with his knights and fair ladies, the courtly poetry of the seventeenth century, the heroic poem of the end of that century (much coarsened by now), and goes underground at the beginning of the eighteenth century to re-emerge not long afterwards, first with pseudo-mediæval stuff like Horace Walpole's *Castle of Otranto*, then with the " horror " novels of Mrs. Radcliffe and " Monk " Lewis and the younger Shelley, and finally joins up with many other currents to flow into the main stream of the so-called "Romantic Revival." The realistic tradition of the *fabliau*—apart from its underground activities—gives us Elizabethan fiction such as Nashe's *Unfortunate Traveller*, and then broadens out to become a more general influence having an effect on fiction from Defoe to George Gissing and beyond. This tradition is less easily isolated, for it joins up at a fairly early stage with realism as a general tendency. Yet we can see in the two opposite kinds of mediæval literature, in romance and *fabliau* (taking romance to include dream allegory), the two moods which are to alternate in their dominance over European literature for centuries to come.

It is in the work of Chaucer (*c*. 1340–1400) that we see the best examples of the different kinds of English mediæval literature. Chaucer's great achievement on the technical side was to bring English prosody up to the level of French. We have noted the tendency to "refine" English literature that went on throughout the fourteenth century. It was Chaucer who finally made English poetry, in ease and suppleness and varied regularity, the equal of any in Europe. But he is equally important in that his work gives us a collection of specimens of different mediæval literary species, each one of the best of its kind. In *The Book of the Duchess* we have the dream allegory; in *Troilus and Criseyde* we have the courtly romance, though told in a way that is Chaucer's own; while other kinds are represented in the *Canterbury Tales*—the more conventional type of courtly romance in the "Knight's Tale"; the coarse, realistic *fabliau* in the tales of the miller, the reeve, and the cook, and the animal-story type in the "Nun's Priest's Tale"; the popular romance (parodied) in *Sir Thopas*; and we have religious literature represented, too, with the saint's legend, the moral treatise and the sermon. Most types have more than one representative, and there are different varieties of the same species.

Chaucer's handling of material, which was to a large extent traditional and conventional, illustrates what happens when a man of real genius comes on the scene. We lose sight of the special audience for which his work was originally written, and the problem of the social function of literature seems for the moment to be irrelevant. The work of a lesser writer is more easily analysed from this point of view. It is easy to deduce the type of reader for which Lydgate wrote; we can without much difficulty put a minor Elizabethan dramatist in his place in contemporary life. But Chaucer, we feel, wrote for us, and Shakespeare is not to be explained by reference to the society in which he flourished. We remain undisturbed when we are told that the work of some obscure mediæval writer owes all its characteristics to social, economic, and other similar factors. But a description of Shakespeare as, say, essentially a " bourgeois " writer we feel at once to be in itself of very limited relevance. If this distinction has any value at all—and few will deny that it has—it must be because there do exist ascertainable standards of literary worth which can be applied to a given product independently of its origin. A present-day writer, visiting a depressed area, may be moved by contemporary social conditions to write a vivid description of life in these areas. Yet the resultant work might have value, not only as a social document referring to specific facts in social life, but as a moving picture of human life lived under unfavourable conditions, and thus a permanent account of certain aspects of human experience which, in greater or less degree, are always present. One can reach out through the " particular " to the " universal ": the great writer can sum up all human misery in the description of a blind beggar he saw in a London street on a particular afternoon. The social historian who explained to us just why that blind beggar was a beggar and through what economic forces he was driven to seek his living in that way would be giving us useful information which every intelligent person would be glad to have, but the information might be totally useless in helping us to decide just why this account of a blind beggar was good as literature. And so, in dealing with Chaucer's *Canterbury Tales* we cannot explain their literary *quality* on any except literary standards: and the whole question of the existence and nature of such standards we are reserving for a later chapter. We can, however, learn many other things about Chaucer's work from a consideration of social conditions before and during his time. We can see why he worked within a certain tradition, why he chose to describe certain types of character rather than others, why he makes certain of his characters say certain things, why his own views (if we can find any) on certain social and other questions are what they are, why he was enabled to receive the education he did, why he had leisure to write, and innumerable other questions of this kind. In other words, we can find out by such methods almost everything about his work except its literary quality.

To a social historian, then, a bad piece of writing may be more illuminating than a good. Processes, influences, conditioning factors, stand more clearly revealed in a work which is poor in literary quality than in a masterpiece. For literary worth is, ultimately, just that universality that makes a writer talking to his own generation at the same time a man talking to men.

In the case of Chaucer, however, this rule does not fully apply, for the simple reason that in the *Canterbury Tales* Chaucer has given us a deliberate picture of a large part of the contemporary social scene, and we thus have direct evidence of what we generally have to deduce indirectly. Chaucer's pilgrims provide us with a view of society with the two extreme ends—the very highest and the very lowest—cut off. We see neither lords nor villeins: the highest up in the social scale is the knight, and the furthest down is the ploughman.

We do not see the pilgrims in their everyday activities; they are on a pilgrimage, on holiday, and though many references to their daily work occur in their conversation they are naturally in a mood of which escape from normal workaday life is the keynote. We see them, therefore, as individuals rather than as units in a social pattern. And Chaucer is only concerned with them as individuals, although the result of his characterisation may produce at the same time a good picture of the type. Chaucer took the characteristics a man would have as a member of a particular profession in order to enrich his portrait of him as a man; thus his knight is courteous and well mannered, his monk is fond of field-sports, and his doctor rarely opens a Bible. The atmosphere of the whole pilgrimage is, if anything, middle class, though the presence of so many representatives of the clergy—a much more ubiquitous and diversified class then than now—makes it difficult to speak in terms of modern class divisions. None of the pilgrims suffer from undue poverty; even the ploughman was able to pay his tithes " ful faire and wel " and could afford a horse. Characters like the merchant, the franklin, the five members of trade-guilds, the wife of Bath, the miller, the manciple, are all solidly " bourgeois." The knight and the squire alone belong to a higher social stratum, but it is to be noted that the knight is described as a thoroughly ideal figure in an age when his class was on the decline and the whole practice of chivalry had degenerated. To some extent, both knight and squire are " throw-backs." The shipman stands somewhat apart, as an independent adventurer outside the ranks of chivalry. The yeoman comes below the squire in the dying feudal hierarchy. The doctor and the serjeant of the law are middle-class professional men, and the same description would apply to the reeve, whose function is the management of an estate on behalf of its lord. The clerk is a poor student (all students having, at this time, some ecclesiastical connection) who is being helped to support himself in his studies by contributions from friends and charitable persons: he is still on the look-out for a benefice, and is probably the poorest of the company. The cook might be described in modern terminology as " lower middle-class " and mine host himself would be but little above him in social status. The representatives of the Church range in rank from the prioress, who is a "lady" in the Victorian sense, to the poor parson, a humble parish priest who lives off his tithes (if they have not been appropriated by a neighbouring monastery).

This is a very different picture from that which we would expect from a feudal society. We can see from the Prologue to the *Canterbury Tales* alone how feudalism has decayed and the comparatively new town life is becoming more and more important. The courtly and the popular tradition are at this time rather mixed up. We can see reflected in literature what has been happening in society. Chaucer's own career illustrates the changing social ideas. The son of a vintner whose financial prosperity seems to have enabled him to aspire to considerable heights socially, Chaucer started his career as a page in the household of the Countess of Ulster (the wife of Prince Lionel). In later years he was engaged in diplomatic activity, and seems to have had a close connection with the court. He received the appointment of Controller of the Customs in addition to his other work, and altogether his career seems to have been a mixture of court office, diplomatic service, and civil service. Similarly, but on a very much greater scale, the unscrupulous Richard Lyons, the wealthiest London merchant of his day and financier of John of Gaunt's gang, obtained considerable control in the affairs of government. Commercial prosperity was beginning to replace noble birth as a qualification for high place: with the decay of the feudal system, to give place to a money economy, the importance of wealth becomes increasingly recognised, and eventually we have the commercial aristocracy fostered by Edward IV and the Tudors.

So the society which gave birth to the courtly tradition has changed. The *fabliau* element has now grown stronger than the romance. While the pure courtly romance and dream allegory still exist, and are to exist for some time yet, there are growing up hybrid types, where popular, urban, and courtly traditions are united. Chaucer was the son of a merchant, yet he had a courtly education. He had served at a prince's court, and was brought up in French polite literature, yet his last position was Clerk of Works. The very range of the *Canterbury Tales* is symptomatic of this new union between the world of business and the world of polite idleness. And if Chaucer's successors, like Lydgate, returned to a more purely courtly tradition it is because they were less in touch with contemporary society, not being men of affairs, as Chaucer was.

The fourteenth century, with the latter half of which Chaucer's career coincides, was a time of rapid change.

The growing tendency for the commutation of labour service for money-payment combined with the results of the Black Death to cause the decay of villeinage and to increase the independence of the labourers, who, left small in number by the ravages of the plague, were able to set their own price on their labour. In vain the governing class tried to stop the rise in labourers' wages by Statutes of Labourers. The clock could not be put back, and the results of the Black Death in depopulating the countryside put the labourers in an extremely favourable position. Villeins slipped away from the land to which they were legally bound to offer their services to the highest bidder. With harvests rotting for lack of workers, landowners were forced to pay in wages what was asked. In addition to the unrest produced by this problem, there were many other causes for general dissatisfaction in the last years of Edward III's reign and the beginning of Richard II's. England was being governed by a selfish and corrupt clique, who were letting France slip away without striking a blow; English supremacy at sea was being steadily destroyed; the glory of Crecy and Poitiers had departed and—worst of all—the country was being taxed almost out of existence in a vain endeavour to win back the lost power and glory. English commerce depended largely on the maintenance of English sea-power, and the revival of French might by land and sea was more than a military question. Amidst this general discontent the Peasants' Revolt broke out in 1381. Change was in the air, and to a contemporary it might well have seemed to be decay. Chivalry had become a farce. Every kind of magnificence was to be seen in the state of the small minority who had the power in their hands, while disease and misery prevailed all over the countryside. The State had grown lop-sided. When the Black Prince took Limoges in 1370 he massacred all the citizens, including hundreds of women and children, yet he treated the few knights who were in the town with exaggerated kindness and courtesy. In 1377 the Black Prince died, but the spirit exemplified in his action seven years earlier prevailed now more than ever before. The practice of knighthood had degenerated into a stupid pageantry: the old order was breaking up, with all the usual symptoms produced by the working of unrecognised economic forces. And in the Church, too, corruption was reaping an unpleasant harvest. Wycliffe was a portentous symbol, and the connection of the priest John Ball with the rebellious peasants, however much Wycliffe may have disapproved, was no accident.

It was in this world that Chaucer lived and wrote. Yet in his one work where he deliberately sets out to describe contemporary society, or at least a fair number of its representatives, we see very little of this social change and economic conflict. The pilgrims who ride carelessly on their way to Canterbury are real enough men and women, but Chaucer achieves this reality by concentrating on their characteristics as human beings —their humour or kindliness or smuttiness or vanity or rascality or sensuality or long-windedness or pomposity or heartiness or human frailty of one kind or another—and to some extent averting his attention from that background against which their daily lives were lived. We have already suggested that the literary quality of the *Canterbury Tales* cannot be assessed by any analysis of this background: it is equally true that the literary ability of the author cannot be judged from the degree to which he was articulate about the social forces at work in his day. To return to our earlier example of a writer describing a blind beggar in a London street: just as knowledge of the economic factors which made the blind beggar what he is provides us with no criterion by which to judge the description as literature, so the display of such knowledge by the writer will not necessarily help him to produce a better literary work. The writer's duty is to *keep his eye on the object* in a special sense which we shall discuss later, and keeping your eye on the object is not the same thing as keeping your eye on the forces that produced the object, although in many cases the one implies the other. A description of a crystal could give a brilliant and vivid picture of its appearance, while a detailed account of the chemical processes that went to its formation might convey to the reader no idea whatever of its appearance, of the crystal as it is in human experience. The sun is one thing to the astronomer and quite another to the sun-bather. The whole problem of causation in works of art is a delicate one; but if art has a separate function in human life distinct from that of science—and who will dispute it ?—this point at least is clear: the artist speaks as a sun-bather and not as an astronomer.

Is then our attempt to discuss the place of literature in society condemned to failure from the outset ? If we were attempting to judge literary quality by an analysis of contemporary society, our attempt would indeed be bound to meet with failure. But we are attempting nothing so stupid. We are concerned with two questions: first, the nature of the relation of literature to the society in which it is produced, and, second, the function of literature in society as a human activity considered in relation to other activities. We hope to derive data from a brief historical sketch of what literature and society and their relations to each other have been in the past; but adequate discussion of the real questions at issue can only come with an examination of the data we have collected. We have only entered this *caveat* at this point because it is in a consideration of the work of a writer like Chaucer—work which paints a large social canvas yet reflects so little of the social conflicts of the time—that we come up against the fact that literary genius does not necessarily imply social sensitiveness.[1]

Chaucer is the type of the tolerant ironist: the defects in the society of his day are not separated, for him, from the defects in human nature, and he has learned to tolerate human nature, to stand outside it, as it were, and look on, half sad, half amused. In such a mood he paints what he sees, selecting those features of the scene which in combination will give the picture as it presents itself to him. If his mood shifts, his selection of detail changes. The importance of *selection* in literary art is shown when we come from Chaucer to his contemporary Langland and consider *Piers Plowman*. Here the same social scene is viewed through very different eyes. Langland is very conscious of the changes going on in society, though he does not understand their significance.

[1] On the other hand there are times when the insight of the artist must bring with it a realisation of the nature of social forces. This is especially true when the state of social organisation threatens the artist's function. The reader might compare what has been written here with chapter five.

He is a moralist, not a mere ironical observer, and he describes in order to condemn or—less often—to praise. The form used by Langland is the dream allegory, but the allegory is not used consistently, with the sustained subtlety of a Guillaume de Lorris: the field full of folk that the poet sees when he falls asleep on Malvern Hills is filled not only with characters like Holy Church and Lady Meed (that is, bribery) but with living flesh-and-blood characters from mediæval life. What distinguishes Langland perhaps most of all from Chaucer is the sense of movement in his work. There are masses of people, moving to and fro; the individual is lost sight of in the crowd. Langland looks at the contemporary scene with two purposes in view, (1) to point out the wrong that he sees there and suggest how it can be righted; (2) to find out, as a more personal matter, what really is the good life.[1]

Langland's policy to remedy the wrongs he sees in contemporary society is not in the least revolutionary. He believed that if everyone performed his traditional function in society conscientiously all troubles would be gone for ever. A man must not try to remove himself from the station into which it had pleased God to call him. The desire for better food which the labourers, now enabled to demand and to receive higher wages, were beginning to show was condemned as seeking after idle luxury. Piers Plowman is the type of the free labourer (though he takes on more mystical functions as the poem proceeds to its close), doing his allotted work and not seeking to go out of his class. Throughout the

[1] I am accepting the view of Bright, as against that of Manley, that *Piers Plowman* has a single author.

poem there is a great deal of denunciation of the many iniquities in contemporary Church and State. Corruption of one kind and another is denounced again and again with great bitterness—and justifiably, for corruption in high places was largely responsible for the bad times. We have less sympathy with the author when he treats the demand of the labourers for a rise in the standard of living as mere evidence of laziness and vagabondage. But he displays a kind of *laissez-faire* attitude, asserting that Hunger will by a natural law starve the wicked and the lazy into working like decent members of society. Some of the best parts of the poem are the realistically drawn interiors, such as the picture of Gluttony turning aside into an ale-house on his way to church, to drink his " galoun ale " till he has to be carried off to bed.

From Chaucer we would never guess that the old order was changing: but in Langland we see it in decay, with Langland endeavouring to restore the *status quo*. Chaucer stops the clock while we look at the scene: Langland tries to put the clock back, being a social reformer only in the sense that he thought the best way to banish evil was to bring back the " good old days." We might call Langland a reforming reactionary, while Chaucer was concerned only with human nature as it manifested itself in the society he knew. He described but passed no judgment, though he had his own views. Chaucer was no " pure artist " in the sense that he described things *in vacuo*, with no beliefs or standards of his own. He accepted the beliefs and standards of his day, and they provided him with a vantage point from which to observe life.

In *Piers Plowman* the allegorical form is used in a

Es

moral and satirical work of a kind very common—in a more direct form—throughout the Middle Ages. But the treatment of contemporary social and other problems on such a large scale by a poet of such quality is not found again in this age. Social or religious satire combined with a general didactic element is common enough, but not in the form Langland uses. He has made the discussion of contemporary abuses in the Church and in society a full-time job. The tradition in which he writes is neither the courtly, nor the urban, nor the popular. It combines some features of each. Didactic poetry had always tended to keep itself outside these categories, having the simple function of instruction, not a combined one of " profit and delight " nor yet one of delight merely. Yet we may see in *Piers Plowman* indications of the same association of different traditions that we noticed in Chaucer. The scene with Gluttony in the tavern is in the best *fabliau* tradition; the falling asleep on Malvern Hills at the beginning is in the manner of the courtly dream allegory; and much of the direct satire and abuse is in the popular tradition.

For what kind of audience did Chaucer and Langland write? *Piers Plowman* is sometimes referred to as a popular poem, but popular in the sense of being written for the common people, the labourers, it certainly was not. His readers were probably the same as those who read Chaucer. Langland was not speaking for the people to the people. He satirises no one class more than any other. He is a conservative moralist, talking to any who will listen. There is, it is true, a certain difference in class between Chaucer and Langland:

the latter was a poor priest, while the former mixed with the most powerful in the land. Yet there was only one audience for literary works at this time—works, that is, that were not suitable for recitation, and few works are less suitable for recitation than *Piers Plowman*. It was for this single audience that both Chaucer and Langland wrote. How far their works were memorised and spread abroad in garbled extracts is very difficult to say. But however different in appeal these two poets are, those who read their works must have been drawn from the same limited class of readers. The exact limits of this class is, again, not easy to determine. " The great majority of lay people were . . . illiterate, and unable to read or write. . . . Most of the evidence as to the education of lay people, or their power of reading in after life, applies only to the upper social classes, a very small section of the whole population. There was, in the Middle Ages, a career open to talent: and those of lowly birth, like Grosseteste, sometimes rose to great positions: but the career lay through the Church, since the student must at least be in minor orders. Those of the lower classes who gained an education did not remain lay people [this would apply to Langland himself]: and those who became really proficient in Latin seldom remained merely tonsured clerks, without proceeding to the priesthood. The majority of lay people were small farmers, farm labourers, personal servants, members of great households, soldiers, and the handicraftsmen of the town: some, but not most of them, might go to a small local ABC school as children, but they had no further acquaintance with books. There is almost no evidence that little girls attended the

ABC schools at all, though it is possible that in some cases they did do so. Book-learning was no concern of most English people, before the fifteenth century at any rate."[1] We can, however, at least say of the reading public of Chaucer's day that it was not so confined to a single class as it had been in the days of the early courtly romances.

We must pass over Gower, Chaucer's accomplished contemporary, in whose *Confessio Amantis* the courtly tradition is cleverly combined with a religious element. And we can spare little time for the fifteenth century, when the allegorical romance and the allegorical didactic poem held the field. The fifteenth century was one of confusion and civil war, and literature had to beat a rapid retreat from the facts of contemporary life. The side of Chaucer represented in the *Canterbury Tales* found no followers. The association of the *fabliau* tradition with the romantic tradition which we noticed in Chaucer is broken: writers produce purely " escapist " allegories again, or else they become mere

[1] M. Deanesly, *The Lollard Bible* (Cambridge, 1920), pp. 206–7. Cf. above, p. 28. As to the actual possession of manuscripts by lay people, Miss Deanesly concludes: "Judging by wills, and the ownership of surviving manuscripts, very few of the laity possessed books of their own at all, before Wycliffe's day, except a few princes, great nobles, and noble ladies. The number of lay people who bequeathed books was very small compared with that of priests, because the latter possessed breviaries, and sometimes other service books. This is shown clearly in the two largest printed collections of wills, those of London and York. The London wills are mainly those of lay people, merchants and others, and only roughly one will in a hundred bequeathed a book at all. The York wills are those of northern nobles and squires, with a very large proportion of cathedral dignitaries and canons; here, one will in every three or four bequeaths books, generally service books." (Ibid. p. 220.) Chaucer and Langland lived at the very end of the pre-Wycliffite period, and by their time some increase in the reading public is probable. But we must not assume that no book-learning meant no knowledge of literature in the Middle Ages.

long-winded preachers. Literature becomes a matter of formulæ—we notice, for example, Lydgate's lack of independent observation, his use of stock phrases and clichés, in comparison with the clear-eyed descriptions of Chaucer and Langland. Literature becomes conventional, didactic, diffuse, unreal, boring.

The so-called " Scottish Chaucerians," who flourished at the end of the fifteenth and the beginning of the sixteenth centuries, are more interesting. We find romance and *fabliau* side by side in Dunbar (*c.* 1460– *c.* 1520), in whose poetry are the two strains of coarse and vivid realism and " aureate " politeness. There is no fusion of the two traditions; they remain quite separate in his work, which is notable also for the personal and " occasional " note of many of the poems. Dunbar was in contact at once with the popular urban life of Scotland and with the court (which was never so aloof in Scotland as it was in other European countries) : his poetry has two separate backgrounds. The other Scottish Chaucerians carry on the mediæval romantic and allegorical tradition, Henryson making a valuable contribution of his own. The *Kingis Quair*, attributed to James I of Scotland and thus considerably earlier in date, marks an important development in the conception of romantic love, which we shall discuss when we come to deal with the history of this conception in literature from the end of the Middle Ages.

In the fifteenth century the old ruling class was too busy dying to have any creative influence on literature. True, the chivalric ideals enjoyed an Indian summer towards the end of the century, but this was an artificial revival brought about by men of letters rather than by men of action. It had no roots in contemporary life. Caxton, our first printer, came under the spell of the revived courtly ideal and was in part responsible for the revival of the courtly narrative romance which for almost a century had been displaced by the allegory. But, apart from this short revival, we see the polite tradition in fifteenth-century literature in a state of decay. It has no basis in contemporary society, in which the bourgeois element was steadily rising. While the last flare-up of chivalry was providing the dukes of Burgundy with a backward-looking culture which spread to England and had a certain amount of influence there, the real forces that were to dominate English life and thought were rapidly developing. But it was a long time before changing society settled into the kind of equilibrium necessary for the production of works of literary value. The decaying feudal and ecclesiastical tradition had a stranglehold on literature from the top, while a reaction in the form of coarse, satiric realism came from below. Neither produced literature worthy of the name until a new amalgamation, a new balance (of the kind we found in Chaucer, but not in his successors) was achieved.

Until 1485, when the Tudor despotism began, it is difficult for us to have a clear view of the relations between literature and society. We must wait, as it were, until the smoke clears before we can see what has been happening. With the end of the fifteenth century we see the economic power of the new bourgeois class firmly established, the old aristocratic landlord class in decay, and the power of the monarchy consolidated above the old nobility and above the Church. The modern national State has come into being: the mediæval community of ideas has disintegrated. The old world, with all its conventions and habits of mind, existed *formally* throughout the century of change: literature continued in the old grooves and for this very reason became largely stereotyped and lifeless. But new influences were coming to prevail even among the conservative ecclesiastics into whose hands literature had fallen in those difficult times, and already we can trace the beginning of a new attitude.

We see a change in the allegory as treated by Hawes in his *Pastime of Pleasure* (1506). This poem is a thorough mix-up of courtly allegory, romantic adventure, bourgeois satire, and religious didacticism. The hybrid in literature is nearly always a prelude to a new synthesis. But Hawes is still mediæval in spirit: he represents a man not very sure of his place in society trying to make sure that he will appeal to *somebody* by using in combination almost all the known literary themes and modes. We see from Hawes that literature has not yet found its feet again after Chaucer, not yet rediscovered its place and function, and is still largely didactic in purpose. Yet we note an enlargement of scope that holds promise.

The new bourgeoisie was not a class of idealists: it had, in fact, at this stage no ideals at all. Its attitude to most things was negative, and it thought of little but commercial prosperity and financial power. At first the humbler (and the more vocal) elements of this class expressed their antagonism to the old social order in crude and often ribald satire of everything for which the old order stood—the Church (in its institutional, not its theological, aspect), the feudal ideas of chivalry and courtly love, military ardour, loyalty, idealism of every kind. This new satiric impulse carries on many of the older mediæval satiric modes, but with a new content. Its most valuable feature is its contact with life—low life, as a rule, in reaction against the effete and artificial courtly tradition (which was to come alive again later, nevertheless, under new stimuli), but real life, however exaggerated and however interlarded with stock figures of fun. This satire gets mixed up with other influences, so that in a poet like Skelton (*c.* 1460-1529) we get coarse—and most effective—realism together with satire of the court and of the " new learning." And as the Renaissance comes to England via Italy we get new methods of satire, as well as new themes. Alexander Barclay (*c.* 1475-1552) brings in the eclogue as a vehicle for satire (from ancient Rome, ultimately, but via contemporary Italy) as well as a more rollicking idea from Germany—the ship of fools. And as the national State with its national king and its new national polity becomes established, we find the king's court beginning to replace abuses of the Church as a stock object of satire. From Skelton to Spenser and Donne the folly—if not worse—of court life is lashed directly and indirectly.

With the establishment of ordered government under Henry VII the threads begin to tie up. The middle class acquires some ideals and some education. A new kind of " courtliness " is evolved, to which the new social order contributes. Economic individualism and the spirit of self-seeking acquire an idealism in which to root' themselves. The country, however, was not to settle down into a period of economic peace. The new class who replaced the old feudal landholders were if anything more unscrupulous in dealing with their tenants than their predecessors. We hear little more of villeinage, and the right of the labourer to work for whatever wage he can get is no longer contested, but we begin to hear for the first time of rackrenting. As Latimer put it, addressing the landlords in one of his sermons, " That which herebefore went for twenty or forty pounds by year—which is an honest portion to be had gratis in one lordship of another man's sweat and labour—now is let for fifty or a hundred by year." Under the feudal system the landlord had at least some responsibility to his tenants, and he could not take more out of them than was fixed by custom. The new class was bound by nothing save financial expediency. A much greater cause of economic discontent was the increasing habit of enclosing land for sheep pasture. Wool was becoming an increasingly profitable product, and arable farming less profitable. The peasants who were turned off their farms as a result of this movement had great difficulty in finding other employment, and right throughout the sixteenth century, in spite of a certain amount of opposition to enclosures on the part of the State, this problem was acute. The change in the rural economy of England was not completed till the eighteenth century, with the disappearance, for all practical purposes, of the yeoman freeholder.

But these movements went on below the surface, and did not affect those who took part in the literary revival which we generally attribute to the Renaissance. English literature is, in fact, becoming increasingly written by Londoners for Londoners. The courtier, the citizen, the 'prentice, the groundling—these are the types with which we are most familiar in Elizabethan literature. Civilisation and culture are coming to be concentrated more and more in the capital, and literary men feel exiled outside London. Consequently the relation of literature to society is the relation of literature to *urban* society, whereas literature in a feudal organisation does not come into contact with urban elements at all until quite a late stage.

There were many forces making for the social synthesis which rendered possible a new efflorescence of literature. The barriers of the mediæval world were breaking down, in the physical as well as in the intellectual sphere. With the growth of commerce, men travelled about more. Even ordinary citizens made short journeys fairly near home to an extent unknown in earlier times. And on a larger scale there were the great explorers driven by commercial interests to discover new trade routes. Though the impetus behind the discoveries was provided by the exigencies of trade in a Europe seeking an escape in the west from the encroachments of the east, their results had repercussions on every kind of activity. This increase of movement and widening of outlook acted as a kind of solvent which dissolved a great deal of the lumber which had come down from an earlier social system. On the intellectual side, there was the flood of new ideas coming in from Italy and the Continent generally. The "revival of learning," the widening of intellectual interests and breakdown of intellectual barriers, transformed western culture. Travel played its part here, too. Young men went abroad, to France and Italy, to complete their education, and brought back new fashions not only in clothes but also in art and literature. Gradually the new influences were defined, the new activities were organised, and the new world took shape.

CHAPTER II

THAT COMPLEX MOVEMENT we call the Renaissance presents the historian with a bewildering number of aspects. To attempt even a definition would be hazardous, and for that we shall refer the reader to those history text-books where bold simplification is employed in the interests of clarity and coherence. We must confine ourselves only to certain aspects of the movement, though even then we shall have to simplify and generalise if we are to see any pattern at all in the life and work of men at this time. With the decay of the mediæval world almost every kind of human activity becomes less strictly defined, less uniform, and more multifarious; and in describing any movement we have increasingly to make allowances for exceptions and irregularities. Both the physical and the mental world have become larger and more heterogeneous.

The Renaissance was, of course, the rediscovery of Latin and Greek culture, the opening out of men's minds to embrace fresh ideas and engage in novel speculations, the desire to explore both new ways of thought and new continents, the break-up of the exclusiveness of the mediæval Church, and many other things besides. Already at the end of the fifteenth century these new influences were making themselves felt and by the middle of the sixteenth it is a new world that faces us. Perhaps the one feature of this new world which might be isolated and regarded as the most characteristic is its individualism. This individualism is seen in three quite distinct spheres—the economic, the artistic and the religious. The rise of the new bourgeoisie which we have noted at the end of the last chapter is responsible for the growth of economic individualism: the influence of the Church on " business ethics " began to wane rapidly, and the conception of individual profit-making as something quite justifiable and valuable with no connection with religious ideas at all gradually grows up. Eventually it leads to the view that money-making is good or bad according to the character of the person who is employed in it, so that a " good " man could amass wealth to the greater glory of God: but this is not articulate until the eighteenth century. The mediæval idea that it is fundamentally immoral to buy in the cheapest and sell in the dearest market is disappearing. Artistic individualism, if we may use the phrase, is seen in the new desire to write poetry for the expression of purely personal emotions, and in the new view of a work of art as something which will perpetuate the fame of the artist for all time.[1] Individual noblemen began to write and sing their own poems; everyone of any education was anxious to show what he could do and produce a personal work. The writer's immediate audience was his personal friends among whom he circulated the products of his inspiration (shunning, for a time, the

[1] This is a new attitude in English literature but not, of course, new in the history of literature generally (every schoolboy knows Horace's lines " exegi monumentum ære perennius "). Throughout this essay " new " must be taken to mean " not known—or at least not general—in the earlier periods of that European culture which began with the end of the dark ages." Classical literature lies outside our scope.

new and vulgar printing press as an ungentlemanly apparatus) and his ultimate audience was posterity. In spite of great individual artists like Chaucer, mediæval literature was essentially anonymous. It was the handling of common material in a manner more or less fixed by tradition. We do not know, for example, the names of the authors of the mediæval narrative romances. But with the coming of Renaissance influences this tradition of anonymity disappears, and we get both the desire for self-expression and the desire for personal fame. Finally, individualism in religious matters is seen in many of the aspects of the Reformation which is, from one point of view, the setting up of individual judgment against an ecclesiastical tradition. The search for personal salvation that we find carried on with such intensity by seventeenth-century Puritans represents religious individualism at its most extreme.

It is in the work of young noblemen moving in the court circle that the new movement shows its first authentic literary products. Thus the beginnings of Renaissance literature in England are courtly in a new sense. With the Tudors court life became an important social phenomenon, influencing all the bright young people of the day. Mediæval courtly poetry was the work of professional writers; the gentlemen who moved in the court of Henry VIII regarded writing as an accomplishment which every well-bred young man ought to possess. Men like Sir Thomas Bryan, Lord Vaux, Lord Rochford, and—two greater names—Sir Thomas Wyatt and the Earl of Surrey are poets of this new type. Writing poetry is for them a mere side-line in an active and often dangerous life. Yet these men took even their pastimes seriously. Contemptuous of the mediæval tradition they turned with eagerness and enthusiasm to every new source that was available to them. They sought inspiration in Italy, in France, and in the Latin and Greek classics. They experimented in new forms and new metres. Just as, two centuries earlier, Chaucer, under French influence, " refined " English poetry and brought into his versification an ease and suppleness hitherto lacking in English literature, so these men, under Italian and French influence, sought once again to discipline the language which had changed so much since Chaucer's day that his achievement had to be undertaken anew.

With literature being practised amid the bustle of court life the tendency to idealise the countryside as a place of pleasing retirement where the simple and virtuous life could be led comes into prominence. We see it in Wyatt's satires and even more in Surrey. This strain derives largely from Horace, with his praise of the life of the country gentleman, but it soon joins up with the tradition of the Greek and Latin pastoral which had already made itself felt in English, coming via France and Italy. The pastoral tradition of the idealisation of the countryside remains a force in English literature reaching its height of artificiality in the first half of the eighteenth century. Once literature becomes anchored to urban life the country becomes an escape, an antidote, an idea representing all the primal simplicity of life that has vanished with the coming of a sophisticated civilisation. Wherever the pastoral exists as a conscious literary form we may be sure that literature is confined to cities. Earlier literature, which was not exclusively urban, never thought of idealising the countryside and its inhabitants: one does not feel home-sick for the place where one is living.[1]

A feature of sixteenth-century poetry was the miscellany, an anthology of poems by different contemporary authors. We nearly always find such anthologies in an age of experiment and new ideas—we might compare some contemporary publications. In the first of these anthologies, *Tottel's Miscellany* (1557), we have a good selection of the different types of literature that are coming into favour. The tone of the book is courtly and "occasional," that is, the poems are not so much objective studies of great themes as verses thrown off on particular occasions in particular moods. Yet there is a certain stiffness about most of the poems which shows that they are still largely exercises in a not too familiar mode; the ease that comes with complete mastery of form and content is not yet apparent.

This is the literature of a class, written by and for the court circle. Its themes were chiefly love, court life, and the countryside (in the pastoral manner). The courtly love of the Middle Ages had undergone a change. In Italy, Dante and Petrarch had refined the whole conception, bringing it into relation with religion and divine love. Dante's love for Beatrice leads him, under the guidance of Beatrice herself, to God in whom all love is made perfect. The religious language which had

[1] The reader may cite Wordsworth against this truism, but Wordsworth's idealisation of the country was something totally different: it was not a conventional idealisation of what he had not got and perhaps really did not want (as the pastoral tradition tends to be) but a philosophic interpretation of what he knew and loved.

been used of love in the courtly romances almost by way of parody is here taken seriously: the spiritual side of love is quite dissociated from the physical. And later, with the influence of neo-Platonism, again coming from Italy, the idea that earthly love is merely an embodiment of the Idea of divine love contributes its spiritualising influence on the whole conception of the relations between men and women. But it took a single-minded genius like Dante to make the transition from the physical to the spiritual with perfect confidence and without any sense of unresolved conflict. Other poets —even Petrarch himself—could not look on the matter with such intense simplicity, and the conflict between the *Romance of the Rose* and the *Divine Comedy* is visible in English literature until the end of the seventeenth century, by which time a satisfactory, if on some views rather shoddy, compromise had been attained. We see the conflict in Sidney, in Spenser, in Donne and in many others. Sometimes the poet, after idealising love and celebrating his mistress, breaks off and exclaims, as Sidney did:

> *Leave me, O love which reachest but to dust;*
> *And thou, my mind, aspire to higher things.* ...

The bridge between earthly and eternal love often breaks down, and the whole courtly love tradition in the fifteenth and sixteenth centuries is in rather a confused state. But amid this confusion we can trace the dissociation of romantic love from adultery and its grafting on to the conception of marriage, which is so important for literature and for society.

Already in the *Kingis Quair* by James I of Scotland

F3

(1393-1437), we see the goal of courtly love regarded as marriage. This poem is written (or supposed to be written, if we disallow the authorship of James) by a husband celebrating his courtship of his wife. We can see at once how far removed this is from the idealisation of adultery embodied in the Rose tradition. Even in Lydgate (1375-1449) there are traces of a linking up of ideal love and marriage, and by the time of Hawes's *Pastime of Pleasure* (1506) it is quite definite. But Spenser's *Faerie Queene* (begun in the 1580's and left unfinished at his death in 1599) is the first major work of English literature where the association of romantic love with marriage is emphasised. Yet Spenser's romantic love is not entirely the courtly love of the *Romance of the Rose*, for Spenser treats also of a false kind of love which he shows up in his allegory as vicious and harmful, and it is this false love which belongs more directly to the Rose tradition. The true love of Spenser is a compound of many different elements—the spiritual side of the old courtly love (for it did have its spiritual side),[1] the conceptions of Dante and of Petrarch, the neo-Platonism of Ficino, the Puritanism of Cartwright—and in many ways is a literary curiosity. We have to wait some time yet before we find romantic love linked with marriage with

[1] If I may be allowed a minor criticism of one whose knowledge and understanding of the whole history of courtly love (as of literature generally) is so much greater than mine, I would suggest that Mr. C. S. Lewis, in holding that Spenser definitely rejects the idea of love " as understood by the traditional French novel or by Guillaume de Lorris " (*Allegory of Love*, p. 341), momentarily forgets that courtly love had two sides; it had its spiritual side, its conception of service for its own sake, and it was this side that Dante heightened and spiritualised and Spenser reconciled with marriage. Spenser rejects one side only of the courtly love tradition, splitting it clearly in two and showing up the evil part.

a more solid foundation in life and practical morality.

It was the Puritan writers of the seventeenth century who removed all the sophisticated clap-trap from the courtly love tradition and made romantic love, in its simple, more natural form, fit to be associated by the ordinary man with marriage. " This simpler, more natural, popular, or bourgeois love-poetry has nothing in it of the metaphysical strain of courtly love-poetry, of the high duties of patience and sleeplessness and secrecy and the avoidance of ' villainy,' or still less of the transcendental doctrines of the mystical identity of love and the relation of spiritual to sensuous love, or of the cynical reactions from these extravagances. But it was a conception of love which might be reflected on and developed by those who, while condemning the extravagances of Petrarcan worship and the sensuality of Latin poetry, classical and of the Revival of Learning, were not at all inclined to an ascetic exaltation of virginity. Puritans could be lovers like other people. Mrs. Hutchinson tells the story of her wooing with a naïve and somewhat priggish vanity. And there were Puritan love-poets."[1]

These Puritan love-poets, like George Wither and the great Milton himself (for Milton had a great deal to say about love) tie up love with marriage once and for all. And so we come to the conception that romantic love in itself is neither good nor bad, but can be either according to the aim in view. Combined with marriage romantic love is a good thing; outside marriage it is bad. We shall see later how this conception becomes

[1] H. J. C. Grierson, *Cross Currents in English Literature of the Seventeenth Century* (London, 1929), p. 148.

vulgarised until, in the latter half of the eighteenth century, we have in the novels of Samuel Richardson a view of love and marriage which amounts to little more than a recommendation to young ladies to sell their virginity in the dearest market.

We make no apology for spending so much time on the history of love in literature because, at this period at any rate, love in one or other of its aspects is easily the most popular of literary subjects, except perhaps in the drama. And the history of the literary treatment of this commonest of human sentiments can throw some light on the social conventions of the time— though we must be careful here to distinguish between those works which are bred from literature and those that are bred, at least in part, from life. Obviously, once the feudal conditions which produced the courtly love of the troubadours and of the Rose tradition had passed away this conception would be bound to change. The decay of feudalism, the rise of the middle classes (by which is meant the adequately nourished townsfolk and the trading communities), and the growth of Puritanism altered both society and men's view of society. One might see in the new attitude to love and marriage another aspect of the rise of individualism which we have discussed, but perhaps that would be to see too simple a pattern in events. But there can be little doubt that the practice of commerce tends to give men a vulgarly realistic outlook on life, and that a " nation of shopkeepers " faced with an artificial and sophisticated tradition such as the mediæval idea of courtly love will *either* abandon it altogether *or* seek to rid it of its more artificial elements preparatory to grounding it on material facts. That the conception of romantic love was not altogether abandoned seems to be due simply to the fact that it had sunk too deeply into the emotional life of at least one section of the people. There is no economic reason why the conception of love that prevailed in ancient Greece and Rome should not have returned. But the romantic conception of love had, for all its artificialities and stupidities, touched a new chord in the human heart, reached out to a new deepening of human experience, which could not be easily forgotten. The Provençal poets had stumbled on something greater than they knew, and their legacy, however altered in the course of its transmission down the generations, looks like being a permanent one. For, even with the rise of psycho-analysis and the knowledge it brings of the processes at work when one "falls in love," it does not appear that romantic love is going to die completely. At least, a view of contemporary fiction would not suggest that.

But we have wandered far from the young noblemen at the court of Henry VIII who circulated their verses in manuscript among their friends. The new outburst of literature which their work heralded is seen in all its richness in the latter half of the sixteenth century. New influences kept constantly coming in. The Petrarcan modification of the courtly love tradition, with its idealisation and conflict, obtained a firm hold on the minds of poets, and much subsequent literature is development of and then reaction against this. With Platonism and Puritanism, too, a new seriousness came into literature, while at the same time a light-hearted lyrical impulse was encouraged by the gay life of the court and the increasing prosperity of the country. These movements became more pronounced under Elizabeth. The national State, now stabilised and rooted in popular feeling, fostered a nationalism both in citizen and courtier which added the motive of national pride to the existing stimuli that helped to produce literary work. English was a language in which everything that had been done in other languages could and must be achieved at least as successfully. The Italian poets, Boiardo and Ariosto and Tasso, were read and admired, and the Italian romantic epic became another model for the zealous English poet. Spenser wrote his *Faerie Queene* in an endeavour to "overgo" the *Orlando Furioso* of Ariosto.

And with Spenser we may pause, to consider what his great unfinished allegory has to tell us of the relation between literature and society in his day. A consideration of Spenser's work is likely to be particularly profitable because it embraces so many traditions and embodies so many influences. It sums up, as well as any single work can, one aspect of the Renaissance in England. It is only one aspect, because Spenser is a courtly poet writing for the court, and is out of touch with the popular literature which maintains a separate and parallel existence at this time. Literature at the end of the sixteenth century is quite clearly divided into two classes, of which one is the work of the cultured, serious poets and is, socially speaking, the descendant of the courtly literature of the Middle Ages, and the other is the work of hacks and playwrights and its ancestors are the popular amusements of bear-baiting and cock-fighting. As Chaucer combined the two traditions in his day, so Shakespeare combined the two in his; but Spenser had his eyes fixed on the court and his work is narrower in scope. Yet even so it illustrates a fusion of different traditions to an extent that no other single work of the time does: the Middle Ages, the Renaissance and the Reformation all meet in the *Faerie Queene*.

The mediæval view of society exists as a vague background to Spenser's thought. The conception of the community as rigidly divided up in a hierarchy of which each grade has its own special function can be seen right through his work. He was not aware—nor could he have been expected to be—of the new social forces developing around him. He also inherited the tradition of mediæval courtly allegory, though by now greatly modified under Italian and classical influences. The second strain in his thought is the humanism that came with the Renaissance. Humanism does not imply only the study of Latin and Greek literature: it has its wider aspect, denoting also " a due respect for human nature in all its fullness (therefore including our natural desires and instincts) as distinguished from the claims of the divine, of the other-worldly, religious inhibitions when the latter are exaggerated so as to overshadow the former unduly or entirely."[1] This interest in the free play of the human spirit, this joy in light and colour and sound, this enthusiastic desire to make full use of all the faculties of mind and body, was a feature of the court of Elizabeth, and it was at the court that Spenser became infected with the humanist spirit. But before he came into contact with court life

[1] H. J. C. Grierson, *Cross Currents*, p. xi.

the very different spirit of the Reformation had also exerted its influence on him. At Cambridge he had come into contact with the Puritan preacher Thomas Cartwright, and his high seriousness and other-worldliness had touched another side of Spenser's nature and left a permanent mark upon him. Spenser, therefore, was tempted at once to renounce the world and to glory in it, and he compromised in the *Faerie Queene* by using the allegorical form where eternal truths could be conveyed indirectly in rich poetic language with all the sensuous resources at his command. In allegory the message of the Reformation could be delivered through the means discovered by the Renaissance. So Spenser composes his ambitious tale of knights and fair ladies, of trials and combats, of wanderings and halts by the wayside, of giants and sorceresses and heroes and princesses. And if to the modern reader the means seem to obscure the end, that is partly because we have lost the habit of allegory and partly because the conflict in Spenser's own mind was never quite resolved and the world of sense was always getting the upper hand of the spirit.

With all these new influences pouring in on English culture and society the predominant desire of thinking men of the time was to stabilise things, to define their ideals and determine how they might be realised. And so we get a great interest in education, which is already visible in Hawes's *Pastime of Pleasure*. Writers concern themselves with the right method of training a gentleman, and we get " courtesy books " and all kinds of educational tracts. Spenser's aim in writing the *Faerie Queene* is best set forth in the words of his letter to Sir Walter Raleigh:

" The general end of all the book is to fashion a gentleman or noble person in virtuous and gentle discipline: which for that I conceived should be most plausible and pleasing, being coloured with an historical fiction, the which the most part of men delight to read, rather for variety of matter, than for profit of the ensample, I chose the history of King Arthur as most fit for the excellency of his person, being made famous by many men's former works, and also furthest from the danger of envy and suspicion of present time. In which I have followed all the antique poets historical, first Homer, who in the persons of Agamemnon and Ulysses hath ensampled a good governor and a virtuous man, the one in his Ilias, the other in his Odysseis; then Virgil, whose like intention was to do in the person of Æneas; after him Ariosto comprised them both in his Orlando; and lately Tasso dissevered them again and formed both parts in two persons, namely that part which they in philosophy call Ethice, or virtues of a private man, coloured in his Rinaldo, the other named Politice in his Godfredo. By ensample of which excellent poets I labour to portray in Arthur before he was king the image of a brave knight perfected in the twelve private moral virtues as Aristotle hath devised, the which is the purpose of these first twelve books. . . . "

We see here two important features of Renaissance literature—the educational aim, and imitation of classical and Italian literature.

Spenser was concerned with the education of gentlemen only. However much he may be tempted on occasions to praise the simple and virtuous life of the country swain, he remains at heart a courtier and a snob. It is curious that at a time when the old nobility had almost completely died out and the existing noblemen were all fairly recent creations with bourgeois antecedents Spenser should have laid so much stress on gentle birth (he was anxious to vaunt his connection with the Spencers of Althorp, which seems to have been very remote), but he had no clear insight into the social conditions of his time. His eyes were fixed on an ideal past, which he was always liable to identify with the present. Chaucer had fixed his eyes on real men without worrying whether they satisfactorily performed their duties in society; Spenser, on the other hand, contemplated ideal men and worried very much whether they performed their duties in the ideal society he created for them. Yet the social background of the *Faerie Queene* is not wholly unreal, and behind the castles and woods and plains we get an occasional glimpse of Elizabethan society as it must have appeared to Spenser. And in Book V of the *Faerie Queene* especially we see Spenser's ideas about the nature of society and of social justice.

Spenser spent a great deal of his life in Ireland, where the Tudors were then busy holding down the first of England's colonies. He went out in 1590 as private secretary to Lord Grey of Wilton, just appointed Lord Deputy of Ireland, a man who " set himself with unflinching sternness to execute his conception of duty," as a modern critic puts it. What " unflinching sternness " meant to an Elizabethan nobleman governing an unruly country for the benefit of his own class at home can be imagined. "Through the length and breadth of Ireland he passed like a scourge, hanging and mutilating the rebels, burning the crops, reducing the wretched inhabitants to surrender by the terror of famine and the sword."[1] Spenser represented the English official class, with their imperialist aims and thorough methods, and he supported Lord Grey's policy whole-heartedly. He wrote a *View of the Present State of Ireland* defending Grey and explaining the best method of " reducinge that salvage nacion to better gouerment and cyvillitie," and in the fifth book of the *Faerie Queene* he gives us the adventures of Sir Artegall, representing Justice and Lord Grey.

Sir Artegall's adventures are instructive, for they show us the other side of the idealist Elizabethan gentleman. But we have space only to refer to Sir Artegall's dealings with the giant whom he meets sitting on a rock preaching communism. The giant has " a huge great paire of ballance in his hand " and he boasts:

That all the world he would weigh equallie,
If ought he had the same to counterpoys.

As a result of his preaching equality " the vulgar did about him flock . . . in hope by him great benefit to gain," and this is too much for our noble knight, who reproaches the giant for endeavouring to weigh the world anew and " all things to an equal to restore " and after an argument in which " the righteous Artegall " is unable to convince the giant that equality is wicked, he sends his iron-clad page Talus to cleave

[1] E. de Selincourt, Introduction to Oxford edition of Spenser's *Poetical Works*, p. xxiv.

the giant from the rock and cast him into the sea (Artegall gets most of his dirty work done for him by Talus), and the poor giant is battered to pieces against the cliff before he falls in mangled fragments into the water. The deluded multitude show signs of resenting the death of their hero, whereupon Talus mows them down with his flail. Artegall, after watching Talus dispose of the " raskall rout " turns away and strolls to a neighbouring castle for a refreshing cup of tea, or its Elizabethan equivalent.

Such is Spenser's justice, waging ruthless war against those who attempt to destroy the existing social hierarchy. The Tudors having stabilised the State after years of civil war, the idea of order becomes fixed in men's minds as the basis of all other virtues. Again and again in Spenser we find stress laid on social order: we find it in Shakespeare, too. The commonest metaphor is taken from nature, where sea, land, and air each have their own proper place and chaos would ensue if they were to usurp one another's function. Like Langland, Spenser urges the common people to know their station. The new intellectual and social riches that the Renaissance brought were only for the nobleman, the gentleman:

> . . . *the brave courtier in whose noble thought*
> *Regard of honour harbours more than ought.*

The brave courtier—he runs right through Elizabethan literature. Sometimes he is contrasted with the upstart courtier, the man not really of gentle birth and breeding. Culture is the property of the aristocratic coterie; the court is the poet's only audience. When Spenser arrived at the court of Elizabeth in 1590 this spirit was at its height. Not only was there the queen's court, but individual noblemen had their own brilliant circles. Women, too, presided over literary coteries, and the Countess of Pembroke influenced nearly all the poets of the time, including Spenser, Ben Jonson, Daniel and Donne.

So Elizabethan courtly poetry moved in a glittering circle of its own, out of touch with popular life and lacking the invigorating influences of popular art. We weary of the innumerable sonnets written in the courtly Petrarcan vein, of classical imitations and polite exercises. We weary of high Platonic moralising, of transplanted Italian fashions and ideas, and of the number of flattering references to Queen Elizabeth. This terribly serious generation of aristocrats (whose credentials as regards noble blood could not have stood too great scrutiny) regarded themselves as educators and cultural pioneers, but they sought only to educate each other, and those who most needed education were required to know their place. We see in Sir Philip Sidney's *Arcadia* this same indifference to the working and peasant classes, the same cold contempt for the mob that Sir Artegall showed and that even Shakespeare sometimes displayed, though he was not confined to the courtly tradition. Poets could idealise the country dweller as a shepherd or piping rustic swain, but when they saw him in his pattern in society idealisation abruptly ceased. They might satirise the court and the evils of court life, but if they had to leave it they regarded themselves as going into exile.

This writing only for gentlemen infused a didactic

spirit into Elizabethan courtly literature. Critical theory at the time tended to regard the function of literature as a gilding of the moral pill. The poet's duty was to teach delightfully. As Sir Philip Sidney put it in his *Apologie for Poetrie*, " It is that fayning notable images of vertues, vices, or what els, with that delightful teaching, which must be the right describing note to know a poet by." He puts it even more clearly in a later passage: " For if it be as I affirme, that no learning is so good, as that which teacheth and mooveth to vertue; and that none can both teach and move thereto so much as Poetry: then is the conclusion manifest, that Incke and Paper cannot be to a more profitable purpose employed." This is no new theory; it goes back to the classics and it is found in the Middle Ages; in its essence it is a distortion of Aristotle's *Poetics*; but it is significant that at this time, the great budding-period of humanism in its wider sense, courtly English poets should have stressed the didactic function of literature. A closer acquaintance with popular feeling and popular forms of literature might have enabled them to evolve a more adequate literary theory, or at least one which fitted the facts better.

Spenser and the other courtly poets write as conscious representatives of their class, and when they allow us to see what is going on behind all the pageantry we are rather shocked. We do not feel the dualism so much in early mediæval courtly literature, for there the background of common life, when it does appear, is treated in a calmer and more matter-of-fact way. Early mediæval social theory was quite static, and, before the troubles of the fourteenth century, writers were not worried about the function of different classes: they took such matters quite for granted. But theories of government and of society were in the air at the time of the Tudors. The communist theories first seen in the preaching of John Ball at the time of the Peasants' Revolt had never been entirely disposed of, while the coming struggle between King and Parliament which was carried to its extreme point under the Stuarts was already foreshadowed in the interest in political theory which writers displayed at this time. There is therefore an argumentative and even militant note in the references to social conditions that we find in this literature. Like Langland, Spenser finds it necessary to defend the state of things against which some were murmuring: both writers find their solution in the restoration of the *status quo* when everyone would be content with his station in life and perform the function of his class. If this theory was already beginning to be out of date when Langland wrote, it represented a peculiar blindness on Spenser's part, for by his time wealth was coming to be the sole criterion of social status, and to talk of a preordained differentiation of function was nonsense. Shakespeare made enough money to settle down and buy a coat of arms for his family, and thus become a real gentleman. The glaring contradiction between the antiquated theories of " gentilesse " put forward by the Elizabethan courtly poets and the facts of contemporary society is patent to the later historian looking back on events, though it was not so easy for the poets themselves to see it. The glitter of the Elizabethan court diverted men's attention from an examination of the facts of social history.

But there was another besides the courtly tradition in Elizabethan literature. The drama, which grew to maturity within a generation, had twin roots, one of which was the crudest kind of popular entertainment. The development of the drama from the crude miracle and morality plays of the Middle Ages—where biblical stories and primitive moral allegories were simply conveyed—to its maturity with Shakespeare is one of the most interesting and illuminating chapters of literary history, linking up as it does with so many other aspects of the life and thought of the time. With the Renaissance came the direct imitation of the Latin plays of Seneca, and a serious, learned drama arose side by side with the popular moralities. The scholarly drama was stilted and boring and left to itself must have proved sterile, or at the most productive of another artificial, courtly type of literature. But fortunately the two traditions amalgamated—the popular tradition, going far back into the Middle Ages and connected with every kind of vulgar amusement, and the self-consciously learned Senecan convention, a product of the Revival of Learning. We cannot pause to dwell in any detail on the development of the drama after this amalgamation; we can only note that with Marlowe (1564-1593) came at once a richness in the handling of blank verse and a passionate interest in certain types of character, and then Shakespeare broadened the whole basis of the drama both as regards form and content so that it became a vehicle for treating poetically the most diverse aspects of human experience.

The popular tradition that gave so much vitality to

the drama was essentially an urban one. The citizen, the 'prentice and the rabble constituted a large part of the audience at an Elizabethan play. But it was not they alone who supported the drama. As well as public theatres, such as the Globe, there were private theatres frequented by court circles only, where more sophisticated and learned plays were put on. But the public theatres are the more important, for their audiences included both court gallants and town riff-raff, as well as young men from the inns of court representing the professional classes. As Sir Herbert Grierson has pointed out, the idle rich and the idle poor generally have many tastes in common, and the audience at an Elizabethan theatre might be compared with the attendance at a race-course to-day.[1]

We can blame the groundlings of the Elizabethan theatre for much of the triviality and playing to the gallery that we find in even the best of Elizabethan drama, but we must not forget that it was its roots in popular tradition that gave it that remarkable vitality which distinguished drama from other forms of literature at this time. The courtly poets alone could not have produced a living drama. The growing number of Puritans regarded the drama and all forms of entertainment as the Devil's work, to be avoided by all men who sought salvation. The Puritan community of London, which was large, made continued attacks on the theatre and did to some extent succeed in hampering its developing even before the theatres were closed by Parliament in 1642. It was the ordinary city populace that made the art of a Shakespeare possible,

[1] *Cross Currents*, p. 173.

in the sense that they gave it opportunities for development on its own lines which both courtiers and Puritans would have denied.

If we look in the Elizabethan drama for light on the social conditions of the time we are likely to be disappointed. The "Romantic" drama of Shakespeare (1564–1616) is not concerned with the direct influence of social conditions on human behaviour. Shakespeare's aim is to deal with aspects of human experience which cut across social divisions and social problems: if the fashion is for characters in a play to be kings and princes he will cheerfully make them kings and princes, because he is concerned with those aspects of their behaviour which are independent of social position. Had his achievement been less "universal" and his dramatic ability less overwhelming his apparent complacent acceptance of the social conventions of the time might have hampered him. Or, to look at the question in another way: Shakespeare's aim was, *given* such and such social conditions and conventions, to show how people would behave when faced with certain fundamental human problems. Whenever people live, they are bound to work within a certain social framework, and no writer can be blamed for portraying his characters within a given framework; still less can he be blamed when in doing so he lays his finger on permanent and universally recognised aspects of experience and human nature. If the writer allows his class prejudice to distort the facts of life which he is endeavouring to record, if, for example, he portrays the rich as invariably virtuous and the poor as invariably vicious (to put it very crudely for simplicity's sake), he is to be blamed, and the critic must apply his knowledge of social conditions of the time as a corrective. But with Shakespeare this does not happen: there are occasions when he puts into the mouths of his characters distortions of fact due to class prejudice, but, in the first place, these passages are never long or important enough to affect the tone of his work, and secondly, they are not uttered by the author himself but by the character speaking in accordance with his nature as the dramatist portrays it. The dramatist, if he has any genius at all, is least likely to fall into the traps that await writers who have class prejudices, because his method enables him to record with complete objectivity what he sees, letting the characters speak for themselves. However much we may disapprove of monarchy as an institution, no one can deny the interest and importance of knowing what an actual king does and feels and thinks, and if in addition the portrayal of the actions, thoughts, and emotions of the king reaches out to certain fundamental aspects of human experience, the resultant work is of artistic as well as psychological importance.

But in the lesser Elizabethan and Jacobean dramatists we can see the influence of social conditions at work. Ben Jonson (1573–1637), portraying stock types of human folly, makes his contribution to "citizen comedy," and in a play like *Bartholomew Fair* we have all the swarming life of London spread out before us. There are other playwrights who deal more simply and directly with London life at the time. Of these Thomas Middleton (*c.* 1570–1627) is important as illustrating (in his comedies) a transition to a more bourgeois society—a transition "between the aristocratic world which preceded the Tudors and the plutocratic world which the Tudors initiated and encouraged."[1] " In the Tudor times birth still counted (though nearly all the great families were extinct); by the time of Charles II only breeding counted. The comedy of Middleton ... is intermediate ... Middleton marks the transitional stage in which the London tradesman was anxious to cease to be a tradesman and become a country gentleman."[1] Eventually the citizen, instead of aping the nobility, becomes proud of being what he is.

This " citizen comedy " has its counterpart in prose writing in the pamphlets of Greene, Nashe, and others. This type of literature has something in common with the *fabliau* of mediæval times, for, like the *fabliau*, it is coarse, realistic, and often satiric and humorous. It is in the main the work of educated young men who have not got on in the world; sons of poor tradesmen or professional men who have ambitions to climb in the world of letters but who have not been able to make much out of their work. Living in poor circumstances, they come into contact with the colourful low life of the city, and in their more exuberant moods they give us extraordinarily vivid pictures of the lower strata of London life. Sometimes these writings are personal and polemical, like Greene's *Groat's-worth of Wit*; sometimes they are fiction, like Nashe's *Unfortunate Traveller*; sometimes fierce satires like the same

---

[1] T. S. Eliot, *Elizabethan Essays* (Faber Library, 1934), p. 98. Mr. Eliot takes his points about Middleton from the thesis put forward by Miss Kathleen Lynch in her book *The Social Mode of Restoration Drama*.

writer's *Pierce Penilesse*. And just as we have the courtly and the popular strains in the drama, so we have both in fiction, and Thomas Lodge's *Rosalynde* is an example of what the courtly strain in fiction produced at this time. This was written in the Euphuistic tradition begun by John Lyly's *Euphues*, written in a highly artificial balanced style. Sidney's *Arcadia* is another of the courtly prose stories which shows the lengths in artificiality of style and matter to which an idealistic soldier-courtier could go under the influence of the Renaissance and the Elizabethan court.

The courtly writers were gentlemen who regarded literature as a polite accomplishment, but the dramatists and the realistic pamphlet writers were professionals, for whom literature was a means of earning a living. It would be interesting for those who maintain that the amateur is the type of artist who produces the greatest work to compare the work of Shakespeare, a professional dramatist and actor, with that of, say, Sir Philip Sidney or even Spenser, whose literary work was done in moments of leisure in an active life. Sidney was a soldier and a courtier; Spenser was an upper-class civil servant. But the status of the professional writer varies greatly in different times. Chaucer was in a position comparable to that of Spenser, yet he was not out of touch with popular life as Spenser was. It is difficult to lay down general rules as to when a writer can write best.

Just as Chaucer's successors lost that synthesis of courtly and popular which gave such a richness of quality to the *Canterbury Tales*, so the Jacobean and Caroline dramatists retired one by one to a world of their own until by the time of closing of the theatres in 1642 an extraordinary degree of artificiality and decadence had been reached. One reason for this was that, with Puritan opposition growing in the cities, the drama became more and more the exclusive interest of the courtly groups, and the aeration of popular art was again lost. Sentimentality, sophistication, conventionalisation—we see these faults already in the plays of Beaumont and Fletcher. Later playwrights show the same tendencies, and the decline went on—in spite of brilliant incidental flashes—until the Puritans, taking advantage of the Parliamentary victory over the King, administered the final blow. This increase in unreality, in flippancy, in melodramatic subtlety and dramatic artificiality, which brought the decline, was also due to a certain inbreeding among the dramatists. But, " after all, the blame does not rest entirely with the dramatists. Those must bear their share who, by their intransigent fanaticism, their preoccupation with high doctrines of eternal decrees and imputed righteousness, would not allow them to give to this great national tradition a larger scope and higher purpose."[1]

In addition to the courtly poets, the dramatists and the pamphleteers (the last two were often the same people), there existed another class of writers at this time—those who had studied at the universities or the inns of court and had come in contact with the courtly tradition without accepting it. Some of the dramatists were of this class, sons of tradesmen or of professional men who tried to rise into the court circle through

[1] H. J. C. Grierson, *Cross Currents*, p. 129.

their reputation as wits or as men of letters. Ben Jonson, beginning life as a humble bricklayer, won his way through sheer erudition and ability and to the end scorned the court as well as the ignorant populace. Another, and a very different writer was John Donne (*c.* 1572–1631), the son of a prosperous London citizen: he also tried to work his way up by his learning and literary ability. We cannot pause to go into the lives and social background of these two writers; we have mentioned them because they represent, each in his own way, a reaction against the Petrarcan courtly love tradition which was long due. It was not a reaction from the popular side; popular literature was too much separated from this artificial literature to bother about it at all. It was a reaction from the side of learning and common sense in the case of Jonson, and of realistic passion in the case of Donne. These two men between them blew up the Spenserian tradition.

So long as culture and education were confined to court circles, the cultured and educated writer was bound to accept the conventions current in those circles. But when it was possible for outsiders to acquire all the learning and education possessed by the aristocracy, a revolt to realism and spontaneity was bound to come. The Renaissance had reached England through the pioneer work of courtly ambassadors like Wyatt and Surrey, but once it had come to stay others could use the material it brought for their own ends.

John Donne reacted against the conventions of courtly love literature in favour of a frank naturalism. He was interested in his own passions and experiences and put them into poetry with a vigour and a realism that is quite absent from earlier Tudor and Elizabethan love-poetry. " For God's sake hold your tongue and let me love!" he exclaims at the beginning of his poem *The Canonisation*, and this line is typical of one side of Donne's poetry. Donne had a learned and subtle mind, and he tended to express his ideas in far-fetched analogies and obscure, though supremely logical, images. But the aspect of his work that concerns us here is his naturalism. He did not shrink from describing as honestly and passionately as he could the varied moods of love, and his poems range from the cynical and sensual to the tense and impassioned. They are not easy poems; in expression they are often contorted and involved, for Donne could never forget his learning, both in mediæval philosophy (he was brought up as a Catholic) and in contemporary literature, yet this should not blind us to the fact that his work is, in one of its aspects, a protest against the Petrarcan and Spenserian tradition of the courtly poets. Donne is really concerned with the truth of his emotional experiences. He thus represents the liberating effect of coming to literature from outside the courtly tradition.

Ben Jonson reacted in a different way. Like Donne, he was learned, but his learning was more even and balanced. He knew the classics but was little concerned with the mediæval scholastic literature which had so much influence on Donne. His ideal was the classical one of moderation and good sense. He brought into his lyrics a calmness and sobriety lacking alike in Donne and in the courtly poets: he writes with ease and common sense. His poetry is courtly in a sense, for it is polished and graceful, yet it embodies none of the artificial conventions that the Petrarcan school of poets employed. It is significant that Jonson's verdict on Spenser, with his artificialities and archaisms of language, was that " Spenser writ no language."

So we see Donne, the educated, unattached individualist, and Jonson, the learned bourgeois, representing the non-courtly cultured elements among the writers of the time. Each in his own way rebelled against the Petrarcan-Spenserian tradition, and founded movements which were influential throughout the seventeenth century. The characteristics of Donne that were taken up by his imitators were not, however, his passionate realism and psychological frankness so much as his intellectual subtlety and ingenuity of metaphor; and thus he became the leader of the so-called " metaphysical " school of poetry. Ben Jonson's grace and polish was transmitted to the school of " Cavalier poets " (" sons of Ben " the earliest of these called themselves); but though their literary work was thus influenced by him, socially they were descendants of the Elizabethan courtly poets. The old courtly tradition having been blown up, later courtly poets turned to the new modes initiated by Jonson and Donne. The gentlemen poets who wrote in the seventeenth century combined the influences of these two. The later Cavalier poets were both " metaphysical " and Jonsonian; but they were never Spenserian. Spenserian influence went into two channels—allegory and pastoral, and in neither of these was anything of real importance produced at this period.

With the seventeenth century we enter on a period when the output of literature is so great and its character so diverse that in a brief study such as this no attempt at anything like a complete account is possible; we are endeavouring only to trace some kind of pattern in the literary activity of the time, and to illustrate by some particular examples the relation between literature and society. There are other aspects of the work of even those few writers whom we do discuss, and from the point of view of literary criticism these aspects may be more interesting and important. But we must limit discussion to those points which most forward our inquiry.

So we may turn from the Elizabethan and Jacobean scene to consider briefly the Civil War in its social and literary implications. In the Civil War, Puritanism, economic individualism, social progressiveness were all on the rebel side; but humanism in the wider sense, the belief in the free play of the human spirit in all its aspects, was on the side of the Royalists. The two currents which came in at the Renaissance, Puritanism and humanism, were separate from the beginning and antagonistic from a very early stage. We have seen how Spenser endeavoured to unite the two, but they were never united and time and again came into open conflict throughout the seventeenth century. Humanism sought refuge with the court, where leisure and education offered fertile soil in which it could flourish; Puritanism took roots among the urban trading classes and the freeholding yeomen. Thus those kinds of literature which we might call humanist—the graceful lyrical strain that the new courtly poets inherited from the learned bricklayer Ben Jonson, and the daring intellectual and emotional qualities which the " metaphysicals " got from Donne—were on the Cavalier side. But Donne in his later life was also a religious poet, and the " metaphysical " mode influenced the religious poetry of all sects, Catholic, Anglican, and Puritan alike, though mostly the first two. So the literature of the Puritans was not entirely composed of theological and controversial literature—though there was an enormous deal of that, and on the Anglican side as well —but it had its poets too. Yet on the whole we are justified—in spite of the special pleading for the Puritans put forward by some modern scholars—in the generalisation that humanism and the cultivation of the arts were on the Cavalier side. Milton, of course, is the great exception to this as to almost every other rule, but the egotism and individualism of Milton put him in a class quite by himself. Milton was on the Puritan side because he was anti-Royalist rather than because he was pro-Commonwealth. His theological and political ideas were all his own; so sensitive, in fact, was his individualism that every little incident that happened to him in his own life he used as material with which to erect a complete system of government and of morals. Milton fits into no pattern; all his thought derives from the particular circumstance of his own life. And in any case it is very doubtful if Milton could be called a humanist in the sense in which we are using the term: certainly, once his youth was over, his mind narrowed and his artistic sympathies contracted.

So, with the exception of Milton, the best poets of the

period found themselves on the Royalist side. Not that they were very clear about the issues at stake—they were not mere reactionaries or supporters of the divine right of kings. They were for the most part sensitive and talented writers to whom all that was of immediate concern was that the Puritans, with their practical economic interests and intellectual other-worldliness, held forth no encouragement to the artist, while the Cavaliers did. We must not forget that the greater part of non-dramatic literature had been associated with the court since the beginning of the sixteenth century. And though Jonson and Donne, representing non-courtly elements, reacted, each in his own way, against the courtly tradition as they found it, they did not break this association of literature with the aristocracy.

It might be asked why the industrial and commercial classes favoured Puritanism, and why the *fabliau* tradition that had come down from the Middle Ages and had so recently manifested itself in the prose writings of men like Nashe and Greene did not take root among the middle classes and produce a new realistic fiction. The connection of Puritanism with trade and commerce can be partly explained by the fact that the insistence on the uselessness of " good works " without prior " election " to grace, the emphasis on inner assurance rather than on outward shows of conduct, that were features of Puritan doctrine, paved the way for a complete divorce between religion and social and economic ethics, thereby liberating the business man to pursue a policy based on the view that " business is business " and enabling him to seek financial gain without troubling his conscience too much about the methods used. But this implication of Puritanism did not manifest itself till fairly late. " To contemporaries the chosen seat of the Puritan spirit seemed to be those classes in society which combined independence, education, and a certain decent pride in their status, revealed at once in their determination to live their own lives, without truckling to earthly superiors, and in a somewhat arrogant contempt for those who, either through weakness of character or through economic helplessness, were less resolute, less vigorous and masterful, than themselves. Such, where the feudal spirit had been weakened by contact with town life and new intellectual currents, were some of the gentry. Such, conspicuously, were the yeomen, especially in the freeholding counties of the east. Such, above all, were the trading classes of the towns, and of those rural districts which had been partially industrialised by the decentralisation of the textile and iron industries."[1] In time, however, it became clear that the Puritan attitude involved an attitude of *laissez faire* to social and economic problems. We can see now, looking back on history, that one aspect of the Reformation meant the withdrawal of the Church from any interest in and influence on social and economic life. The individualistic doctrine of the inner light and salvation by faith and election destroyed the conception of the Church as a universal institution with a right to control the relations of man to his neighbour in every sphere. This was by no means the intention of the early reformers, who—witness Calvin in Geneva—provided a more rigid and ubiquitous

[1] R. H. Tawney, *Religion and the Rise of Capitalism* (London, 1926), p. 202.

discipline than the mediæval Church ever contemplated. But in time the implications of the other side of the Reformation prevailed, until by the eighteenth century the activities of the Church were restricted to an unreal, theoretical, " spiritual " dominion which in practice meant nothing.

Puritanism once rooted in the trading classes, it was extremely unlikely that a new outburst of literature would arise from them. In the first place, Puritanism frowned on " entertainment " of every kind, and any but a severely didactic literature found little encouragement. We have already noted the attitude of Puritan London to the drama, and the closing of the theatres in 1642. Secondly, this class was still young and struggling for dominance; its energies were concentrated on purely practical matters, and it could as yet afford little leisure for the arts. The infant bourgeoisie of the Middle Ages had not yet embarked on the struggle, and the adult bourgeoisie of the eighteenth century had already emerged victorious; but in the sixteenth and seventeenth centuries the trading and business classes were on the offensive, and literature was frowned on as a distraction.

The Restoration of 1660 meant the failure of Puritanism as a political force, but not the decline of the class which sponsored it. The old Cavalier class, consisting mostly of the landed gentry, the country squires and landowners, realised that they were too weak and too few in numbers to regain their influence without some sort of alliance with the now powerful merchant class. Whatever the superficial evidence to the contrary, the Restoration did mean such an alliance. True,

Puritanism was persecuted for a time, but that was only to be expected in the reaction against the rule of the saints and the coming to power of the backward-looking Earl of Clarendon. The alliance between squire and trader held good until the beginning of the eighteenth century, by which time the landed gentry—represented by the Tory party—did not need, or thought they did not need, the help of merchants and financiers. In the meantime, economists preached religious toleration as being good for trade.

The immediate reaction of a society starved for nearly twenty years of all concessions to human frailty was towards licence and dissipation. The Cavaliers were back, enjoying an Indian summer in political alliance with a class that would share none of their pleasures or recreations. A sense of irresponsibility, of unreality, overtook the court and its hangers-on. Below the surface respectable citizens were busy carrying on trade and making money; on the top the returned exiles amused themselves by trying to re-create a lost world. There was thus something bogus about Restoration courtliness: it was not so much the product of the cultured leisure of the governing classes as a self-conscious attempt to create a society of gallantry and fashion. The type of activity popularly associated with the Restoration was something quite inorganic, deliberately superimposed on society rather than a spontaneous product of it.

It is not, then, at all surprising that that most social of all literary forms, the drama—for of course the theatre came into its own again with the political defeat of the saints—should at this time have been at once more artificial and more the self-conscious product of one class in society than it had been in the first half of the century. In tragedy, we have the Heroic Play, rhetorical, bombastic, preposterous: here the romantic courtly love tradition that descended from the Middle Ages reached its *reductio ad absurdum*; the romantic love of the eighteenth century is chastened and rationalised, and it is as though Restoration writers, aware of the inevitability of Queen Anne and the dominance of bourgeois morality, determined to have a final fling. In Restoration comedy we have a species that has become a by-word in text-books of literature for its flippant and cynical treatment of social problems. In tragedy the dramatist escaped from life; in comedy he remained in the society of his day but refused to treat it seriously.

The aristocracy, freed from the threat of "levellers" and equalitarian doctrines in politics and religion, were anxious to make their own lives distinctive for "elegance" and sophistication. They had to be different from the respectable bourgeoisie, whose habits they disliked and whose growing power they feared. But the aristocracy were no longer a genuine class at all; they were a hang-over from an earlier order, and had lost their integrity and function in society, the real rulers of which were rapidly coming to be a plutocracy embracing both the old upper and middle classes. So the attempt to produce a new aristocratic literature failed conspicuously. Gradually the bourgeois element penetrated. The first of the Restoration writers of comedy, Sir George Etherege (*c.* 1635–*c.* 1691), a man of brilliant wit, cynical worldly wisdom, and perfect elegance of manner, wrote his plays to amuse himself and his friends. He belonged to the society he wrote of. But William Wycherley (1640–1716), whose cynicism is even more pronounced, is looking at society from the outside: he is a realist, and paints a picture of an unscrupulous and selfish society striving to be " gallant," with such faithfulness that its hollowness is shown up by sheer observation. His almost brutal writing implies that there are other standards besides those implicit in the behaviour of his characters: Etherege was not brutal, because he saw nothing wrong and had no other standards. Congreve (1670–1729), the next in the line, is the most self-conscious of the Restoration dramatists. He is the professional writer catering for a taste and doing his work with superb technical skill (though he, like Etherege and others of the time, would not consider himself a professional writer, but a gentleman who wrote in his leisure). The society Congreve paints is already passing away; wit and gallantry and cynical irony have become literary fashions and the world described becomes an ideal one—it is, in a way, a wish-fulfilment world for the wits of the time. Perhaps this description could apply to the whole of Restoration comedy. It was not an aristocratic literature; the actual lives and opinions of the bourgeois majority put these writers on the defensive, while a true aristocratic literature is more spontaneous and unself-conscious.

So the attempt made at the Restoration to produce a new courtly life with its new courtly literature failed. Restoration tragedy was on the whole bombastic and stupid; Restoration comedy was brilliant enough, witty and cynical, yet turning out eventually to be coarse rather than courtly, brutal rather than polite, and, at bottom, empty, shallow, superficial. A graceful gallantry that is the reflection of something deeper in the life of the time—as, with all its faults, the mediæval ideal of chivalry and courtly love was—is born and not made, like a poet. It is born out of social conditions, and cannot be superimposed on conditions which are unfavourable. For the fact is that the self-conscious rakishness of this literature represented neither the will of society nor the real state of society. What people really wanted after all the troubles and upheavals of the century was peace and quiet, not debauchery and swashbuckling. The court of Charles II and everything that is popularly associated with the Restoration represented a temporary reaction. With the " Glorious Revolution " of 1688 that period was over. In 1698 Jeremy Collier published his *Short View of the Profaneness and Immorality of the English Stage*, and English society settled down into respectability. The bourgeois victory was won.

Peace and quiet, order and rationality, clarity and common sense—these were the ideals which the townsmen and the intellectuals sought after at this time. If we turn aside from the drama to look at the other activities of the age we see a very different prospect. In poetry, the excesses of the later " metaphysicals "— their tortuous and far-fetched images, their eccentric versification and unusual subjects—had produced a reaction in favour of smoothness and clarity. Waller and Denham were praised by eighteenth-century critics as the " reformers of our numbers ": they had actually revived the clarity and ease of Jonson and his immediate followers and taken over the stopped couplet from France. Regularity and clarity were the order of the day. In philosophy, the calm empiricism of Bacon was reinforced by the contemporary works of Hobbes and Locke, those eminently sensible, rational, and not over-profound thinkers. The empirical spirit was making itself felt, too, in the sciences. In 1660 the Royal Society was founded. This had its influence on English prose, for papers read before the Society had to be written in a clear and vigorous style. The elaborate poetic style of the earlier Anglican preachers was deprecated. Bishop Spratt, writing his *History of the Royal Society*, denounced metaphors and other meretricious tricks of style. In every sphere of life " enthusiasm " was discouraged: things were to be inquired into calmly, rationally, empirically.

This was the spirit that was rising at the very time when the wits and gallants were roistering about London, and it was more representative of the wishes of society than they were. The reaction against the Commonwealth brought with it a distaste for any kind of zeal or fanaticism. Violence in religious opinions was sneered at. Satire, which had flourished in the controversies of the Civil War (Samuel Butler, in his great *Hudibras*, having the last word on the anti-Puritan side after the Restoration), became disciplined and moderated into the forceful argumentation of Dryden's *Hind and the Panther.* There was at the same time a certain amount of anti-court satire during this period—the mildly Puritan poet Marvell was outstanding in this field—which was more or less in the old style, but on the whole the movement was from violence to wit, from abuse to irony. In all respects society was settling down, and the middle classes sighed with relief as they turned with renewed hope to their shops and counting-houses.

As the seventeenth century draws to its close, and the civilisation of the country becomes centred in its town life, a new social pattern emerges. Aristocracy in the old sense is dead, and wealth becomes the main motivating power in society. The old idealisms are gone for ever; men are more civilised, more calculating, more complacent, more rational, more self-seeking, more respectable. Those who have not the minimum of income to allow them to mingle in urban society remain out of sight and out of mind as far as the great majority of the thinkers and talkers of this period are concerned. Poverty is regarded, not as a challenge to the existing social order or even as an argument in favour of doing something about it, but as a guarantee that the working classes will continue to work. Economics and ethics are finally separated. A shallow optimism, which takes for granted that " whatever is, is good," begins to make its appearance. The new economists—their field is " Political Arithmetic "—prove to their own satisfaction that the individual desire to make money can produce in the long run nothing but good, and poverty can only be the result of idleness. Society refuses to take responsibility for those of its members who fall by the wayside.

This organisation of society and of social theory in the service of the middle-class town-dweller produces

LITERATURE AND SOCIETY 117

an urbanisation of literature as of other activities. London dominates the intellectual life of the country to an unprecedented extent. The coffee-house replaces the court as the meeting place of men of culture. The journalist makes his appearance. Gossip and tittle-tattle make their way into print. Poetry becomes social and familiar. There is a sort of conspiracy among writers and readers to say what they are expected to say, not to startle or shock by extending their observation or their speculation too far. It is a small world —smaller than that of the previous century—and everyone knows everyone else.

At the end of the last chapter we saw the bourgeois element in society slowly coming to the fore, with wealth replacing noble birth in the new aristocracy of the Tudors. It took over two centuries for this process to be completed. Pausing on the threshold of the eighteenth century we can see the end of one epoch and the beginning of another. The new class has won its victory, but it is still comparatively uneducated socially. The town has defeated the court, and has rejected the court's standards in manners and morals: it has now to find its own standards, to root itself in a social and ethical code. It has to define its attitude to its writers, determine the function of the literature it produces, and make up its mind about the permitted and the prohibited. It needs educating in the trivialities of life, which hitherto has been the property of the court. The education of the Elizabethan aristocrat had included everything from Platonism to deportment. The new society had its Hobbes and Locke and its rationalising clergy (Toland's *Christianity not Mysterious*,

1699, proved that Christianity was just common sense which it needed no revelation to justify), but it had as yet neither monitor nor dancing master. We shall see how the periodical literature at the beginning of the eighteenth century supplied this deficiency.

CHAPTER III

IN THE PERIOD between the beginning of the eighteenth century and the beginning of the industrial revolution towards the end of that century, the tradesmen of the towns come to play a more and more important part in the life of the country. We have seen how the class they represent developed in numbers and influence in the two hundred years between the coming to power of the Tudors in 1485 and the Glorious Revolution of 1688. But the middle classes were not yet the actual governors of the country. The political rulers were the landed aristocracy, the country gentlemen and big estate owners, though they ruled only with the permission of and in alliance with the commercial interests. When the alliance was broken not long afterwards, it was broken only in a formal political sense, for by this time the landed aristocracy had become so absorbed in the upper strata of the middle classes that their interests had become identical. The long period of Walpole's rule lulled the squirearchy to sleep, and when they awoke they found themselves indistinguishable from upper middle-class gentlemen. The fusion of interests was complete. Eighteenth-century England shows the working of democracy in this sense, that during this period no social exclusiveness was shown by the ruling class in relation to those who could come forward with money in their hands; money was the solvent of all social differences; all who had money were equal. So wealthy merchants bought seats in Parliament and purchased the estates of bankrupt landowners, and aristocracy developed into plutocracy.

This process continued throughout the century, and we can see it taking place in the pages of Defoe's *Tour Through England and Wales* (1724–6). Defoe is in many respects a typical representative of the middle class at this time. He was a Nonconformist, an individualist, a trader who would sell his literary talent as well as anything else that he had at his disposal, a plain, observant, rational man who differed from other members of his class only in being the possessor of an extraordinary visual imagination and a consummate gift for journalism. *Robinson Crusoe* shows us the economic individualist at his most ideal. " Robinson renounced the past and prepared to make his own history, he was the new man who was ready to command nature, his enemy. Robinson's world is a real world, described with a vivid and understanding feeling for the value of material things. The storm is a horror which puts in peril the ship and its cargo, men are pirates and mutineers, cruel and merciless to their fellows, but Crusoe's faith in himself, his naïve optimism, enable him to overcome both his own folly in risking his fortune, the cruelty of nature and the savage hostility of his fellow men, and to found his ideal colony beyond the seas. . . . ' Here my partner and I found a very good sale for our goods . . . and dividing the produce, my share amounted to three thousand four hundred and seventy-five pounds seventeen shillings and threepence. . . .' Robinson's life, like that of Odysseus, is the story of a strange journey, and like that of Odysseus it ends—' in retirement, and the blessing of ending our days in peace.' But the whole aim of Odysseus is to return from the war at Troy to the island home, while with Robinson it is the outward, and not the homeward, trip in his voyage which is important. He is the empire-builder, the man who challenges nature and wins. His reward is calculated down to the last threepence, and is well earned."[1] And, as Edmund Gosse pointed out to George Moore, Defoe does not even let Robinson sit down to write his narrative till he has exhausted every profitable occupation he can think of and has tied up the last fruit tree.[2]

But Defoe, with his vigour and realism and plain forthright style, did not write for the cultured. He wrote for the new reading public, small tradesmen and shopkeepers who had no pretensions to gentility and knew nothing and cared less about the canons of taste. The upper middle classes preferred a more " genteel " literature, which was not only polite in style but helpful in its subject-matter—something that might, while entertaining, give them some hints on correct social behaviour and some proper ideas about literary appreciation. For they were a rather bewildered company, these prosperous citizens with their wives and daughters. They had kept aloof from the courtly life of the Restoration, with its licence and debauchery, and now that that had gone and correct conduct in a metropolitan society was coming to be a concern of their own they felt awkward and ignorant, and wanted

[1] Ralph Fox, *The Novel and the People* (London, 1937), pp. 37–8.
[2] George Moore, *Avowals* (Ebury Edition, London, 1936), p. 9.

advice. The town had defeated the court, and now the town had to be educated up to its new position.

It was to these men and women, anxious to be educated in taste and manners, that Addison and Steele addressed themselves in the periodical essays of the *Tatler* and the *Spectator*. They deliberately set out to educate their readers in the superficialities of life. Steele began the work first in his plays, but eventually found a much more effective instrument in the periodical essay, in the production of which he soon obtained Addison's collaboration. We may note here that the drama at this time was in a state of complete decadence. Collier's attack on the viciousness of contemporary drama had served only to make ordinary folk very self-conscious about play-going and eventually to confine interest in the theatre to the more " rakish " town element. He had aroused his readers to a sense of the faults of the drama, but instead of this producing a new efflorescence of healthy comedy it drove those who could have helped in such an efflorescence away from the drama to other forms of literature. So comedy continued to be immoral without the saving graces of brilliance and wit: it became merely silly and not very popular.[1] It was only with Goldsmith and Sheridan later in the century that a revival came. Tragedy laboured under different disabilities; it was as a rule dull and artificial, suffering from the mechanical application of rules derived from French and classical drama. So it was not in the theatre that the bourgeoisie received their instruction, but in

---

[1] There was, however, an attempt to create a moral sentimental comedy, of which the plays of Steele and Colley Cibber are illustrations. But the attempt was premature and produced very little.

those chatty essays that were written for them in the coffee-house and read by them at home over breakfast.

The method of Addison and Steele was gentle irony, insistent suggestion, and, to a less degree, plain preaching. Steele was more of a sentimentalist, and dilated on the humanising influence of good women and the compatibility of good manners with good morals. Addison, with a more delicate style, was more of a satirist: he poured subtle ridicule on every kind of social extravagance and nonconformity. The subjects dealt with ranged from fashions in dress to literary criticism. Not only were the readers told what to wear and how to wear it; they were instructed in the appreciation of the arts, told what literary works were good and why, and presented with character sketches of social types as object lessons. It was a complete education for a drawing-room civilisation. The elements of psychology, of æsthetic theory, of moral and political philosophy were conveyed in a sufficiently " easy " and superficial form to be capable of assimilation by the most simple minded of readers. There was no deep thinking, no profundity, no real insight into fundamental questions, but always a graceful, easy rationalism which would make the reader feel at home and flatter himself that he was a man of sense and understanding. Addison and Steele are talking down to their readers in endeavouring to raise them up to their own level. They found it all the easier to do this because their own thought was superficial and their own interests identical with those of their readers.

A comparison of the " courtesy books " of the

Elizabethan age—such as Castiglione's famous *Courtier* —with the essays of the *Tatler* and the *Spectator* reveals the difference between the ideals of an aristocratic society, where culture and noble birth go together, and those of a plutocratic society, where wealth means social position and social position requires a minimum of drawing-room conversation and knowledge of the world. We may applaud the increasing democratisation of society, yet we are appalled by the amazing superficiality of eighteenth-century popular culture compared with the aristocratic culture of the earlier age. The sixteenth-century Platonic idealists may have been wrong in their ideals and confused in their metaphysics, but at least they thought hard about fundamentals and devoured all the philosophic and literary material they could obtain. The readers of the *Spectator* were not allowed to look below the surface in any subject; they were treated to charming and graceful platitudinisings about life and literature, so that they would know what to think without the necessity of actually doing so. It is a perfect example of the influence of the audience on writers and thinkers. For it is not as though the eighteenth century was more ignorant than the sixteenth. Newton and Galileo, to mention only two out of many great names, had given the products of their thought to the world in the interval, and the Cartesian philosophy had started a tradition that had already culminated in Spinoza at one end and Locke and Berkeley (if their work can be called a culmination) at another. No, it is not that there was no material for profound thought, but that profound thought was not required. Society needed polishing, and the aims of polishing are smoothness and plausibility. And neither smoothness nor plausibility are conducive to profundity.

But Addison and Steele were not aware that they were not qualified to give adequate instruction on the profounder aspects of philosophic and critical questions. And perhaps it is well that they undertook their task with such confidence, for it did enable them to do what they set out to do. They did provide rules in manners and in taste for those of the townsfolk who wished to move in society, and this is what the age required. The Cavalier tradition had proved itself a failure, and the Puritan tradition needed to be humanised if it were to be able to take its place. Critics have regarded the achievement of Addison and Steele as the humanisation of the Puritan tradition, and, if we take the term " Puritan " in a sufficiently general sense, this sums up the matter very adequately.

That Addison was able to reach the class of readers for whom he wrote and to hold their interest and attention was largely due to the ease and clarity of his prose style. The reformation of English prose style which was begun by men like Spratt and Tillotson in the Restoration period was permanently effective. Dryden was the first great writer to use the new medium: the vigorous prose of his essays marks an important development in English literature. Bunyan, too, in his *Pilgrim's Progress* and other writings, used a plain, direct conversational style, and Defoe wrote similarly, though in an even more popular manner, more in the style of the new class of journalists of the day, with whom he had a close connection. By the time Addison and Steele arrived on the scene the new tradition was established. Steele wrote fresh, straightforward English; Addison's style was more graceful, more polished, more elegant, but still possessing the virtues of simplicity and clarity. This was an age of prose, when calm reasoning and elegant conversation were the order of the day. The whole tone of society was in accord with the tendency towards ease and simplicity in writing.

Ease and simplicity, rationalism, " enlightenment," toleration: these are the keynotes of the civilisation of the early eighteenth century. This was the self-styled " Augustan Age "—to be compared, that is, with Roman society under Augustus—when in the eyes of the cultured dilettanti and the gentlemen citizens civilisation had reached a higher peak than ever before. There was an extraordinary complacency about the age. Society was regarded as having reached a point where it was to remain static. The optimism of the nineteenth century meant belief in perpetual progress towards an ever more glorious goal, but at this period the limit of progress was regarded as having been already reached. Past ages were looked back on as " barbarous," past literature as crude and unrefined, or, at best, the product of wild geniuses who wrote by the uncertain light of uninstructed intuition instead of following the precedent and example of the classics. The classics of Greece and Rome, in particular the works of Homer and Virgil, were regarded as the models which all men of taste were to follow, and French writers like Boileau, who insisted (though not so dogmatically as critics like Chapelain) on a rigid classicism and the necessity of refining literature by the application of rules derived from the practice of the " ancients," were very influential in England. The " ancients " referred not to the authors of Renaissance and mediæval literature but of the Latin and Greek classics. There could be difference of opinion as to whether modern literature—that is contemporary eighteenth-century literature—had not improved on the classics and was not the last word in literary achievement: the controversy between the " ancients " and the " moderns " of which Swift's *Battle of the Books* is a monument centres on this question: but no third element might enter the discussion. There was little perception of the organic nature of either literature or society. The former was regarded as something whose nature and excellences remained constant throughout history, so that what was the best way of writing poetry in the Greece of Homer's day was the best way in the Rome of Augustus and the England of Queen Anne: if the Middle Ages and the fifteenth and sixteenth centuries had produced different kinds of writing, the only conclusion to be drawn was that these kinds were inferior, less polished, less refined, less civilised. It never occurred to Pope that his own rendering of Homer was itself a forceful argument against this view; that Achilles was no parallel to a coffee-house wit and an interpretation of Homer in terms of eighteenth-century thought and society was itself proof that different ages produced different types of literature. But, though many realised, with the great classical scholar Bentley, that Pope's *Homer* was a good poem but not Homer, few if any contemporaries saw the implication, that the advice to follow the classics was illogical and based on a superficial view of literature as a human activity. Literature, in fact, was not regarded as an *activity* but as a *thing*, whose characteristics, qualities, and criteria could never change. Similarly, the view of society that prevailed during this period was inorganic and therefore inadequate. No one saw the historical processes which had produced the " Augustan Age " and that would in time cause it to dissolve (and it dissolved very rapidly) to bring a new society in its place. It was regarded as good in an absolute sense; civilisation had been finally achieved, and must be maintained.

This satisfaction with the metropolitan civilisation of London did not prevent critics and thinkers from appealing to " Nature " as the great criterion of fitness and propriety. Christianity is defended (in its less doctrinal aspects) by an appeal to " natural religion "; the state of society is justified by pointing out the relation between natural and civil order:

> *Order is Heaven's first law; and, this confessed,*
> *Some are and must be greater than the rest.*[1]

The rules of literary critics are but " Nature methodised ":

> *Nature, like liberty, is but restrained*
> *By the same laws which first herself ordained.*[2]

The literary critic finds that Nature and Homer are the same. Nature is common sense, reason, what one is used to and familiar with, and when Pope says to the critic:

> *First follow Nature, and your judgment frame*
> *By her just standard, which is still the same,*[3]

[1] Pope, *Essay on Man*.　[2] Pope, *Essay on Criticism*.　[3] Ibid.

he is merely urging him to be sensible and reasonable. The deprecation of " enthusiasm " is part of the same attitude. Moderation, self-control, are ideals never to be lost sight of. That is one reason why the literature of this period has often been regarded by later critics as " unpoetical " : writers never let themselves go, never abandoned themselves to their emotions. They never thought of following nature as implying an abandonment to instinct and impulse: to follow nature was to be correct and reasonable, And in the use of language, too, the writers of the time show their " unpoetic " attitude by relying on the " denotation " rather than the " connotation " of the words they use, that is, they confine themselves to the strictly intellectual meaning of the words, paying little attention to their emotional associations, their numerous overtones and suggestions, as nineteenth-century poets did. Deep emotional feeling was only allowed to be presented indirectly, sometimes even in a half comic or apologetic tone. When the poet John Gay turned from the artificial pastoral to write of the thoughts and habits of real rustics he wrote in a deliberately burlesque manner. The concentration on the " denotatory " rather than the " connotatory " aspects of language—a natural result of the general attitude of the age—makes it, as Matthew Arnold insisted, essentially an age of prose. The poetry of the time from Dryden to Pope is rhetorical (in the best sense), polished, witty, rather than passionate, emotional, evocative. It is a poetry of statement, of brilliant rhythmic argument and epigram.

The nature of literature in the early eighteenth century was essentially *social*: it was agreed that the proper study of mankind was man and what man did in a metropolitan civilisation. People in cities, not individuals searching their souls in garrets, were the poet's inspiration. Every age which has created a polite urban culture for itself and feels complacent and self-satisfied about its civilisation is liable to suffer from autophobia: people like to get together and point out to each other how grand everything is and take comfort from seeing other people do what they are doing. This emphasis on the social nature of literature is responsible for the "familiar" school of poetry which flourished now. Just as Addison and Steele were bringing criticism and philosophy out of cliques and libraries to dwell in coffee-houses and among ordinary citizens, so poets like Prior and Gay introduced a "familiar" style of poetry which would appeal to the unpoetical reader. They succeeded in making "verse speak the language of prose without being prosaic" as Cowper put it. Pope was read by dilettante gentlemen, amateur philosophers, and pretenders to culture, but Prior and Gay had a wider appeal. Their poetry was more "chatty," less formal and official than Pope's. Yet Prior could be elegant enough, and in his *vers de société* he produced a type of poetry that was the very embodiment of the social life of the age—polite, graceful, trivial. The "familiar" poets produced poems that varied in diction from the purely colloquial (like Carey's *Sally in Our Alley* or Gay's *Molly Mog*) to the refined and classical, as in many of Prior's. But there is an ease and familiarity about all these poems, even when they talk about Chloe and Euphelia.

Pope (1688–1744) is in many ways the ideal

representative of the civilisation of his day. He writes as a gentleman for gentlemen, a man of taste and culture writing for an audience of his own class and habits. His poetry has all the wit, all the polish and brilliance, that we would expect from a metropolitan civilisation of that kind. As a critic, he is the typical neo-classic; that is he takes example and inspiration from the "ancients" without binding himself to too slavish an allegiance. His criticism is directed to form rather than to content. For in an age when there is a common body of thought, when the " right " opinion about almost everything is settled and accepted, what matters most is the *treatment* of this common body of thought, not the discovery of new thoughts. The poet of Pope's day is one who gives poetic form to the material which he has to hand. Pope took the superficial thought of his time and treated it poetically. In his *Essay on Criticism* he strings together, in brilliant epigrammatic couplets, the ideas on literary criticism that were prevalent at the time. In his *Essay on Man* he takes the current facile philosophy of his day and does exactly the same thing. His ideas are all second-hand, most of them coming from Bolingbroke and Shaftesbury, both of whom were rather specious thinkers. The moderate scepticism of Bolingbroke and the shallow optimism of Shaftesbury provide the basis of his thought. The poem sets out to be a complete account of the " state and nature of man " with respect to nature, to man as an individual, and to society, and concludes with a discussion of happiness. Right through we hear the voice of a self-satisfied dominant class speaking, assuring itself and the world that the present order is best and everything if left to itself is going to work out in the best possible way. It is a doctrine of complete moral and social *laissez faire*, which can be best summed up in the concluding lines of the first part:

> *All Nature is but Art, unknown to thee;*
> *All Chance, Direction, which thou canst not see;*
> *All Discord, Harmony not understood;*
> *All partial Evil, universal Good;*
> *And, spite of Pride, in erring Reason's spite,*
> *One truth is clear, WHATEVER IS, IS RIGHT.*

And at the conclusion of the whole poem he emphasises his view

> *That REASON, PASSION, answer one great aim;*
> *That true SELF-LOVE and SOCIAL are the same.*

Such a creed can only be that of one class, never of society as a whole. The crude, facile optimism which asserts that if a man acts consistently on purely selfish motives he is best doing his duty to society, and that any evil which exists is really good if looked at in the right way, can only be maintained if a complete blind eye is turned to the condition of the vast mass of people whose labour makes the lives of the bourgeoisie and landed aristocracy so comfortable. We can readily see how Pope's thought is but another aspect of that *individualism for the prosperous* which was so important in contemporary and later economic theory. The practical applications of such a theory can be seen in the way the age treated, for example, the questions of enclosures and pauperism. Earlier social thinkers had been deeply concerned with these problems and endeavoured to pass some practical measures to remedy matters: but the eighteenth century sat tight, letting things go their own way because " whatever is, is right " and the " partial evils " of poverty and misery were part of the " universal good "—the good of those who were neither poor nor miserable. Already in the previous century a minister had asserted that " it is an undeniable maxim that everyone by the light of nature and reason will do that which makes for his greatest advantage. . . . The advancement of private persons will be the advantage of the public."[1] No longer was any stress laid on the social character of wealth and the responsibility of ownership. A study of the administration of the Poor Law in England from this time onwards would be an illuminating commentary on Pope's *Essay on Man*.

One of the characteristic products of early eighteenth-century literature is satire, and this fact again is another indication of the spirit of the age. A civilisation which is *static*, which has arrived at a point where everybody agrees that the peak of progress has been achieved and all effort is directed towards maintaining conditions as they are, will be more likely to ridicule those who disagree with its standards and differ from the majority in taste and habits than a civilisation which is dissatisfied with itself and looks forward to change and further progress. What the age does is right, and anyone who does not conform is an obvious subject for the satirist. Ridiculing the unconventional is the sport of a

[1] Joseph Lee, *A Vindication of a Regulated Enclosure*, 1656. Quoted in Tawney, *Religion and the Rise of Capitalism*, p. 259.

complacent society, and if a man can be made out to be different from others the case against him is complete. In an age which is dissatisfied with its condition and wishes to change things we get quite the opposite phenomenon—the satirist here ridicules the conventional, holds up to the light the commonly accepted standards to show people what they really amount to. The difference between Pope and Bernard Shaw as satirists (apart from the fact that Pope was often inspired by personal venom and Shaw never was) is the difference between the man who accepts society as it is and sneers at those who do not conform to its standards and the man who is concerned with the faults and weaknesses of the society of his day and sneers at those who do conform to its standards. It is the difference between a static and a dynamic view of society.

The polish and gentility of the early eighteenth century did not prevent a certain amount of " low life " from coming into literature. Defoe's *Moll Flanders* (1722) and Gay's *Beggar's Opera* (1728), both deal with the criminal classes. Defoe, however, is outside the rank of socially acceptable authors of his day: he is a journalist, a hack-writer, a pamphleteer, who will sell his pen to the highest bidder. His work represents an undercurrent of realistic writing which was to appear in more acceptable form in Fielding and Smollett. But *The Beggar's Opera* is realistic in a different sense: it is a self-conscious realism, treating of something that exists, but so far removed from the world of the gentlemen who read and wrote as to refer to another world. The story of the lives of pimps and bawds and highway robbers will amuse the gentlemen, as stories of pirates amuse children: they are too far away to be dangerous, and, being wrongdoers, their fate is too deserved for any tale of their sufferings to make the readers feel uncomfortable. Such realism was, in small doses, acceptable, but it is doubtful if a realistic account of the lives of the ordinary lower middle and working classes would have found any favour at this time. So long as it is held that poverty arises from vice or laziness and prosperity in the upper classes is socially necessary and to that extent implies virtue, the portrayal of " low life "—of the adventures of thieves and prostitutes—can be allowed. But the sufferings of the virtuous poor are another matter—to portray this as the lot of a class, determined by the state of society, could never have entered the minds of early eighteenth-century writers.

The work of Jonathan Swift (1667-1745)—whose prose provides perhaps the best of all examples of that plain forthright style which was characteristic of much early eighteenth-century literature—illustrates quite another aspect of the spirit of the age. While Pope's work was a symbol, Swift's is a symptom: that is, Pope symbolises the age as it saw itself while Swift is the symptom of its inner weakness. Swift was a conservative, a Tory, firmly believing in the stratification of society as he found it. But the world that he saw left him thwarted and angry, and some of his greatest work is his denunciation of the human race which had not come up to his preconceived standard. Swift is the inverted sentimentalist: starting with an idealist, sentimental view of life, he becomes angry when he finds that life does not accord with his *a priori* conception of what it ought to be, and lashes out in savage satire at the weaknesses of men in general. This is not the typical satire of the age, no mere sneering at social nonconformists, but the obverse of a complacent society. In one sense, Swift's work is a disillusioned comment on an age of "enlightenment," as the nineteenth-century Samuel Butler's is on an age of progress.

With the growing importance of Parliament and party politics the writer becomes important as a potential propagandist. Not only is the political journalist active, but even the higher grades of writer often associate themselves with a political party and give support to the Government or Opposition. Swift wrote in support of the Tory party: Prior was given a job in the Whig Government; Addison had a political career as a Whig and ended by marrying a countess. The politician was regarded by the author as a likely patron, and a promising young writer could look forward to a government sinecure when the party he supported came to power. Thus in the early years of the eighteenth century the relation between politics and literature was close, and professional writers were encouraged by the Whigs and Tories alike, because they were useful.

With the death of Queen Anne and the subsequent decline of the Tory party, the situation changed. In the first place, the development of parliamentarianism was making it more and more necessary for politicians to look out for men who could command votes rather than for men with literary gifts. Secondly, the establishment of the Whig supremacy, especially the long period of over twenty years during which Walpole was in power, made the literary propagandist to a large extent unnecessary: the Whigs did not require him and the Tories had no opportunity of using him. Thus the political patron gradually disappeared from English literary life and the author was left to fend for himself. The pamphleteers and hack-writers who in Queen Anne's time might have made a tolerable living by writing Whig or Tory propaganda were now in a bad way: their services were not needed by the dominant Whig party and were useless to the temporarily shattered Tories.[1] And so we begin to hear more and more of " Grub Street "—the realm of hack-writers and starving poets. The ambitious young writer had nowhere to turn for certain employment, and after a time was ready to do anything to make a living. For not only was political patronage decaying, but the patronage of men of letters by the wealthy was also rapidly decreasing as the wealthy increased in numbers and became less and less of a small privileged caste with established customs and traditions. The booksellers—at this time also publishers—were quick to take advantage of this situation, and began to employ these stranded writers in all kinds of hack work. Impecunious writers were thus employed by booksellers (who often housed them) to translate foreign books, compile or abridge treatises or works of reference, correct proofs and revise old publications, or do any kind of marketable literary work. The typical eighteenth-century picture of the starving writer

[1] It is not true that there was no political pamphleteering between 1714 and 1742. But there was, comparatively, much less of it than in the age of Queen Anne. The political patronage of authors, of the kind that got Addison or Prior their jobs, declined steadily.

working in the bookseller's garret is not altogether without foundation.

Yet the growing power of the booksellers did mean that there was employment (though irregular and ill enough paid) for anyone who wished to take a turn at quill-driving. So we find not only gifted writers, like Johnson and Goldsmith and Smollett, starting in at Grub Street and gradually working their way up, but also many other less qualified persons taking to the profession of letters because they could not make a living in any other way. Unsuccessful tradesmen might turn to hack-writing as a last resource, and every kind of impecunious adventurer was liable to end up in Grub Street. But it was not long before conditions improved for writers of ability, who were able to escape to better circumstances, though often leaving weaker brethren languishing in the bookseller's garret. The rise in the level of middle-class education bringing an increased demand for popular books of instruction in history, geography, natural history, science, and literature, and for all kinds of compilations and abstracts, gave dependable employment to the competent hack-writer.

The famous letter of Dr. Johnson to Lord Chesterfield (1755), when, after struggling on his own and achieving success, he refused the latter's belated offer of help, is often taken as one of the causes of the decline of patronage. But patronage was in decline before this, and Dr. Johnson's letter merely illustrates what had been going on for some time. Johnson's whole life provides a good illustration of the place of the author in society from, say, 1730 to 1780. Like Smollett and

LITERATURE AND SOCIETY 139

many another writer of the time, he graduated from Grub Street. After difficult early days he became known for his contributions to periodical literature (he was Parliamentary correspondent of the *Gentleman's Magazine* for some time) and eventually built up the reputation which has become almost proverbial. His two periodicals, *The Rambler* (1750-2) and *The Idler* (1758-60), show some of his characteristic qualities as a writer: didactic, serious, even dictatorial, he wrote in order to instruct and improve his readers. Unlike Addison, he was concerned with morals rather than with manners. Addison's job had been to educate the bourgeoisie in social behaviour, and he had done his work well. The " Addisonian settlement," as we may call it, put literature and society in their places for over a generation. Johnson is no rebel against the Addisonian settlement—indeed it had become too much part of the order of things for anyone at that time to have even been conscious of it as an imposed order—but he goes behind it and beyond it, seeking for a profounder purpose in literature and a profounder comment on life. The underlying melancholy of Johnson's temperament may have had purely personal, psychological origins, yet it cannot be treated as an isolated and insignificant phenomenon. The facile optimism of a complacent society, that had been voiced by Pope, was beginning to disappear, the inevitability of goodness was more and more questioned and the necessity for intellectual and moral effort realised. Goldsmith, in *The Deserted Village*, deplores the evils brought about by the depopulation of the countryside and attacks " the increase of our luxuries." " For twenty or thirty years past," he says in his introductory letter to Sir Joshua Reynolds, " it has been the fashion to consider luxury as one of the greatest national advantages. . . . Still, however, I . . . continue to think those luxuries prejudicial to states by which so many vices are introduced, and so many kingdoms have been undone." Johnson, in his *Vanity of Human Wishes*, expresses more general grievances and points to the defects in human nature and the ills of human life (though he never joined in the attack on luxury common to so many writers of the time). A discontent was abroad, not so radical as Swift's (and Swift is rather in the nature of a special case), but in strong contrast to the spirit of Pope's *Essay on Man*. Yet the remedies proposed were intensely conservative. *The Deserted Village* looks backward to the time when the " bold peasantry " was unspoiled and uncorrupted; Dr. Johnson,[1] for all his melancholy, was an almost fanatical Tory, a hater of Whigs and all reformers, a firm believer in established authority and things as they were. It is as though a sense of coming change and disintegration made men cling all the more firmly to tradition and long established institutions.

Johnson emerged from Grub Street to become almost a literary dictator, and his emergence coincides with a certain improvement in the lot of Grub Street writers generally. The professional writer was acquiring an independent status, and if he had real ability he could count on earning a living and making social contacts.

[1] One might compare the rather unreal abuse of London in Johnson's poem *London* with his statement that " When a man is tired of London he is tired of life."

At the same time the upper classes become less interested in literature and less active in its production. If Horace Walpole—son of Robert—has a taste and a talent for writing, he indulges it only half seriously; it is his recreation, his pastime, his method of amusing himself. He is not a " professional " writer, but a gentleman amateur. The consolidation of the writer's profession produced a feverish desire for amateur status on the part of the " gentlemen." " We, my lords," said Lord Chesterfield in an often-quoted speech, " may thank Heaven that we have something better than our brains to depend upon." We are reminded of the early Tudor courtly writers, to whom the writing of poetry was an accomplishment to be indulged in in leisure hours for their own and their friends' amusement. But there is this important difference: in the sixteenth century this was the attitude of those who were producing the best literary work of the time, while in the eighteenth it was the attitude of the minority of the upper classes who merely dabbled in literature and produced little of real importance. Literature had become essentially a middle-class activity.

This separation of the professional from the " gentleman " writer helped to produce a dilettante spirit among the latter. Horace Walpole, with his sham Gothic castle at Strawberry Hill, is perhaps the most typical representative of this side of eighteenth-century culture. In history, antiquities, literature, painting, and natural scenery Walpole shows the superficial interest of a leisured curiosity. Throughout the century we find virtuosi and men of " taste " collecting *objets d'art* and discussing the picturesque. Earlier in the century there had been a close association between gardening and landscape painting; Pope and the dramatist Vanbrugh were notably interested in these associated arts. But the formal, classical garden of Pope's time succeeded to a more " natural " variety, where the gardener aimed at merging his work into the surrounding countryside. The whole question of landscape gardening in the eighteenth century, its relation to the changes in " taste " and its significance for the development of æsthetic theory is full of interest, but we cannot pause to discuss the matter further.[1] The point to be made here is that the growth of the dilettante and the virtuoso among a class of " gentlemen " voluntarily debarred from professional literary or artistic activity provided a nursery for ideas about nature, history, and literature which, when full-grown, were to become incorporated in the " Romantic Movement." The love of nature, the mediævalism, the love of the strange and the picturesque, the interest in ruins and in antiquities generally—these are features of the " Romantic Movement " and they are to be found, though only superficially, in the habits and hobbies of mid-eighteenth-century country gentlemen. Once again we find that most common phenomenon of literary history—a leisured and cultured upper class providing rich material for a later generation of a different social class to utilise and develop.

As yet the middle classes had not achieved any

---

[1] Readers who are interested are referred to the chapter on " Taste " by Osbert Sitwell and Margaret Barton in the second volume of *Johnson's England* (ed. A. S. Turberville, Oxford, 1933) and to the bibliography appended there.

distinctive literary form. As they rose in influence and importance they took over and developed the literary traditions with whose origins they had so little connection. Bunyan produced a middle-class Puritan allegory in *The Pilgrim's Progress*, thus revealing new potentialities in straightforward allegorical story-telling, and Defoe wrote long narratives in a simple and direct style, but neither writer can be said to have founded a new mode of writing. Addison and Steele (the former especially not writing as a member of the middle class, but writing *for* the middle class from above) had given us the prose sketch in addition to their development of the essay. But it was Samuel Richardson (1689-1761), the most bourgeois writer (in the popular sense) who ever lived, who gave us the first modern novel and thus founded a literary species which might be described as the great middle-class contribution to literature.

The prose tale was no new thing. It was produced sporadically by Elizabethan writers as different as Thomas Nashe, the realist, and John Lyly, the courtly gentleman. And the seventeenth century had seen the flourishing of the heroic romance (that last direct descendant of the courtly romance of the Middle Ages) as well as a certain amount of miscellaneous prose narrative. But these do not give us the modern novel, any more than does the fifteenth-century *Morte Darthur* of Sir Thomas Malory or the prose fiction of Greece and Rome. The work of Bunyan and Defoe, Addison and Swift had added much to the art of prose narrative, and these writers are regarded in all reputable textbooks of English literature as " anticipators " of the novel. But they are no more, because none of these writers treat prose narrative as a means of presenting a single complete and unified picture of one or more aspects of life. This is what Richardson achieved in *Pamela*, his first novel. It is because he is at once the most perfect example of his class—its habits of mind, its morality, its assumptions, its limitations—and, for all practical purposes, the founder of a new literary mode, that he is important for us in our present inquiry.

With the Addisonian settlement, literature had become " classical " and moral. The innate Puritanism of the middle classes would allow no compromise with the culture that went together with gentility unless the whole conception of the non-morality of art was abandoned. Thus the diluted Puritan ethics of the bourgeoisie came into literature. That art should have a moral purpose was no new claim: it was implicit in such literary theory as the Middle Ages produced, and Sir Philip Sidney had voiced it eloquently in his *Apologie for Poetrie* at the end of the sixteenth century. But these early theorists had demanded a moral background for art only in the broadest and most general sense. The moral ideas in early eighteenth-century literature were more detailed, more restricted, more petty, even. Robinson Crusoe must spend time evangelising Man Friday (" after the evangelisation of Friday I've forgotten if Crusoe taught Friday his catechism and his prayers; if he didn't the oversight is incomprehensible "):[1] the Vicar of Wakefield and his family found that in the long run it paid to be virtuous

[1] George Moore, *Avowals*, p. 8.

("all my cares were over, my pleasure was unspeakable" is how he describes his condition in the last paragraph of the book): Pamela, by refusing to have sexual relations outside marriage, eventually secured her wealthy but rakish pursuer in bonds of legitimate wedlock. Richardson comes a good while after Defoe, and Goldsmith some time after Richardson. When the first part of *Pamela* appeared in 1740 the Addisonian settlement was already beginning to break up. And when Goldsmith published *The Vicar of Wakefield* in 1766 we are well into the "Age of Johnson." So we must endeavour to put the moral element in Richardson in its place in the development of the relation of literature to social morality from Addison onwards.

Addison and Steele had advocated what might be called a classicism without paganism. But as time went on the negative aspect of this doctrine became increasingly positive and the positive aspect tended to disappear; so that classicism lost its force as a vital literary creed and "without paganism" came to mean *with* a certain restricted kind of Christian morality. (It would be unfair to call it simply Christian morality, because it was merely one version, and that not the most representative.) Pope and those who had more affinities with the upper classes than with the middle classes preserved the Addisonian balance, and the popularity of deism at this time shows in what a vague and general sense the negative side of Addison's teaching was interpreted by a certain section of the people. But that section did not include the bourgeoisie, ever growing in affluence and influence, whose morality was something more defined and worked out in detail. Both upper-class deists and middle-class moralists (to make a bold generalisation) based their ethics, whether consciously or not, on an individualist, *laissez-faire* principle. We have already noted the emergence of this principle among the trading classes of the seventeenth century: it was developed in the eighteenth century for the simple reason that it was found to work. Richardson was a prosperous printer, having started as an apprentice and, after marrying his master's daughter in the approved style, setting up for himself and flourishing. He thus came from a class that combined a narrow and perhaps rather mechanical morality with a determined individualism. Addison, in his campaign to make gentlemen out of tradesmen, had necessarily taken some view of society as a whole, for it was with the remoulding of society as a whole that he was concerned. He did consider, however superficially, questions of social, as distinct from personal, ethics: he tried to see a pattern in society and to make sure that it was the most desirable pattern. But the true bourgeois has not even that much social conscience. The work of Richardson is, in one of its aspects, an indication of how Addison and Steele's reconciliation of gallant and shopkeeper eventually only made the shopkeeper more articulate and more independent. It was, after all, a uniting of two very unequal forces and the stronger was bound to predominate sooner or later.

So Richardson, the moral, bourgeois individualist, presents us with a picture of the individual isolated from society. The subtle analysis of character which is possible in this kind of writing is not necessarily vitiated by this isolation. But it is interesting to observe the social causes of Richardson's choice of the psychological novel. The search for personal salvation had always been characteristic of Puritanism, and Puritanism, as we have noted, was still dominant (in a rather diluted form) among the middle classes. Seventeenth-century Puritan literature is full of personal introspective records, searchings for the light. The sense of stability in the eighteenth century together with the economic forces at work combined to strengthen this individualist attitude and to weaken the sense of social responsibility. So that there is a curious resemblance between Pamela's frantic efforts to preserve her virginity until she had secured her man and the seventeenth-century Puritan's search for personal salvation. There is a lack of background, a lack of any consciousness of social obligation, a narrow insistence on a purely personal and mechanical code of behaviour, whose origins are to be sought in the social, economic, and religious history of the previous hundred years.

Saintsbury has summed up the themes of Richardson's works with justness and conciseness. " *Pamela, or Virtue Rewarded*, gives the history of a girl of low degree who, resisting temptation, marries her master, and in the second and less good part reclaims him from irregular courses; *Clarissa* (1747-8), that of a young lady of family and fortune, who, partly by imprudence, partly by misfortune, falls a prey to the arts of the libertine Lovelace and, resisting his offers of marriage, dies of a broken heart, to be revenged in a duel by her cousin; *Sir Charles Grandison* (1753-4), that of a young man of still higher family and larger fortune, who is almost faultless, and constantly successful in all his endeavours, and who, after being the object of the adoration of two beautiful girls, the Italian Clementina della Porretta and the English Harriet Byron, condescends to make the latter happy."[1] The gradual rise in social status from Pamela to Sir Charles Grandison is interesting and instructive. Richardson, the apprentice become master printer, is feeling his way up into high society, and is less and less at home the further up he goes. Richardson's greatness, however, does not lie in his descriptions of society, but in his " insight into the human heart." His studies in feminine psychology are convincing and sound, and if the type he describes is appallingly limited in outlook and ideals that only means that Richardson has kept his eye on the object and described with faithfulness what he is most familiar with. The narrow world he lives in is a real world, and the very fact that he cannot see outside it enables him to present it to us unspoiled, with the narrator being ultimately a part of what he narrates. Richardson " had not an idea beyond those common to his class; he accepted the ordinary creeds and conventions; he looked upon free-thinkers with such horror that he will not allow even his worst villains to be religious sceptics; he shares the profound reverence of the shopkeepers for the upper classes who are his customers, and he rewards virtue with a coach and six."[2] In letting us see the woes of Pamela and Clarissa through their own

[1] G. Saintsbury, *Short History of English Literature* (London, 1898, etc.), pp. 599–600.
[2] Leslie Stephen, *English Literature and Society in the Eighteenth Century*, p. 159.

eyes (his novels are in the form of letters written by the characters) he presents us with a perfect picture of a certain class of eighteenth-century woman. It is because he sympathised and understood that he depicted so well. Richardson *knew* Pamela: her views were his views and her actions were natural and right in his eyes. Unconsciously, Richardson endowed his heroine with " the implicit utilitarian qualities of a Puritan temperament devoid of nobleness " (in Professor Cazamian's phrase) because those were the predominating qualities of his own class. The sentimentalism, the dwelling on emotions such as grief and despair for their own sake, that we find in Richardson, is the tribute paid by the materialistic and self-seeking bourgeois to the spiritual and emotional side of human nature.

Richardson's work is didactic, even, in a sense, religious. And it is a fact that the more mercenary the lives and habits of a class the more inclined it is to moralising and the enforcing of a rigid practical moral code. It is the simple working of the law of compensation. The *laissez-faire* individualist who claims that his seeking for private gain can only be productive of public good, and who repudiates all social responsibility, is liable to restrict morality to a sphere where it is incapable of interfering with his way of life. And that is why morality in the eighteenth and nineteenth centuries came to imply sex almost exclusively. An immoral book was a book that dealt too frankly with sexual matters, while a book which described extortion or exploitation, which treated in great detail of some abuse of social trust, or of any other kind of non-sexual vice, would never earn that adjective. Words like " delicacy,"

" decency," " propriety," came to have a purely sexual connotation. So it need not surprise us that Richardson, the narrow-minded bourgeois tradesman, should be so anxious to introduce a " moral " purpose into his work; a certain type of Puritan morality is not incompatible with commercial individualism. We see both in Pamela, and it is because we can see these qualities so clearly and naturally in this and other characters of Richardson's that he has a right to be regarded, with all his limitations, as a great literary artist. He has painted one aspect of human nature and conduct to perfection.

The sentimentalism which we find in Richardson's *Clarissa* and to a greater extent in later eighteenth-century writers has its social and economic causes, though these would not explain it entirely. Sentimentalism might be described as indulgence in emotion as a luxury, for its own sake, without adequate attention being directed to the cause of the emotion, and sometimes without there being any objective cause for the emotion at all. When men withdraw into themselves to contemplate and indulge their own feelings as it were æsthetically there must be some reason why they prefer this to contemplating the outside world in a purposive and practical manner. The literary artist can be either didactic, objectively descriptive, psychologically descriptive, or purely introspective. Shakespeare's *Hamlet* gives us a psychological description of a certain type of character placed in certain surroundings, and as such it is interesting and valuable to the student of human nature quite apart from its more formal literary qualities. Spenser's *Faerie Queene* is, in intention at least, didactic, pointing out what right conduct ought to be by allegorical description and practical example: it has also simple descriptive elements. And—there is no need to dwell on examples—these different elements can be combined in different proportions to produce works of varied interest and appeal. But introspective indulgence, such as we find in Sterne's *Sentimental Journey* (1768) and Mackenzie's *Man of Feeling*, presents a much less obvious method of writing. It seems to imply a deliberate lack of contact with reality, a refusal to seek emotional satisfaction in normal relations with people and things, a literary auto-eroticism which is fundamentally unnatural and unhealthy. Can we see in this an indication that the economic individualism of the time was gradually limiting the field of application for the generous human emotions, such as pity and admiration, and forcing writers to indulge them in a masturbatory manner? Introspection and luxurious wallowing in self-induced emotion are normal enough human activities in moderation, but when they become the characteristic of an age we are justified in looking for their causes to the state of contemporary society. If a man wishes to weep literary tears he can always visit the slums and write about the miseries of the poor. But *laissez-faire* economics would refuse to admit that there was anything to weep about in the existence of slums and poverty, and the lachrymose emotions had to be turned inwards. It was only in the nineteenth century, when the " condition of England question " roused writers to a sense of social injustice, that these emotions could once more find normal—as well as more useful—outlets.

But we have jumped well ahead of Richardson, in whose novels sentimentalism is less conscious and much less marked than it is in later writers of the century. The qualities of Richardson that aroused the anger of his younger contemporary Henry Fielding were his priggishness, his mawkishness, and his narrow conception of morality. Fielding began by parodying Richardson, but was soon led to produce great and original work of his own. *Tom Jones* (1749) is at once his most important and his most characteristic work, and has particular interest in virtue of its social background and ethical standpoint, both so different from those of Richardson. Fielding came of an aristocratic family, and it must be at once admitted that his connection with the landed gentry encouraged a breadth of outlook and a generosity of feeling of which the petty tradesman or prosperous merchant, with his prudential morality and restricted interests, was incapable. How far Fielding's view of men and society arose from his own character and how much it owed to his social origins is impossible to tell, but the fact that he was never subjected to the narrowing influence of commercial individualism and had an altogether different background from that of Richardson must account to some extent for his freedom from the shams and artificialities, from the smug and calculating virtues, that we find in Richardson. Fielding's positive virtues were, however, his own: it would be ridiculous to maintain that anyone who came of a non-bourgeois stock was bound to have a generous outlook and a tolerant view of life.

In his mock-epic invocation prefaced to Book XIII

of *Tom Jones* Fielding asks for the support of Genius, Humanity, Learning, and Experience. To Experience he says: " Come, Experience, long conversant with the wise, the good, the learned, and the polite. Nor with them only, but with every kind of character, from the minister at his levee, to the bailiff in his sponginghouse; from the duchess at her drum, to the landlady behind her bar. From thee only can the manners of mankind be known; to which the recluse pedant, however great his parts or extensive his learning may be, hath ever been a stranger." Fielding had a knowledge of society from the duchess to the landlady and did not scruple to bring into his story everything that he knew. He thus has a catholicity which appalled Richardson, who regarded " low life " as something inadmissible to a novel. Fielding's pictures of the lower strata of society are in a different style from, say, that of Defoe in *Moll Flanders*. Defoe indulges in picaresque narrative for its own sake, dwelling on scenes and facts which he thinks will interest and amuse the type of reader he has in mind. But with Fielding everything is subordinated to an organically constructed plot, so that he takes us from one stratum of society to another naturally and unself-consciously. He is trying to see the man of his time in his social background and at the same time to indicate what human characteristics he regards as good and what he regards as evil. He does this by following the adventures of certain main characters, the nature of both the adventures and the characters being such that a large canvas is necessary and many subsidiary characters and events are brought in, yet the story being kept firmly in control so that it never becomes merely a string of interesting events, as earlier narratives tended to do. We get from Fielding's works, and in particular from *Tom Jones*, a view of eighteenth-century society, both rural and urban, completer than that given by any other fiction writer of the century.

Fielding, unlike Richardson, had a well-developed social conscience. His experience as a Bow Street magistrate must have helped to strengthen this, and to give him a knowledge of aspects of human nature and conduct which did not come into Richardson's ken. He is as much a moralist as Richardson, but in a very different way. He is concerned to stress the fact that goodness of heart, generous instincts, and practical sympathy are the chief virtues, while hypocrisy, deceit, selfishness, and cold calculation are the worst of vices. Sins of the senses are to be forgiven, if they are the result of a too free and kindly nature. To Richardson (and to the middle classes generally up to this day) sins of the senses are the only sins that really count, and immorality refers only to these. To Fielding they are nothing beside the sins that arise from cruelty, harshness, and cunning self-interest. So it is not altogether surprising that Richardson remarked of Fielding that " the virtues of his heroes are the vices of a truly good man." The ideal good characters of both writers are not so very dissimilar (Squire Allworthy has more than a slight resemblance to Sir Charles Grandison), but their conceptions of ordinary practical goodness in the workaday world differ completely.

From one point of view, Fielding's work can be said to represent the protest of the surviving pre-bourgeois humanism against the commercialising of virtue and the interpretation of righteousness in terms of a narrow ultra-individualist philosophy. But Fielding's own view is as much open to the charge of sentimentalism as that of Richardson. To identify virtue with " goodness of heart " is ultimately unrealistic and romantic in the bad sense. If we assume that goodness of heart always leads to generous action and prohibits all real wrongdoing we might be able to accept Fielding's criterion; but there are no adequate grounds for such an assumption. We have no instrument to gauge a man's sincerity or to test his motives (as Lenin pointed out in a famous passage): we can only judge a man by his actions, and a man leads a good or a bad life in accordance with what he does, not necessarily with what he feels. So there is something in the contention of the eighteenth-century critic of Fielding that " goodness of heart, which is every day used as a substitute for probity, means little more than the virtue of a horse or a dog." Ideally, Fielding is right: if men's actions were always the accurate reflections of their characters there would be no fault to find with his conception of morality. But, unfortunately, no such simple correlation is possible, the complexities of human nature being what they are. Yet Fielding had more right than Richardson, and his protest was natural and timely. Fielding widened the scope of morality and did something to clear up the confusion between manners and morals, between mere good form and real virtue. The confusion goes back at least as far as Addison, whose teaching was concerned with the superficialities of life, with " proper " social conduct rather than with right and good action either in the private or the social sense (and ultimately private and social morality are one). If the doctrine of the good heart was taken up and vulgarised by later writers, we cannot blame Fielding. The sentimentalism which we have already noted as being to some extent the turning aside of moral impulses into non-practical channels (because to put them into practice would have meant taking cognisance of social and economic evils that could not be comfortably contemplated) owed a great deal to this doctrine, just as it owed much to the "sensibility" of Richardson and the parading of emotion characteristic of Sterne and Henry Mackenzie, but to discern sources and influences is not always to apportion responsibility. Burns was much influenced by Fielding's view of morality, and he was no bourgeois.

Fielding has importance apart from his opposition to Richardson on moral issues. His realistic view of objective reality[1] gives him a high place among those who developed the novel as an instrument for the description of and comment on life in epic fashion. His work represents the antithesis of all "escapism" in literature. His contemporary Tobias Smollett was equally objective and realist in his approach, but as a rule wrote in a more frankly picaresque manner, without a unifying purpose underlying the whole. The tradition which Fielding founded was not taken up immediately because the changes in thought and in society were

[1] Realistic in one sense only: we must remember that Fielding, like the other writers of his time, never considered that the social order as he saw it could or should be other than it was. It never occurred to him to consider the part played by social and economic conditions in producing the kind of immorality he deplored.

becoming increasingly rapid and momentous, so that the latter part of the eighteenth century presents a picture of swift disintegration and reintegration within which events do not fall in easily ordered succession or phenomena appear in obviously related groups. The diversity of the literature produced at this time is but a reflection of wider changes. What textbooks call vaguely the " beginnings of the Romantic Movement " comprise no simple group of connected works.

It is time we paused to inquire into the nature of the reading public during the eighteenth century. At the beginning of the century readers of books were still comparatively few and largely confined to the capital. The flood of controversial pamphlets that had been let loose by the Civil War had long abated, and only the idle rich and the scholar provided a potential public for the writer. For the former class there was little except outmoded romances; for the latter, mostly dull theological writings. Poetry was read by a very small circle: its readers have never been numerous in any age (unless we include in the term " poetry " doggerel narrative verse, indecent rhymes and all kinds of indifferent topical versifying). There was as yet hardly any " polite " light prose literature, which for two centuries has been the staple of the ordinary intelligent reader. With the development of the periodical essay by Steele and Addison this gap began to be filled. Not only was material provided for those who desired to read, but those who had the leisure but not, hitherto, the inclination were brought into the circle of readers. In " bringing philosophy out of closets, schools, and colleges, to dwell in clubs and assemblies, at tea-tables, and in coffee-houses " (to use his own phrase) Addison broke down the barrier between the professional reader and the ordinary leisured middle-class public. By the time the *Spectator* ceased publication a new middle-class literature had been created—a literature, that is, that was neither scurrilous and, in the bad sense of the word, popular, nor learned and "highbrow." For, apart from the small group of those genuinely interested in literature, it was into these two extremes that reading matter had been tending to divide. Economic causes were producing an ever growing middle class with sufficient leisure and opportunity to indulge the reading habit, and the conscious efforts of Steele and Addison provided the material for it. And once the reading habit was formed the material was produced in increasing bulk, so that action and reaction helped to produce more books and a larger public. Within the first twenty years of the eighteenth century the sale of every kind of fairly popular literature increased enormously. The first impression of *Gulliver's Travels* sold out in a week, and even poetry—especially poetry of the more popular type, such as Gay's *Fables* and his two operas—found a ready market of a size hitherto impossible. The reading public was growing rapidly as the middle classes acquired education and social ambition.

Periodical literature advanced steadily throughout the century, and we find, too, increasing numbers of miscellanies, collections and anthologies. Those who would have found the reading of complete books tiresome dipped into magazines, newspapers, and "elegant extracts," and thus acquired at least an ability to talk in knowledgeable fashion about current literature. An increasing number of people came to regard familiarity with books as a social asset. With the development of the novel the reading public was further widened. " Novels," says a publisher in a play published in 1757, " are a pretty light summer reading, and do very well at Tunbridge, Bristol, and other watering places; no bad competition either for the West India trade."[1] The spate of stories, sketches, travel-tales and novels which poured forth from the middle of the century onwards is a sure indication of the growth of light reading. Subscription libraries began to make their appearance, and fashionable young ladies, meeting in the street, would discuss the latest books they had borrowed. Gradually, too, literary centres arose beyond London. In Scotland, Edinburgh, as the capital, had long had a literary tradition of its own, and in the second half of the century the intellectual life of the city attained a degree of vitality never equalled before or since. Here as in London there were lending libraries and booksellers, literary coteries and tea-table talk about books as well as (what London had not got) philosophers, historians, and economists. The growth of manufacturing towns produced, in Manchester and Liverpool, in Glasgow and Birmingham, centres which became in some respects miniature Londons, with their own social and literary activities. The concentration of culture in the capital, which had been going on for centuries and had reached a climax

[1] Quoted from Foote's play *The Author* in A. S. Collins, *Authorship in the Days of Johnson* (London, 1928), p. 244.

in the reign of Queen Anne, began for the first time to give place to some degree of decentralisation.

The growth of popular education helped to increase the reading public. The Society for the Promotion of Christian Knowledge, founded at the very end of the seventeenth century, proceeded, in the beginning of the eighteenth, to found charity schools for teaching children to read at least the catechism. Though still sporadic and irregular, means of teaching the ABC in parishes and villages throughout the country increased as the century proceeded. And towards the end of the century we find a fair amount of specifically juvenile literature being produced by enterprising publishers, though most of it intended as much for "improvement" as entertainment.

It was ultimately the growth of the public that enabled the author to survive the decline of patronage. As long as the class of readers remained small, the author required a patron to back him and introduce him to society, but when the reading public became large enough to guarantee a certain circulation the author was at last able to stand on his own feet. He did not acquire independence suddenly, however: the apprenticeship of Grub Street had to be served first. The booksellers became the intermediaries between the public and the writers and for long prevented the two from having any direct contact. The public demand was estimated by the bookseller, who ordered what he thought would be profitable from the author. And it must be admitted that the shifting of the dependence of literature on to popular demand did nothing to raise its quality—at least, not immediately. As long as the author had a patron to back him he could produce, within limits, what he thought fit (though if he had a political patron he would require to turn out propaganda as well when it was needed). But the public taste ran to spicy stories and breathless adventures, as well as compilations of all kinds and equivalents of the modern " outlines." After the decline of the political patron with some abruptness in 1714 the social patron continued for some twenty years or so to play an important part in literary life, and under the patronage of the cultured rich the author's position was most favourable of all: he was guaranteed financial independence and he could exercise his genius freely without worrying about a public. But complete lack of consideration for the reading public probably does more harm than good to literature and, in spite of its encouragement of third rate popular writing, the emancipation from patronage eventually produced much more good than harm. The eventual result was the appearance of authorship as an independent and " respectable " profession. No longer was the writer a mere hanger-on at court, a low-grade civil servant, a humble sycophant at the tables of the rich, or a political hireling: gradually he began to take an honoured place in the community, until with Sir Walter Scott he becomes the hero of a generation. Dr. Johnson is one of the earliest examples of the man of letters achieving independence and prestige, and his position in the intellectual life and in the society of his time was rendered possible by the development of the reading public.

Though cultural activity throughout the century

was confined to towns, and to London in particular, we must not forget that the majority of Englishmen before the industrial revolution were country dwellers. In addition to agriculture, crafts and industries were carried on in villages to a large extent. The typical English gentleman of the time was a country squire, who only came up to London for " the season," and something like ninety per cent of ordinary Englishmen had little if any contact with the urban civilisation which we have been discussing. Most country squires were hard-drinking fox-hunting men with no literary interests, while the yeomen, craftsmen, tenant farmers, and labourers were as a rule completely cut off from London cultural and social life. The growth of large-scale farming, part cause and part result of the second enclosure movement in the reign of George III, did a great deal to depress the miscellaneous rural population of England and to cut it off finally from any contacts with urban civilisation. Unlike the sixteenth-century enclosures, the eighteenth-century movement had for its aim the improvement of arable farming, not the conversions of farm land into sheep pasture. And though agricultural methods were greatly improved as a result, the depression of the small landowner, the elimination of small tenants, and the clearing out of squatters and cottagers who had occupied what was hitherto common land,[1] resulted in the formation of a large rural proletariat, many of whom migrated to the cities with the growth of industrialism to take up work

[1] For a documented account of the state of these classes after enclosure, and an explanation of the inevitability of such results, see J. L. and B. Hammond, *The Village Labourer, 1760–1832* (London, 1911), chapter v.

LITERATURE AND SOCIETY 163

on whatever terms were offered. The face of rural England changed greatly during the eighteenth century. The English yeoman, for so long considered the backbone of the country, gradually disappeared altogether. The traditional type of English village disappeared too, with the abolition of the old communal holdings and the concentration of land in the hands of the country gentry. But it took some time for these effects to make themselves felt, and in the period we have been discussing in this chapter there was comparatively little social discontent in rural areas. Squirearchy worked for a time, and we see it working in Fielding's *Tom Jones*—ideally under Squire Allworthy, the type of the benevolent landlord; not perhaps so perfectly, but effectively none the less, under the harsher and probably truer to fact Squire Western.

So the relation of literature to society in the eighteenth century is, on the whole, the relation of literature to urban society only. In spite of the vast growth of the reading public, the improvement in popular education, and the raising of the status of the professional writer, the vast majority of the people lived their lives outside the circle within which this activity was carried on. From the time of the Tudors onwards—indeed from the time of Edward IV and even earlier—the middle classes had been steadily rising in numbers and influence, until in the eighteenth century it was they who were the main producers and consumers of literary and cultural work. This development of the middle classes was to continue further, but with the industrial revolution in the latter part of the eighteenth century the existence of the working class is gradually brought, first to the consciousness and then to the conscience, of the nation. The working class, whether in town or village (and most lived up till now in rural areas), had hitherto been humble, silent, and, on the whole, content. The vast increase in urban population, together with all the other manifold changes that followed in the wake of the industrial revolution, eventually changed this situation.

The Addisonian settlement had enabled bourgeois literature finally to oust aristocratic literature. The bourgeois cultural dictatorship rapidly developed, and continued to develop until it reached its height in the Victorian age. But in the nineteenth century, unlike the eighteenth, the development of literature was not coextensive with that of the bourgeoisie. The ever growing proletariat was beginning to penetrate the world of letters, at first indirectly by means of middle-class sympathisers and finally directly as a result of the extension of popular education, so that the future of culture was not to depend entirely on the success of the bourgeois cultural dictatorship. And that brings us to the modern problem, which is discussed in a later chapter.

One has no sooner mentioned the bourgeois ascendancy over literature and society that emerged in the eighteenth century when another aspect of the contemporary scene presents itself. Was not the aristocratic principle still dominant? Parliament was controlled by the aristocratic landowners, the government was oligarchic and not in any real sense democratic, the bourgeoisie had no real political power. In a sense it is true that the aristocratic principle was dominant in the eighteenth century. But there was no firm line drawn between the middle and the upper classes. The ruling class was not a permanently fixed body, but flexible and ever changing. There was no aristocracy of blood, but only of social and political power, and the way to that was through the ownership of land and the resultant control of votes and general influence over the surrounding country. Aristocratic sentiment was still very strong, aristocratic forms were kept up, but behind everything lay the " cash nexus." Further, it must be remembered that the bourgeoisie were quite willing to leave the purely political power in the hands of an oligarchy provided that they were guaranteed freedom and security to carry on their economic activities. They preferred to let others do the dirty work for them while they consolidated their own power (though there was nothing conscious in this preference and this policy). And they were ready, too, to be genuinely respectful before landed aristocracy. There is nothing fundamentally paradoxical about this state of affairs, which prevails, to a very much less extent, even in our own time. In literature, the power of the bourgeoisie can be seen more simply and more directly. The periodical essay, the novel, the moralising and didactic verse of the middle of the century, the pseudo-learned compilation and popular work of reference, the domestic drama of George Lillo and Edward Moore, the comedy of Goldsmith and Sheridan and the sentimental drama of their dull contemporaries and successors, are all, in different ways, expressions of the bourgeois outlook. Sheridan (1751-1816), perhaps, with his drawing-room wit and irony, preserves as much of the aristocratic as of the middle-class tradition, but such philosophy as there is at the basis of his work consists in a vaguely optimistic trust in human nature guaranteeing its own morality which is merely another side of the bourgeois doctrine of *laissez faire*. The literature of an age can tell us as much about its nature and spirit as the political activity in which it indulges, and Pamela's belief in the morality of getting her dissolute but moneyed pursuer to marry her is as significant as Dr. Johnson's profound veneration for the monarchy. There were many more Pamelas than Dr. Johnsons in the eighteenth century.[1]

By the middle of the century the complacency that we found earlier is beginning to disappear. The corruption of political life, the apathy of the Church, the stagnation of the universities (though not in Scotland) combine with less definable causes to produce complaint and dissatisfaction. A sign of the times is John Brown's *Estimate of the Manners and Principles of the Times* (1757), a book which attacks the corruption and vice of the age, comparing the state of Britain with the state of Carthage before its fall and that of Rome in its final decline, and prophesying her conquest by France if things are not changed. The dominant mood of writers is melancholy: the easy optimism of Pope's *Essay on Man* has gone, and men become, either reformers, desiring change, or passionate conservatives, looking to the traditions of the past to restore the

---

[1] *And* Dr. Johnson approved of Pamela. He remarked (among other things) that Richardson taught the passions to move at the command of virtue.

glories of the past. The appearance in 1762 of Rousseau's *Social Contract* helped to give force and direction to the discontent in Britain as in France. The basic ideas of Rousseau's work were not new to Englishmen: the conception of a state of nature and of a social contract had been frequently discussed in the seventeenth century, and Locke in particular had dealt with them at length in his *Second Treatise of Government*. But Rousseau had much greater influence on political ideas at this time, because he came at a time when these ideas were uppermost in men's minds.

Rousseau is important in English political thought, but he is more important for his influence on imaginative literature. The " noble savage," the " natural man," in literature has a long history, and is to be found wherever the idea of a lost golden age haunted men. The " natural man " of the eighteenth century is rather a species of his own, however, and we see him first, perhaps, in Mrs. Aphra Behn's *Oroonoko* at the end of the previous century. The conception of man, uncorrupted by civilisation, as noble and virtuous to a degree impossible in civilised society, is not, of course, quite Rousseau's, nor did he equate the " state of nature " with the golden age. His theories were less crude than this, though the ordinary reader of the time may have been unable to distinguish between the state of nature as a theoretical controversial concept and the same term used in a much more literal manner. But we cannot pause to discuss Rousseau's social and political ideas: suffice it to note that his conception of an original free and natural society entering voluntarily into a social contract between the people as individuals and the " general will " of the public and thus originating civil government had immense influence in stimulating fresh thought about freedom, personality, and the relation of man to nature. And these are fundamental problems for the imaginative writer. The earlier eighteenth century was concerned with men in cities, equated the natural with the civilised and the urban, took men in groups and crowds and dwelt on the characteristics they had in common: Rousseau was to some extent responsible for the growing tendency to study man in isolation, away from cities and civilisation, against a background of hills and clouds. The result was not only a new attitude to nature and a new interest in natural scenery, but also a new interest in human personality. An increase in the imaginative content of writing logically follows: writers cease to be satisfied with recording in polished verses what men do and say and think, and concern themselves rather with the emotions that arise in the individual in his contemplation of aspects of life and nature, and with the imaginings and myth-making that such emotion encourages.

This is a crude differentiation, and quite inadequate as a definition of those complex changes in the nature of literary activity generally known as the " Romantic Movement." But it may suffice to show the main trend of the movement, which was towards a freer play of the imagination and a less dependence on the standards of everyday urban conduct. Society no longer presented such an attractive and inspiring surface. The stereotyped movements of men in groups began to arouse disgust. Why could not writers retain the suavity of

Addison, the optimism of Pope, the smugness of Richardson ? We can answer that changes in outlook and sensibility are bound to come and always do come at more or less regular intervals. But granted the natural tendency to change, what factors can we discover which decided that the change should have been in this specific direction ? There is, of course, the general stagnation and corruption bred by the long Whig ascendancy, which stimulated men to protest against things as they were and to think again about government and society. The proved incapability of a static and self-satisfied age to provide for the future was making men dissatisfied with the early eighteenth-century way of looking at things. The American War of Independence shook men up a bit, and the French Revolution shook them up a great deal. Writers like Burke might plead for a combination of tradition and expediency in conducting human affairs, but to many thinking people tradition had already proved itself of doubtful value, and expediency found many different interpreters. It is perhaps significant of the profound unrest and deep sense of change that lay behind the late eighteenth century that the political wisdom of Burke was unable to penetrate to an understanding of so many important issues. An age whose fundamental nature is threatened with change does not yield its secrets to the philosopher who draws all his arguments mechanically from past experience, and though Burke was so often right and sensible, as in his attitude to the American colonies, his looking backward instead of forward blinded him to the real nature of the most important issue of his day.

Two aspects of " Romantic " literature are regularly stressed—idealisation of the past and love of nature. Men preferred to avert their eyes from contemporary urban society. Is there a reason for this? It may be an undue simplification to say that with the development of the industrial revolution urban life became more and more ugly, the activity of men in society became more and more unpleasing, so that sensitive writers were driven either to the past or out into the open country. But there is no doubt that changes in society made the earlier eighteenth-century position impossible. The hierarchy of landowner, wealthy merchant, middle class of varying degrees of wealth, peasant, and worker guaranteed a certain permanence and stability in social organisation. There might be considerable fluidity between the two top classes, but society was based on a static and dependable lower class which was, on the whole, cheerful and patriotic. Polite life lived contentedly in its own world very satisfied with the progress that had been made in civilisation and culture, and presenting a pleasant, untroubled picture to the eye of the writer and thinker. The development of machinery, the growth of factories, the depopulation of the countryside, which went on in the last years of the eighteenth century finally upset the social hierarchy on which Addison had founded urban culture for the middle classes, and eventually changed the face of society. New classes were formed which the old order was not capable of assimilating with ease; new social forces came into being; new problems arose. The conception of a static society was abandoned with suddenness, and men faced the future with mingled confidence and bewilderment. It is not to be wondered at that literary men turned their back on this turmoil, as yet undirected and largely incomprehensible.

The industrial revolution was the process whereby Britain ceased to be an agricultural country and became predominantly industrial. The tremendous expansion of trade which went on in the seventeenth and eighteenth centuries and the tendency towards economic specialisation that went with it led to a demand for increased production of easily standardised kinds of goods, and this in turn encouraged mechanical invention and its application to industry. This process went on continuously from the middle of the eighteenth century: markets expanded, mass production rose to meet them, machines and factories arose that could produce more and more cheaply and in ever greater bulk. The transition from mediæval craft guild (decaying already in the seventeenth century under the influence of Puritan individualism) to modern factory involved many stages. With the growth of distant markets and the consequent separation of producer and consumer, the middle-man, supplying the raw material and disposing of the finished article, became increasingly necessary. So there arose (especially in the woollen industry, the most important in England at this time) a system under which the workers still worked in their own homes, but with raw material, and often with tools, supplied by capitalistic middlemen who paid them for their work and marketed the completed product themselves. The differentiation of function between worker and trader-financier became more regular as time went on and by the time machinery came to be applied to industry the now familiar distinction between proletarian and capitalist was clearly marked. It was not, however, until the introduction of machinery that the worker finally lost his independence. Hitherto he had continued in his own home or workshop within which he was subject to no discipline and was more or less his own master: but the use of machinery meant the concentration of workers in the building where the machines were, and their subjection to a common discipline and loss of all independence in method of working followed naturally. Private craftsmen were unable to compete with the mass production of the factories and were driven to seek employment in the towns at whatever wages were offered. The numerous small farmers and squatters who had been ruined by the great enclosures of the eighteenth century also drifted to the towns to form a part of the rapidly increasing urban proletariat. The result of all this was to change the face of both town and country. In becoming the "workshop of the world" Britain lost many of the best features of its village life, lost its independent craftsmen, abandoned social relationships, institutions and organisations which had developed from the earliest Middle Ages, and, in gaining an ability to produce goods with an unparalleled efficiency and in unprecedented bulk, created a new wage-earning class depending for its livelihood entirely on the sale of its labour and free from the threat of unemployment only so long as the market was constantly expanding, and all the other accompaniments of industrialism. In addition, it further strengthened the middle classes, putting more wealth and power into their hands until they were no longer content with economic influence only but demanded and gained the reform of Parliament which enabled them to enjoy also direct political supremacy. Already for some time the relations between the landowning class and business men had been close, and the distinction between the two classes blurred: money could buy squiredom, and throughout the eighteenth century retired merchants would buy estates and settle down as country squires to become in a short time indistinguishable from the other landed gentry. With the coming of the industrial revolution the bourgeoisie were enabled to rule in their own right.

The evils brought into being by the rise of factories worked by an industrial proletariat—depression of the standard of living, appallingly long working hours, the iniquities of child labour—are commonplaces of social history. Beside power-driven machinery human life was cheap: unskilled labour was plentiful and the individual ceased to count. Thus while we find among the bourgeoisie an ever increasing individualism, a tendency (constantly growing from the seventeenth century) to extol private profit-making and regard economic activity as involving no social responsibility whatever, we find their attitude to the working class one which denies all individuality and which refuses to consider the problems of human freedom and personality—to take the case at its most abstract—involved in the system of factory production. That the writers of the time averted their gaze from the industrial scene is understandable on many grounds. In the first place, as we have already observed, such a scene would encourage a sensitive literary man to escape altogether into quite another world rather than to spend time describing or discussing it. Secondly, in most cases the writers simply did not know what industrial conditions were like: like most people who did not come into any contact with the life of the workers and did not live in factory towns, they were quite ignorant of the whole business. Thirdly, the currents of thought stimulated by the French Revolution drew men's minds away from the problems of the industrial revolution towards theoretical problems of freedom and the organisation of government. The situation in France, where a decayed feudal system was being overthrown to give way to the rising middle class, was not at all parallel to that in England, where the process now being achieved so suddenly and painfully across the Channel had long been completed. But the principles and theories which precede and follow any political upheaval are of more general application than the immediate questions involved, and the wider issues raised by the French Revolution were eagerly discussed by English writers. It might almost be said that the American War of Independence and the French Revolution between them side-tracked the English social conscience: they directed the attention of sensitive minds to the rights of man and the life of reason, but drew them away from contemplation of the conditions in industrial centres and the application of theories of justice and equality to the facts of contemporary industrial life. The social ideas of writers at the end of the eighteenth and the beginning of the nineteenth centuries were in many ways lofty and inspiring, but in no case did they take any cognisance of the problems raised by the industrial revolution. The new working class struggled on, allying themselves when they could with the numerous English radical movements against which the Government, thoroughly scared by what was happening in France, launched a fierce campaign of repression and terrorism. But even these movements, even the predominantly working-class London Corresponding Society founded in 1792 and the kindred societies that sprang up all over the country, did not devote their main attention to the securing of better conditions in the factories and thus improving the lot of the working man: they aimed in a general way at " freedom " by means of the reform of Parliament and the introduction of universal adult suffrage. It was only after the working class had become more self-conscious, had embarked on struggles for the right to form trade unions, and brought their case before the country by means of strikes and other agitation and propaganda, that the indifference of literary men to their lot began slowly to give way to some sense of the reality of the problem. Until then—and it was well into the nineteenth century—the urban proletariat which the industrial revolution had largely brought into being remained outside English literature: they did not read it, nor did they figure in its subject-matter.

One English writer has, however, given us a vivid picture of some aspects of life in village and small town at this time, though he does not deal with industrial conditions. George Crabbe (1754–1832) in his poems *The Village* and *The Borough* deliberately sets out to paint lower-class life " as Truth will paint it and as bards will not ": in *The Parish Register* we have " the Village Register considered as containing principally the annals of the poor " providing a series of sordid stories of village life. Crabbe's aim is not to point to the miserable conditions of the peasantry and so suggest, even by implication, the economic causes and remedies for the evils of which he is only too conscious. He is a moralist: in *The Village* he is concerned to show that the country dweller is every bit as vicious as the rich city dweller, and the anecdotes of *The Borough* and *The Parish Register* are at bottom comments on human nature by one very conscious of man's essential depravity. Crabbe succeeds in painting a most convincing picture of the squalor and dreariness of lower-class life in the village and small town at the end of the eighteenth and the beginning of the nineteenth centuries. There is a sense of hopelessness and decay in the atmosphere he evokes. Looking back from our vantage-point some centuries ahead we can see that Crabbe chose a period, between the great enclosures and the completion of the industrial revolution, when all the old traditions and institutions of village life had been broken down and nothing had arisen to take their place, so that poverty and helplessness prevailed to an unusual degree. But the special circumstances of the time do not explain Crabbe's pessimism and his insistence on the seamy side. There was something in his own character which made him torture himself by concentrating his gaze on ugliness. Like Swift, he is an inverted sentimentalist: he sets his own standards for humanity too high, and when life as he sees it does not come up to his own preconceived sentimental standards he turns round and bitterly attacks it, picking out all its worst aspects, indeed, even fascinated by the scenes of suffering and squalor, and returning to them again and again as a man with a toothache cannot help worrying the tooth that pains him and thus giving himself more pain. So Crabbe is not motivated either by a desire to describe the lot of the poor in order that people may take steps to improve it, nor is he merely painting what he sees with complete objectivity. Nor again is he callously exploiting the literary potentialities of the immoral poor, though there is perhaps something of this in his work—he cannot help seeing what dramatic and tragic possibilities there are in these lives of degradation and despair. But he is primarily a disappointed moralist, describing from the outside a scene of which he is not a part. (It is worth noting that Crabbe owed his success to the help given him by Burke and other patrons. Patronage was not yet quite dead, though very nearly so; Crabbe was the last English poet of any distinction to profit by it, if we except rustic poets like John Clare, patronised largely as curiosities or " phenomena.")

Crabbe's Scottish contemporary, Robert Burns, presented the annals of the poor in a very different manner. Crabbe, though of fairly humble origin, was never really one of the people he described, so that he never spoke *for* the people, but only about them. Burns, however, always managed to identify himself with the people whose emotions and adventures formed the theme of most of his best poetry. A small farmer himself—Crabbe was a doctor, then a minister—this

Ms

identification involved no conscious effort: he knew the ordinary folk of the Scottish countryside. Crabbe remained outside the village pub, pressing his nose against the window and looking in to note with sad disapproval the sordid " goings-on " within: Burns was inside, sitting comfortably round the fire with his cronies, one of them himself, unself-conscious, happy at least for the moment. There had been minor poets of proletarian birth in England in the eighteenth century, such as Stephen Duck (1705-1756) the agricultural labourer who had been patronised by the gentry and was recommended in 1730 to Queen Caroline who granted him an annuity and saw to it that he had some sort of a career in the Church. But Duck was regarded as a phenomenon, and was treated as such: it is perhaps significant that, like John Clare the " Northamptonshire Peasant Poet " (the title is revealing) of the nineteenth century, he went mad before his death: both Duck and Clare were patronised as curious and unique specimens, and their life and work suffered accordingly. Burns was different. Though he was trotted round the drawing-rooms of the Edinburgh gentry, like Clare in London in 1820, he was something more than the Ayrshire Peasant Poet. For at its best Burns's poetry represents the consummate expression of the personal and social emotions of the ordinary intensely-living peasant. Love, conviviality, recklessness, patriotism, boasts of independence, commonsense morality, the supernatural—these are themes that ring true: it is the peasant through the peasant's eyes in his richest moments. There is no need to revive the old legend of the completely uneducated and spontaneous ploughman genius to be able to see in Burns a new development in the relation of literature to society. Here was a poet of humble birth expressing human passions in terms of the humble society with which he was most familiar. Other poets before Burns had risen from the ranks of the poor to a certain success, but only at the expense of accepting the terms of reference of their patrons. Burns, at his best, wrote with reference to the life he really knew. It is not that human emotions are necessarily any more genuine or universal when found in the humble worker, but for the universal implications of such emotions to be brought out by a poet he must be true to the world of experience he knows; he must keep his eye on the object and not distort his vision or falsify his imagination and intuition in order to level up his experience to that of the class for which he writes. And as the life of the farm-worker is harder and more intense than that of the town dilettante, a genuine portrayal of life as the farm-worker lives it is liable to present such emotions as love and patriotism in their more elemental aspects. And elemental does not mean biological: it is not that Burns dwells more on the physical side of emotion than a writer of a higher social station would be likely to do, but that he is able to reach to the bottom of an emotional experience to an extent not always possible to the writer whose capacity for genuine emotion is unconsciously confused by convention and social habit. There was plenty of humbug about Burns: he fell a ready prey to the sentimentalism of Henry Mackenzie's *Man of Feeling* and imbibed many of the French revolutionary doctrines about justice and equality without being at all sure what they really involved and how they were to be applied. But as long as he referred his emotions and his ideas to the lives of those among whom he was most at home he was able to embody in his poetry the truth about human emotional experience to a superb degree. His attraction to Scottish folk-song, which led to his great work in reviving and remoulding traditional Scottish songs, arose from this same sense of the genuine in experience: for the ballad and the folk-song always look at life directly without trying to adapt their vision to some foreign perspective.

But with industrial capitalism establishing itself throughout Britain the standardising of working-class thought and experience—standardisation by reduction to a bare minimum—went on apace.[1] William Blake made his great protest against the mechanistic materialism and the hypocrisy that he saw in the society of the last years of the eighteenth century, and finding himself becoming more and more out of touch with the standards of middle-class life as he saw them, he retired into himself to work out his ideas in a series of mystical utterances barely if at all intelligible to the ordinary reader. But Blake's early work, and even a fair amount of his later writing, is simple and direct, and his message is, in essentials, clear. He preaches in favour of spontaneity, generosity, love, disinterestedness,

[1] In Scotland the decay of feudalism and the expansion of commerce and industry came with a suddenness compared with which the gradual change in England was the slowest of evolutionary processes. See Scott's epilogue to *Waverley* for a vivid reference to changes in Scotland in Scott's own time. The complete collapse of the clan system in the Highlands after 1745 gave rise to special problems unknown in the south.

freedom from every kind of constraint and institutionalism; he is against the form and for the spirit, against the rules and regulations devised by Church and State and for the true morality which such rules ought to, but in practice very rarely do, embody. He revolts against all institutionalising of the things of the spirit because that leads to ossification and, whether consciously or not, to hypocrisy. Blake in fact saw that the organisation of society under the economically dominant middle class had led to the organisation of religion and morality for the purpose of sustaining and justifying the inequalities and iniquities inevitable in such a society. He did not see the social and economic forces at work in subordinating the spirit to the letter in the field of ethics and religion, but he did see that the process, for whatever reason, was taking place, and he protested violently against it. The ethical *laissez faire* associated with commercial activity from the seventeenth century—soon to be reinforced by a consciously applied economic policy of the same kind—had naturally produced every kind of contradiction between moral theory and practice, every kind of justification of social injustice and iniquity, every kind of hypocrisy and special pleading. It was essentially against this that Blake revolted: his keen vision and sensitive nature saw all too clearly the ugliness of the situation, the lack of all spontaneity and moral emotion in the application of ethical theory, the evils of an "unspiritual" legislation. But Blake never established adequate contact with the public, and he was driven into himself more and more, to dwell in a world of private symbolism. To the outsider he was a madman; his visions were the product of a diseased mind; his contemporaries shrugged their shoulders and passed him by.

At the end of the eighteenth century the social ideas of the ordinary thinking man were rather confused. The French Revolution was encouraging radical theories, belief in progress and change towards greater freedom and equality. Reaction was similarly encouraged, and there were many stout defenders of things as they were. Burke, for whom statesmanship was " a disposition to preserve and an ability to improve," stood between the two extremes, though with the coming of the French Revolution he stressed the necessity for preservation rather than the need for improvement. There was still a degree of complacency —observable throughout the century—which assumed that Englishmen had been more fortunate than other men in the development of their political and social institutions and ever since the " Glorious Revolution " of 1688 they had enjoyed a government combining privilege with freedom, and provided with checks and counter-checks, of a kind impossible of achievement by the benighted foreigner. The optimism of the earlier part of the century had not, however, survived in its pristine freshness: we have noted the rise of pessimism in the beginning of the century, and at this time a certain uneasiness as to whether all was really well is discernible in a great deal of casual writing apart from the purely political literature. In the economic sphere Adam Smith had, in his *Wealth of Nations* (1776), advocated the abandonment of government control over economic activity and complete economic *laissez faire*, and this implied a trust in the working of natural forces shared later by Bentham and James Mill: yet this confidence that all was bound to work out for the best is not prominent in other spheres of thought. There are, in fact, two distinct currents in social and political thought at this time, the complacent and the purposive, and we find the two side by side again and again.[1]

While, under the stress of the Napoleonic wars, reaction was hardening in England and the general run of political thinkers were becoming more and more facile and complacent in their attitude to such problems as that of poverty and social misery, a theoretical radicalism was growing which was to have great influence on literary men for more than a generation. Blake's was the emotional protest of the poet looking at a soulless society with little knowledge of social or political theory but with generous instincts and burning intuitions. But there was also growing up a protest from the more purely rational side, represented by such works as Thomas Paine's *Rights of Man* and William Godwin's *Political Justice*. Both sides are represented in the

[1] A combination of optimism and pessimism can be seen clearly in Burke's *Thoughts on Scarcity* which " reflect, on the one hand, the optimism of the eighteenth century which believed that all would be well if ' the simple system of natural liberty ' were given its head and, on the other, that settled pessimism about the future which arose between Malthus's blow at Godwin and the universal acceptance of the classical political economy."—H. J. Laski, *The Rise of European Liberalism* (London, 1936), p. 200. Pope's dictum that self-love and social are the same is still found in Burke, who exhorts the poor farm labourer to acknowledge the justness of the social order " with thankfulness to the benign and wise Disposer of all things, who obliges men, whether they will or not, in pursuing their own selfish interests, to connect the general good with their own individual success." This was too comfortable a view not to be retained by the bourgeoisie in the nineteenth century. Its detailed application to the economic sphere is first explicit in Adam Smith, and the utilitarians gave the theory a new lease of life, basing it on a more general view of human activity.

"Romantic Movement": both the passionate emotion of Blake and the pure reason of Godwin find an echo in the young poets of the time. And so we come to the new movement in literature, moulded by complex and even contradictory forces, completing the change in the attitude and function of the writer which had begun with the collapse of the Addisonian settlement. The change was neither sudden nor complete, but it was radical enough to justify the traditional claim that the romantic poets at the beginning of the nineteenth century wrought a genuine revolution in an important sphere of human activity. The significance of this change for the relation between literature and society is not easy to assess, because literature becomes larger in bulk and more multifarious in kind as the nineteenth century advances. But in the following chapter we shall try to separate out the main lines of development and obtain some view of what is happening even at the expense of drastic simplification.

CHAPTER IV

THE CHALLENGE of the French Revolution in England was met by a stiffening of the reactionary policy of the Government. The struggle of the bourgeoisie against the personal power of the monarchy which George III attempted to restore and against the oligarchical principle of government—a struggle represented by the activity of John Wilkes and the Junius letters—broadened out, first, under the influence of agricultural distress, into a more general reform movement with agrarian reform in the foreground and then, under the influence of the French Revolution, into a still wider radical policy. Similarly on the other side personal and political opposition developed into a more thorough fight on questions of principle and finished up with severe repression on the part of the Tory Government (in power from 1783 till 1830 with only one short interval). In conservative periodicals like the *Anti-Jacobin* every attempt was made to sneer at all reformers indiscriminately and to represent the supporters of the revolution in the very worst light, but there were not lacking literary men on the other side: in fact the knowledge that certain sections of literary men had revolutionary sympathies led to literary criticism based on purely political grounds. While the industrial revolution went merrily on, the young writers, Southey, Coleridge, and Wordsworth were reading Tom Paine and William Godwin and laying plans for the realisation of a theoretically ideal society. Poets began to define anew their attitude to society—not to society as it was, for of that they were largely ignorant, but to society as they would have it. It was the theorists of the French Revolution who were largely responsible for this deflection of interest to theoretical problems. (Even those who, under the influence of the evangelical and philanthropical movements that first arose in the middle of the eighteenth century, fought against the slave trade and concerned themselves with the welfare of negroes, paid no attention to social conditions at home. This fact is not so easily explained. The pious Wilberforce, the great anti-slave-trade campaigner, supported the Combination Acts of 1799 and 1800, which declared trade unions illegal. The attitude of evangelical religion to social misery tended to be similar: acquiescence in an intolerable lot was urged and compensation promised in the next world.)[1]

Tom Paine's *Rights of Man* (1791-2) seems a moderate enough book to-day. It defended the French Revolution against Burke and pled for true democracy and political equality. The book became immensely popular, and was to a large extent responsible for the development of a working-class radicalism. It is perhaps due to Paine that working-class radicalism began as a vague cry for political rights rather than with any serious examination of the causes of social

[1] The reader may doubt this, and wish to judge for himself the attitude of evangelical religion to social questions at the time of the industrial revolution, in which case he is referred to J. L. and B. Hammond, *The Town Labourer* (London, 1918 : Left Book Club edition, London, 1937), chapter xiii, and to a statement of the opposite view in W. J. Warner, *Wesleyanism in the Industrial Revolution* (London, 1930).

evils and their remedies. More influential among literary men was William Godwin's *Enquiry into Political Justice* (1793). Godwin had inherited the sanguine rationalism of the French Encyclopædists: he believed that everything could be achieved by the application of calm reason, and that if people were argued with sufficiently clearly they could not help seeing the truth. He believed in the perfectibility of man: only change people's opinions by reasoning and a new world will appear. In such a world every kind of institution and legal machinery would be unnecessary; everyone would practise justice, benevolence, and brotherly love, and all problems, social and personal, would solve themselves automatically. Godwin would abolish government except local, parochial government with a very limited function and a skeleton State Government for emergency purposes. In other respects " each man should be wise enough to govern himself, without the intervention of any compulsory restraint."

This, of course, is an almost ludicrous simplification of the theme of *Political Justice*, but perhaps it will suffice to show the kind of thought that was influencing young poets at the very end of the century. The enlargement of sensibility, the dissatisfaction with polite urban society as the sole background for literature, the high imagination and serious purpose of the poets whose work marks the full development of the " Romantic Movement " were sympathetic to Godwinism if only because of its rebellious attitude and its bold optimistic imagination. The anti-institutionalism of Godwin found acceptance with the prophets of a " return to nature," and Wordsworth and Coleridge, at the beginning of their careers, imbibed the doctrine with enthusiasm. That there should have been this influence explains in some measure the purpose of the romantic revolt, but it would be a mistake to regard it as primarily a philosophic or political movement. We might learn more of the new attitude by considering for a moment one who, as much as any single man, is its parent: Jean-Jacques Rousseau.

There were three main qualities in Rousseau which impressed the romantic poets—primitivism, individualism, and a certain type of imagination. Primitivism is the belief in origins, the belief that the beginning of the world, as of the individual life, is more perfect, more its natural self, than later processes. We get praise of the "state of nature," of the "noble savage," of the child. The conception of the noble savage and the state of nature does not arise with Rousseau: it is found in the literature of the seventeenth century—it is to be found in a mild form in Locke's *Second Treatise on Civil Government*—and recurs throughout the eighteenth. But with Rousseau the doctrine is central: the contrast between the natural and the artificial is one of the key points in his thought, and it is in his work that it is handed on to the poets. Wordsworth's praise of the child in his *Immortality Ode* (the child is a "mighty prophet, seer blest," but loses its power and insight as it grows older and the "shades of the prison house" close in) and his theory of poetic diction (that the best language for poetry is the ordinary speech of the humble peasant) derive from the primitivism of Rousseau. Primitivism in one of its aspects is at the back of the whole "return to nature" movement associated with Wordsworth and the romantic poets generally. It is in part a revolt against the artificialities of a polite and sophisticated society, in part a self-justification for the socially maladjusted. The desire of the literary man to seek life at its most elemental—in the toil of the peasant, the play of the child—is healthy enough, but the self-conscious seeking of the differentia of the "natural" life implies a certain doctrinaire approach which is not altogether free from artificiality itself.

The individualism of Rousseau is again in part a protest against the conformity demanded by a conventional society. It lays stress, not on those qualities the individual has in common with his fellow men, but on those which differentiate him from his fellows. Belief in and stress on the uniqueness of the individual is valuable in literature: it may produce the lyric of personal emotion, the autobiography, the free expression of personality in any form. But individualism of this kind is most treacherous as a theory of art. We know what it has led to in later nineteenth-century poetry and in literature of our own day—every kind of private eccentricity and monstrosity, and every kind of false æsthetic to justify them. Mr. F. L. Lucas has collected examples of individualistic extravagance in his *Decline and Fall of the Romantic Ideal* (a book whose data we may appreciate without associating ourselves entirely with the views expressed on them), and after reading them we are forced to conclude that individualism in art is liable to the most horrid abuse. And the reason is not far to seek. Self-expression in art has value only if in expressing himself the artist is illuminating some recognisable human experience. We cannot be expected to interest ourselves (otherwise than medically) in a man getting something off his chest unless this process gives us something valuable for its own sake. It is not to be assumed that every reader of poetry is an abnormal psychologist. Romantic individualism contains within itself dangerous potentialities: it is valuable as a reaction from standardisation and conventionality, and at the end of the eighteenth century it did act as a valuable liberating agent on poetry, for which we must thank Rousseau and his followers. Early nineteenth-century poetry is, on the whole, the gainer from Rousseau's individualism. Poets were not yet tempted to express themselves except when their emotion resulted in the expression of something valuable on a humanist standard—valuable, that is, as embodying some experience which is related (however indirectly) to the general experience of men and therefore of objective worth. But we must not blind ourselves to the fact that the Rousseauistic attitude ultimately implies a dissociation of the artist from his public, a denial of the responsibility of the artist to his fellow men, a severance of all connection between literature and society. And to deny any social function to art is to reduce the artist to the status of irresponsible playboy. Some critics, it would seem, are prepared to take this step, but though this extreme view may derive ultimately from Rousseau we must not forget that Rousseau himself asserted the individualistic point of view largely as a protest against the evil effects of the standardisation and lack of spontaneity encouraged by an artificial society.

The romantic imagination is the third inheritance from Rousseau. Here again we must not be too literal in our attribution of this development to Rousseau's influence; there were others before him in whose work this attitude can be clearly seen. But the threads come together in Rousseau's hands, and what we note in different writers as sentimentality, sensibility, extravagance of fancy, we can see here in convenient combination and label the romantic mind. The essential feature of the romantic mind in this sense is perhaps a lack of any sense of responsibility to the real world. If the poet dislikes the world as he sees it, he has a right to retire into a dream world of his own, or, if he cannot do that consistently, cultivate his emotions to such an extent that he is able to extract fullness of feeling from the most trivial and ordinary incident. The first alternative is simply imagination, the second, sensibility. This delight in the unanchored imagination is found everywhere in Rousseau's writings. It is closely associated with the individualism we have just discussed. On one side this irresponsible imagination is a product of revolt—a revolt against a society which rejects him. " Me voici donc seul sur la terre, n'ayant plus de frère, de prochain, d'ami, de société que moi-même. Le plus sociable et le plus aimant des humains en a été proscrit par un accord unanime." This is how Rousseau begins his *Rêveries*. He, the most sociable and affectionate of beings, is alone in the world, without friend or companion, cut off from all social intercourse by a conspiracy of hate. He therefore takes refuge in a world of his own creation, and renounces all responsibility to the society which has rejected him—rejected him because he has rejected it, being unable to adjust himself to its ways.

But there is more to the romantic imagination than that. The romantic poet claims complete freedom for his mental creations, but that is only the beginning of his activity. He is not content with a dream world for its own sake, but endeavours to interpret reality in terms of his dreams. This, at least, is what the greater romantic poets aim at; there are others who seek no more than the dream itself. The mysticism of Wordsworth, his view that in the natural processes of the countryside, in the sights and sounds of the Lake District, or of any unspoilt region of mountain and lake and stream, can be found moral teaching and truth which has significance for the lives of men, shows the combination of primitivism with the romantic imagination to produce a vital and purposive creed. He avoids everyday reality to find a higher reality; he turns his back on the activities of men in order to come back to them, after communing with nature, with a means of interpreting human life. Rousseauistic escapism can be made the basis of something very different.

In turning his back on the life of men in cities the romantic poet has two courses: he may " return to nature " or he may return to the past. And so we get the mediævalism that is so prominent in nineteenth-century poetry. It begins as the most flippant kind of escapism quite early in the eighteenth century. There is Horace Walpole with the sham Gothic castle at Strawberry Hill and his pseudo-mediæval romance, *The Castle of Otranto*. Towards the end of the eighteenth century there arises a whole school of " terror novelists " producing preposterous works like Lewis's *The Monk* and the stories of Mrs. Radcliffe. But mediævalism as a serious movement, having as its motive a genuine desire to reinterpret reality and discover new values in human life, is found in the nineteenth-century poets from Keats to William Morris. As industrialism developed and the face of Britain grew steadily uglier, the past took on ever brighter colours. Movements such as agrarian reform were from the beginning wholly conservative, motivated by a desire to return to the good old days. The crusty Toryism of Cobbett was consistent with reformist activity (of a kind) just because the reforms he wished to see involved a return to the past, to old England as he remembered it, or thought he remembered it, in his childhood. The novels of Sir Walter Scott, with their re-creation of the Middle Ages and, more significant, of the immediate past, had their origin in the same conservative attitude. Scott, as critics have pointed out, did in fiction what Burke did in direct political writing—showed his reverence for tradition, his love of the life that was rapidly passing away, his belief that a nation, to be healthy, must connect with its roots. Scott's success in depicting Scottish life of the generation preceding his own is partly due to his enthusiasm for types of life and of character that were disappearing or had already disappeared. Dissatisfaction with industrialism drove writers to the past, and even those who, like William Morris at the end of the century, preached a constructive socialism as a remedy for the evils they deplored, could not help looking backwards almost as often as they looked to the future.

There is another aspect of the "Romantic Movement" which is summed up in Watts-Dunton's phrase "the renascence of wonder." In a polite, urban society the tendency is to avoid any contact with the unusual and the extraordinary, or at least never to allow oneself to be caught up in an ecstasy of astonishment but always to keep control of one's faculties and emotions. The Horatian *nil admirari* is the ideal of a sophisticated generation. There was another reason besides sophistication which accounts for this determination to be astonished at nothing in the early eighteenth century. An age which has reached, in its own estimation, the pinnacle of civilisation, which looks back on previous ages with scorn and can see no further progress possible in the future, prefers to have the universe "taped," in the modern slang phrase. Everything must be reduced to order, sorted into the proper category, and whatever defies sorting into categories must be ignored. But with the romantic poets a completely changed attitude, which had been developing for some time, manifested itself. The repudiation of urban society, the escape to the world of nature or to the past, bred a new attitude of mind in observation. The poet was seeking new worlds of experience, and even disposed to create them where he could not find them. For this purpose constant curiosity and enthusiasm were necessary, enthusiasm not only for the new and strange but also to seek new meaning in the commonplace. These are two complementary attitudes in the romantic mind—the search for the unknown and mysterious and the desire to invest the most ordinary objects with new and deep significance. We see the first in Coleridge's *Ancient Mariner*

(1798) and the second in those numerous poems of Wordsworth dealing with ordinary incidents in the lives of humble peasant folk. The cultivation of wonder developed throughout the nineteenth century until it reaches its most obvious form in the *Tales of Mystery and Imagination* of Edgar Allan Poe. But with the poets at the beginning of the century wonder was not an attitude cultivated solely for pseudo-æsthetic reasons; it was part of an attempt to reformulate an attitude to life. That it manifested itself in two such opposite ways —in search for the " rich and strange " as well as probing into the ordinary and commonplace—is a tribute to its vitality as a poetic outlook. This attitude did, however, imply a deliberate separation of the poet from other men, leading the poet to regard himself as a prophet whose every utterance is sacred however little it may mean to those who hear it. This had its effect on the poet's conception of his own function. It is not a very long way from Wordsworth's view that the poet creates the taste by which he is to be judged to the view that the poet has no responsibility to society at all, his only duty being to pour forth the products of his inspiration. This lack of responsibility of the poet to his public is one of the most serious results of the " Romantic Movement." It reacted on the public's view of what a literary man ought to do, so that when writers tried to say something of practical importance they were dismissed as merely literary men and their message was not taken seriously. How far the " art for art's sake " theory that prevailed at the end of the nineteenth century was due to " sour grapes " on the part of the artist, and how far it was a genuine descendant of earlier romantic theories, is difficult to discover. There is no doubt that the artist himself must take a large part of the blame for the conspiracy not to take the artist seriously that is such a feature of modern life, even if the blame ultimately rests with the public.

Wordsworth (1770–1850), Coleridge (1772–1834), and Southey (1774–1843) lived to abjure the revolutionary enthusiasm of their youth, but the romantic revolt went on, displaying new characteristics as new writers arose. The revolt against urban artificiality gradually grew into an antagonism to the whole of bourgeois society. The artist tended to become a voluntary outcast, contemptuous of the civilisation in which he lived, acknowledging no principle of control, no norm of conduct, no social function. This movement reached its full development in French literature in the middle and latter part of the nineteenth century, and never became dominant in Britain, though its influence was felt here, perhaps more in criticism than in creative writing. The "Romantic Movement" began as a conscious protest and never lost its attitude of rebellion. But this attitude took two forms. It might mean, as in Shelley, a genuine desire to reform the world, to preach against the evils of contemporary life and paint the ideal in glowing colours. Or it might mean pure escapism, denial of all responsibility and obligation, recognition of no objective standards, complete reliance on emotion and feeling. The decadence of English Romanticism, as seen at the end of the century in the work of Oscar Wilde or Ernest Dowson, produced the theory of the functionlessness of art. Critics rose to meet this theory, and even in our own time we have had writers like H. L. Mencken asserting that the sole function of art is to purge the emotions of the artist, so that literature would become a mere by-product of purgation. Thus the wheel comes full circle: from interpreting society to itself and expressing in beautiful, polished phrases thoughts with which everyone agrees and ideas universally accepted the writer eventually comes to expressing his emotions in the most individual and personal manner possible. To Addison the poet was a man of unusual sense and insight talking in silver tones to his fellow men in the drawing-room; the romantic poet at his most extreme—or most decadent—is a lone outcast talking to himself in the wilderness.

But so long as the romantic remained a rebel with a message he was saved from complete seclusion in the ivory tower. Byron (1788–1824) and Shelley (1792–1822) were both rebels, in a more popular sense than Wordsworth ever was. Byron had a grudge against society, and without being very clear about its real defects and without being at all certain as to how it ought to be reformed, devoted his chief attention to satirising bourgeois life. His heroes were those who had broken the rules of conventional morality—Cain, or Don Juan. He loved to sneer at middle-class respectability, at all that the ordinary man reverenced, but he had no constructive criticisms to offer. His aristocratic birth, of which he was very conscious, encouraged his contempt of a commercial civilisation, and his egotistic and theatrical nature led him to pose as the misunderstood genius, driven out by a society that was too petty and sordid to appreciate him. He is at his best as a satirist, for his habit of mind was almost entirely destructive. Shelley was a rebel of a different kind. He is a descendant of Paine and Godwin, believing firmly in the natural goodness of man, the power of reason to change the world, and the evil influence of institutions. In many ways he is the complete Godwinite, adhering to the principles of *Political Justice* (a book which he admired tremendously) even after Godwin himself had become doubtful of them. His programme of reform is vague and idealistic. Abolish kings and priests, make room for the natural goodness of human nature to assert itself, and a new world will arise. Shelley has not the sophistication of Byron; his nature is generous and ingenuous, and to the end he remains ignorant of the world. This lack of contact with normal human life is his main defect as a poet, besides making him futile as a thinker. He is the apostle of revolt from above. He has no knowledge of social and economic forces, and though he is conscious in a general way of human misery he knows nothing of its detailed causes and believes that the only way to eliminate it is for the thinkers—the Godwins and the Shelleys—to explain why Governments and institutions are bound to lead to oppression and wrong and so pave the way for a conscious and rational revolution. How far Shelley seriously thought such a revolution possible is difficult to determine: his own practical activity was limited to the distribution of pamphlets in Ireland. But in his poetry he is continually stressing the inevitability of man's natural goodness eventually destroying the bonds that enslave the world. He thinks chiefly of the ideal rather than of the means to its attainment, and though later socialist thinkers may look on him as a forerunner

LITERATURE AND SOCIETY 199

he is in no way a political thinker in the modern sense. He has the outlook on life of a sensitive and intelligent child. He never faced the real problems of earthly existence, though on the other hand he never consciously retired into a dream world. If he did spend his life in an unreal world he did not realise it: he thought it was the real world and judged accordingly. That is why Shelley, for all his great lyrical faculty, is a poet whom we find, sooner or later, to be unsatisfying.

While poets were building Utopias in verse, the working classes were struggling to improve the grim conditions under which they lived and worked. A discussion of working-class movements is outside the scope of this book, but brief mention must be made of the activity carried on in the hope of improving industrial conditions. At first the movement was largely agrarian, agitators like Cobbett endeavouring to restore the old days of the peasant proprietor and fighting against the new industrialism. But once it was seen that industrialism had come to stay, and that neither Tom Paine's schemes of " agrarian justice," Cobbett's backward-looking reform movement nor the practice of smashing machinery would alter matters, a more practical outlook developed. When the Napoleonic wars came to an end in 1815 an agricultural depression combined with an economic slump set in, rendering the condition of the workers both in town and country worse than ever before. Wages dropped, factories closed down, unemployment increased. The resultant widespread misery gave an impetus to radical agitation. Demonstrations and riots took place, but these only encouraged the Government in its policy of severe repression. It is probable that in the four or five years after the conclusion of the Napoleonic wars England came nearer to revolution than ever since. But the working class were completely unorganised, and the middle-class radicals on whom they depended had none but the most constitutional aims in view. It was not until after 1820 that some kind of constructive working-class policy began to take shape. Hitherto despair had been the main motive, and an unreasoning desire to get rid of the machines and return to pre-industrial conditions the most obvious feature, in all agitation. But from now on trade unionism developed rapidly, and a rudimentary socialism began to take root. The working class began to make themselves felt in journalism, acquiring organisation, responsibility, and a method of putting their case before the public. They supported the movement which resulted in the Reform Bill of 1832, unaware that parliamentary reform of the kind granted by the Reform Bill was a purely middle-class advantage, putting Parliament directly under the control of the class which had long achieved economic domination and which could no longer be kept from direct political power. But the principle was sound, and universal adult suffrage, once voiced as an ideal, was eventually to lead to more complete reform and thus put a powerful constitutional weapon in the hands of the workers. One of the first reformers to turn his face to the future instead of back to the past was Robert Owen, the founder of the co-operative movement. In accepting industrialism and realising that the machine, if rightly used and controlled, could be of incalculable service to the community, he did a great service to the working-class movement, directing its attention to the possibilities of the social control of industry.

But while the workers' movements made slow progress the dominating force in the country was the middle class with its policy of social and economic *laissez faire*. After the Reform Bill both Whigs and Tories accepted the middle-class franchise as the basis of parliamentary activity, and the country settled down to enjoy complete bourgeois domination. The Tories became Conservatives and the Whigs became Liberals. Liberalism is the most characteristic product of bourgeois thought. Its main purpose was to free the individual from undue government interference, in the firm belief that the free play of individualism always worked out for the best. In the economic sphere, this view had been systematically expressed by Adam Smith in his *Wealth of Nations*, but free trade as a national policy was not put into operation until the repeal of the Corn Laws by Peel in 1846. But Liberalism was responsible for much more than free trade. Bentham and James Mill, whose thought lay behind most Liberal ideas throughout most of the century, were the apostles of freedom in the political and religious as well as in the economic sphere. The individual must be allowed to think and (within wide limits) act as he pleases, for only by the automatic balancing of forces thus achieved can the " greatest good of the greatest number " be attained. Thus the abundant legislation removing restrictions and disabilities of all kinds—such as the emancipation of the Catholics, the abolition of university tests, the establishing of free trade, the granting to Jews of the right to sit in Parliament—were all products of this attitude, whether the particular laws were passed by a Conservative or a Liberal Government. Indeed, throughout the middle years of the nineteenth century there was little if any fundamental difference between the two parties.

There was an ugly side to Liberal individualism. Believing as it did in the untrammelled play of economic forces, it extended the doctrine of non-interference to matters of social distress and industrial conditions. The Factory Acts, abolishing by degrees the iniquities of child labour and overworking, were passed under protest, as it were, after individual philanthropists had brought the appalling conditions to the notice of the public in a way that could not be ignored. Social legislation of this kind—the Factory Acts of 1833 to 1878 (Consolidating Act), the Mines Act of 1842, forbidding the employment of women and children underground, the acts of 1867 and 1873 concerning the employment of women and children in rough agricultural labour, the acts of 1834 and 1864 concerning boy chimney sweeps, even the Public Health Acts of 1871–5—all this legislation was put through under pressure and in the face of strenuous opposition from the individualist and *laissez-faire* point of view. Any interference with the rights of private property, with the liberty of the employer to use his wealth and his employees as he chose, with the natural working of the laws of profit-making, was fiercely resisted. This attitude drew strength from the population theory put forward in Malthus's *Essay on Population* (1798). Malthus's book was originally written as a reply to the optimistic radicalism of Godwin, but it was far-reaching in its effects. It maintained that, as population increased in geometrical progression, the natural checks provided by misery, poverty, disease, and war were necessary to prevent over-population. He urged the danger of "coddling" the people by too generous social services, which would only increase breeding and counteract natural forces, and advocated also "moral restraint" in keeping down the population level. This was an argument which could be brought—and often was brought—against every kind of social legislation. The Poor Law Amendment Act of 1834 was motivated by a mixture of Benthamism and Malthusianism. It was Liberal and Benthamite in that, by stopping outdoor relief and herding the poor together in deliberately unattractive workhouses, it put a premium on self-reliance and independent labour, however ill-paid. The principles guiding the Royal Commission which recommended the legislation were that of "all or nothing"—the recipient of relief to surrender his freedom completely and be entirely dependent on the workhouse or else get no relief at all—and that of "less eligibility"—the workhouses were to be made as unpleasant and depressing as possible, so that no one would seek poor relief unless it was absolutely necessary. Thus the worst kind of job was made preferable to pauperism, and every kind of loafing was discouraged. The law was Malthusian in that it restricted relief to a minimum and recognised the folly of maintaining the poor with comfortable doles: it was argued that the principle of granting doles to the poor in proportion to the size of the family only encouraged the poor to have children and thus added to the danger of over-population.

So we see that there were two sides to nineteenth-century Liberalism. In stressing freedom and the independence of the individual it did good work and produced much wholly admirable legislation; but in defining the rights of the individual as including complete liberty to do what he liked with his own property, even when that property consisted in means of production, it meant that freedom for the working classes was only freedom to work under the conditions imposed by the employers and, if no work was required, freedom to starve. Once the system of industrial capitalism was set firmly on its feet, as it was by the fifties of the nineteenth century, the middle classes could afford to grant concessions and enact social legislation that contradicted the *laissez-faire* principle, but that such legislation was no necessary outcome of their view of society is the gravest criticism of Liberalism. This was seen by John Stuart Mill (1806-1873: son of James Mill) who was brought up by his father as a Benthamite utilitarian but who came to see the limitations of the *laissez-faire* principle. He gradually extended the field within which he thought government interference necessary, and by the end of his life was, to all intents and purposes, a socialist, believing in the social responsibility of the Government and the necessity for interfering with the private ownership of the means of production. Mill never seemed himself quite to realise the extent to which he had departed from orthodox Benthamism or the implication of his final intellectual position. We can see now that it was much closer to that of the Fabian socialists than to the older utilitarianism.

How far was the literature of the time a reflection of bourgeois society and the bourgeois attitude? We have already discussed romantic escapism, and noted that certain sensitive minds found middle-class complacency too much for them and retired into a world of their own. From the end of the eighteenth century we have constantly to reckon with this attitude. Escapism is, of course, very much older than that, but deliberate escape from an uncongenial society becomes a pronounced and constant feature of literature once industrialism establishes itself. It might be complete escape, or it might be temporary escape in order to return with new data for the interpretation of human life. There is too the literature of revolt, often combined with escape as in Byron and Shelley and, later (though to a much less extent), Ruskin and Morris. Keats (1795–1821) had a different attitude again: he refused to concern himself with the obvious activity of men in society but endeavoured, rather, to explore aspects of experience that do not arise directly out of any given set of social conditions. That is always the harder task, and it takes a poet of the finest calibre to succeed. That Keats, like Shakespeare, did succeed, that he did, in spite of his youth, have the insight into certain constant phases of human emotion that enabled him to produce poetry of permanent value, as well as the technical skill to express what he saw, is the reason why he is the greatest poet of his generation. He dealt only with what he knew and understood—not as fact, but as emotional experience—and thus, at its best, his work has a maturity which Shelley never achieved. For most writers, to isolate themselves from society is dangerous if not fatal, but Keats preserved his insight into aspects of reality even when he turned to the Middle Ages for inspiration. Let the reader turn to the fourteenth stanza of *Isabella* and consider the significance of Keats's sudden illumination of the economic background of romantic idleness.

But, in spite of everything, it was only a minority of writers who rejected contemporary society. The novelists in particular looked at the life in the midst of which they found themselves and used it as the material for their work. This was a tradition of the novel from the time of Richardson and Fielding, each of whom had interpreted in their own way the life of their contemporaries as they saw it. Smollett, in his roving novels, had depicted variegated scenes of town and country life at home and abroad, stressing particularly the less savoury elements in which the picaresque novel specialised. Later, Fanny Burney drew material from the social life of the upper classes. The novel had now established its claim to take the whole of social life into its view, and deal with any class from the rogues and cheats found in the pages of Defoe and Smollett to the drawing-room company of *Evelina*. At the very beginning of the nineteenth century Jane Austen (1775–1817) showed what could be made of the narrow lives of upper-class country society. She is the annalist of a decaying class—the landed gentry and their satellites—and her work gives a most vivid picture of English country society in the days when the industrial revolution had not yet transformed the face of the country and the old ways of living and thinking. The picture that emerges from her novels is essentially an eighteenth-century one; the new forces are not yet visible and the old standards still prevail. Her young ladies have all the tastes and enthusiasms and snobberies of a society governed by a landed aristocracy; her heroes are Darcys and Knightleys—country gentlemen of culture and refinement and large estates; her young men, if they are younger sons and do not succeed to estates, buy commissions in the army or, if they cannot even afford that, go into the Church as a respectable and easy profession with considerable material advantages. It is because of her very restriction in scope that Jane Austen is able to write with such delicacy and truth. What she does see she sees so clearly that a satirical note emerges almost without her being aware. There is a certain hard clarity in her picture of society that one does not associate with a female writer, and the result is a crystal clear portrait of one aspect of an age. The working world is not shown at all; at the most we have an occasional glimpse of lower middle-class society which nearly always appears as vulgar and ill-mannered. It is a petty world of ladies and gentlemen and would-be ladies and gentlemen, and the omissions are as eloquent as what is included. The author belongs to that world and knows no other, yet she has the intelligence and the clarity of vision to realise its pettiness, perhaps only half consciously. She writes for a middle-class audience, very much like herself in interests and social position, but whether the same sense of irony that is apparent to us was obvious to her contemporaries is difficult to say.

Eighteenth-century society in disintegration at the beginning of the nineteenth is admirably shown in the novels of Thomas Love Peacock (1785-1866), most of which are satirical sketches—almost caricatures—of upper middle-class society of the time. The hard-drinking Epicurean clergyman, the romantic young lady, the bluff squire, the transcendental philosopher (satire of Kant and Coleridge), the political pamphleteer, the optimistic believer in constant progress (anticipating the typical Victorian view, represented by Macaulay) and the pessimistic Malthusian all make their appearance. There is satire of the universities, dormant and useless throughout the eighteenth century and in the early years of the nineteenth, and of the Church, worldly and sluggish and suspicious of any attempt at reform, as well as of all the ideas Peacock considered new-fangled and ridiculous. Peacock's works are as much an attack on contemporary thought as on society, and the element of caricature that is never long absent makes them not always reliable, but they remain a valuable source for the student of manners and opinions of the time. At times we feel that Peacock is writing as an aristocrat, resenting the intrusion of a new class with its new ideas: at other times he appears as the satirist of the landed-gentry class of his day. The general impression is that he represents the old order, looking with disfavour on the disrupting and disintegrating elements developing in the thought and society of his day.

The Victorian novelists deal boldly with society as they see it and are almost all propagandists of a kind. Dickens (1812-1870), himself of humble origin, is chiefly interested in lower middle-class life and looks on the workers from the lower middle-class point of view at its most sympathetic—understanding, that is, owing to propinquity, rather than insisting on drawing a dividing line that is not at all obvious to the outsider. A considerable amount of his work is vitiated by that sentimentalism which seems in origin to be the compensating factor for middle-class indifference to social misery, though Dickens himself had none of that indifference. Dickens has no doctrinaire view of society, and he is neither the complete anti-Benthamite nor the complete socialist. He deals with life in patches as he sees it, and attacks abuses out of the generosity of his nature rather than from any definite political or social creed. He has a real understanding of certain aspects of lower middle- and working-class life and has the gift of creating a type of character which, though a preposterous caricature in itself, yet sums up a whole world of truth about a section of life and activity with which he is familiar. Most of his books attack some definite social evil: *Nicholas Nickleby* attacks the profit-making private schools; *Bleak House*, the painfully slow and cumbrous working of the law; *The Old Curiosity Shop*, the cruelties of child labour; *Dombey and Son*, the cold, unconscious cruelty and almost megalomaniac self-importance of the zealous capitalist; *Oliver Twist*, the workhouse system; and the other novels have a similar social purpose. Even *The Pickwick Papers*, a book whose essential nature is comic and good-humouredly satirical, gives a grim picture of the debtors' prison and attacks the evangelical preacher in the person of the hypocritical Mr. Stiggins. Dickens writes for a middle-class, even a lower middle-class, audience. In his whole attitude to society he is the lowest in the social ladder of all our novelists up to his time, with the possible exception of Defoe, if he can be called a novelist. He is not describing low life for the amusement of the gentry, as Gay did in his *Beggar's Opera*, nor does his work possess the casual picaresque quality of Smollett's adventurous tales. His characters appear in their own right, and his work represents an important stage in the democratising of literature. The increase in the reading public, which goes on at a rapid rate throughout the nineteenth century, is reflected more, perhaps, in the work of Dickens than in that of any other front-rank writer.

We have mentioned Dickens's attack on evangelical religion in the *Pickwick Papers*, and before proceeding with our discussion of the Victorian novelists it might be well to say something of the evangelical movement, the most influential movement of its kind in the nineteenth century. It began with the Wesleyan protest against the apathy of the Church of England in the eighteenth century, and developed rapidly into a kind of new Puritanism which found ready favour with the middle classes. It was no Puritanism in the historical sense, having little relation to the specific theology of sixteenth-century Puritan controversialists, but it did stress personal salvation, the power of the individual conscience, and the unimportance of institutions compared with the letter of the Bible, in a way that is strongly reminiscent of the Puritans of two hundred years before. This religious attitude had never really died out, and it required only the slightest encouragement for it to become again an important force in English life. Evangelical religion laid stress on decorum and decency in outward life, on avoiding above all sins of the senses, and of maintaining " respectability." It was responsible for a great deal of thoroughly praiseworthy humanitarian and philanthropic activity; from its numbers were drawn a large proportion of those who opposed the slave trade and who organised the philanthropical movements which grew up in such numbers throughout the century. Yet in many ways it was but the complement of Benthamism, of *laissez faire*, of capitalist exploitation. Just as the seventeenth-century Puritans preached an individualist religion and thus freed themselves from all social responsibility and even found it possible to regard material prosperity as the sign of God's blessing and poverty as a sign of spiritual unworthiness, so their descendants in the nineteenth century tended to regard material self-seeking and money-making as entirely worthy and religious pursuits and to consider the poor and the materially unsuccessful as lacking in the virtues of self-reliance and industry and thus to blame for their lack of fortune. It was rarely that the matter was expressed as bluntly as this (though it was done so more often than the modern reader would imagine), but this view was implicit in the Nonconformist attitude. While the *laissez-faire* Liberal advocated a freedom which on examination is found to mean only freedom for one section of the people, the Nonconformist put forward a view of righteousness which was far too narrow to admit of application to society as a whole. The narrowness of the evangelical attitude became increasingly marked as the nineteenth century advanced, growing most noticeable in the second quarter of the century. Edmund Gosse, in his autobiographical record *Father and Son*, has given a vivid picture of the effects on family life of the evangelical creed, and if we realise that Gosse is describing a particularly enlightened character we can understand something of the restricted outlook of the ordinary nineteenth-century middle-class Nonconformist. Yet this attitude spelt " religion " to the great majority of the bourgeoisie in England; it was a force in social life whose strength cannot be overestimated, being the only guarantee of morality of any kind that existed. An age that refuses to believe in any kind of purposive action or interference in social matters and has complete faith in the certainty of unrestricted individualism working out for the best, which has no real belief in any standards except in such as can be reduced to the one standard of personal prosperity, which has no use for a tolerant humanism or a purely scientific outlook, has to fall back entirely on such religious creed as it possesses for every kind of sanction. Evangelical religion was the ultimate sanction behind the activity of millions of ordinary Englishmen in the first half of the nineteenth century, and this perhaps explains why it was unconsciously narrowed down to suit the practical interests of the middle classes. Whatever the reason, there can be no doubt that the bleak atmosphere of Nonconformist Protestantism at this time aroused the anger and the opposition of men as different as Charles Dickens and John Henry Newman —of the former because it appeared to be the result of gross hypocrisy, of the latter from more purely theological motives. Matthew Arnold was another who, on more humanist grounds, led a later revolt against the drab and narrow outlook of the majority of middle-class men and women. A point of view which aroused the antagonism of three such different characters was bound to have very grave deficiencies.

The evangelical attitude was expressed in numerous minor works, in particular in magazine stories and poems. Sermons, too, were more popular than at any time since the seventeenth century. Samuel Smiles's *Self-Help* (1859) gives perfect expression to the practical side of this attitude, extolling thrift, hard work, honest money-making, and the desire to rise in the world. Such a doctrine left little room for the arts or for any non-utilitarian activity; it made of life a means to an end, without giving thought to the question of how the end was to be enjoyed once it was attained. If pressed on points of theology, Samuel Smiles would have admitted that in any case this life was but the prelude to a higher existence and that those who, in spite of everything, remained poor and miserable could have that consolation. For side by side with the urge to rise in the world (" Ever remember, my dear Dan, that you should look forward to being some day manager of that concern ") was the view that one ought to do one's duty in the station to which it had pleased God to call one—but this latter argument was generally addressed only to inferiors.

The first great protest against evangelical Christianity in the form it had assumed at the beginning of the second quarter of the nineteenth century came from the side of Anglo-Catholicism. The emancipation of the

Catholics in 1829, followed by the Reform Bill of 1832, put the Established Church in a minority with regard to political influence. Hitherto the Church of England had represented the religion of the governing classes, however widespread dissent may have been among the people. But the extension of the franchise in 1832 created a vast middle-class electorate which was largely Nonconformist in religion. Church of England men began to talk of the Church being in danger. Feeling was heightened by the bringing in of the Irish Church Bill in 1833, and in the following year John Keble and John Henry Newman (1801–1890) began to bring out their *Tracts for the Times*, appealing to the Anglican clergy to consider the position and realise that they were part of the Holy Catholic Church and not a mere department of State. The " Oxford Movement " was begun. The leaders of the movement were more concerned with theology than with social questions, but their religious position led them to attack the principles of Liberal political economy, which Newman condemned as " a categorical contradiction of our Lord, S. Paul, S. Chrysostom, S. Leo, and all saints."[1] But in condemning the worship of money and the utilitarian view of happiness Newman showed himself as indifferent to social questions as the most extreme supporter of *laissez faire*. If money was evil, the poor were blessed, for theirs was the kingdom of God.

Newman is an important figure in English literature, his *Apologia pro Vita Sua* (1864) being a classic in virtue of its beautiful prose style and sincerity of thought. But

[1] Quoted by M. Beer, *History of British Socialism* (London, 1920), Vol. II, p. 179.

at bottom he is as much concerned with personal salvation as the evangelical, and his message is for men as ideal individuals rather than for society as it is. He takes no account of problems other than those concerned with religion and culture, and he deals with men in abstraction from their environment, so that his movement remained that of a very small minority, with no appeal to those whose problems were of a more practical nature. Kingsley's question, " What is the use of preaching about heaven to hungry paupers ? " would have appeared to him irrelevant, and this fact is sufficient to show that his attitude was not wide enough to take in all the facts. It was not that the Catholic Church did not have a well-defined attitude to social problems (Newman became a Catholic in 1845), though it is doubtful if this attitude would have helped in the nineteenth century, but that Newman himself was more concerned with other matters.

The inadequacy both of the current evangelical view and of the view of the Oxford reformers where social questions were concerned was seen by Frederick Denison Maurice, the leader of Christian socialism in England. This movement had for its aim the application of practical Christianity to politics. Maurice believed that a truly Christian society would have to be socialist in nature, based on understanding co-operation rather than on commercial competition. This view was very similar to that of Owen, and differed chiefly in that its ultimate sanction was religion, not reason. The responsibility for initiating political action lay with the Church: " We want the Church fully to understand her own foundation, fully to work out the communism which is implied in her existence. Church Reformation, therefore, in its highest sense, involves *theologically* the reassertion of these truths in their fullness, apart from their Calvinistical and Tractarian limitations and dilutions; *socially* the assertion on the ground of these truths of an actually living community under Christ, in which no man has a right to call anything that he has his own, but in which there is spiritual fellowship and practical co-operation."[1] The Christian socialists carried on for some years, promoting co-operative enterprises on a small scale and trying to put their views before the public. But the movement fell to pieces, and though many of the points it had raised continued to be discussed and developed, Christian socialism as a coherent creed and organisation did not survive, at least not in the form which its original members had given it. Maurice and his associates had, however, rendered a great service to religious and social thought in stressing the Church's responsibility to society and boldly facing issues that contemporary religious thinkers refused to meet. And Maurice rendered what was perhaps an even greater service: he pointed out the narrowness of conventional evangelical theology, showing the futility of basing ethical conduct solely on a desire to avoid hell-fire, the fundamental immorality of grounding virtue on fear, and the evil complacency bred by such a narrow and selfish view. He was more interested in Christian ethics than in Christian dogma, and attacked the formalistic piety so common in his day—the attitude that regarded

[1] Quoted in M. Beer, op. cit., Vol. II, p. 182, from J. Maurice, *Life of F. D. Maurice*, p. 10.

whistling on Sunday as a greater sin than utter lack of charity. He refused to box religion up into a separate compartment, believing that " God is to be sought and honoured in every pursuit, not merely in something technically called religion."[1] Maurice is thus one of the chief influences in the broadening of the basis of Christianity which went on in the latter half of the nineteenth century. To his contemporaries his life seemed largely a failure, but he achieved more than they or he himself knew.

Among the group of Christian socialists was Charles Kingsley (1819–1875), known to-day as a novelist and an opponent of Newman. Kingsley in his early days was a pamphleteer and an agitator, sympathetic to the Chartist movement and bitterly critical of contemporary working-class conditions. When the Christian socialist movement collapsed he carried on his work in propagandist novels. *Yeast* and *Alton Locke* are two of the most formidable indictments of working-class conditions that have ever come from the pen of an English novelist. *Yeast* deals with the treatment of agricultural labourers by country squires and reveals the appalling conditions of the rural proletariat under the landed gentry. *Alton Locke* deals with industrial conditions, explaining the origins and development of the Chartist movement from 1844 to 1848 by showing the facts which underlay it. Even *The Water Babies*, a rather "slushy" children's book, contains propaganda against the employment of boy climbers by chimney

[1] Maurice was referring to the only effective way of combating the Secularists—by opposing equally the " Religionists," that is those who treated religion as something isolated from normal life. See D. C. Somervell, *English Thought in the Nineteenth Century*, p. 117.

sweeps and a considerable didactic element. *Two Years Ago* gives a grim description of the cholera epidemic of 1849. *Westward Ho!* is the only novel of Kingsley's that is entirely free from propaganda; it is an historical adventure novel of fairly high quality, though even here readers may detect an anti-Catholic bias (of the kind noticeable in J. A. Froude's historical works) which shows his inherent controversialism.

Kingsley had not the intellectual quality of either Newman or Maurice, but of his sincerity and practical energy there can be no doubt. He was interested in the condition of the working people of England to an extent unequalled among British novelists. He firmly believed that true Christianity involved action in social matters and that the Christianisation of democracy would result in some kind of co-operative socialism that would remedy the evils against which he so violently protested. In spite of all his prejudices and limitations he remains a sympathetic figure, a writer of poetic temperament who devoted his life to championing the cause of labour by the most effective method at his command.

Other novelists of the time, their interest awakened by the general discussion of industrial questions that went on inside and outside Parliament in the late forties and early fifties of the century, presented descriptions of industrial conditions in their work, but none so consistently or with such singleness of purpose as Kingsley. Mrs. Trollope's *Michael Armstrong* (1839) gives a picture of factory conditions, and *Helen Fleetwood* by Charlotte Tonna (1841) attacks the whole system of factory labour, giving a grim picture of its cruelties and pleading for action by the community and, in particular, the Church. Disraeli's *Sybil* (1845) presents a picture of society divided into " two nations, between whom there is no intercourse and no sympathy." The early stages of Chartism are traced, and the " wail of intolerable serfage " which Chartism represents attributed to the conditions brought about by the capitalists' worship of Mammon, to the transformation of society in the name of the sacredness of wealth and toil, and to the supplanting of the artisan by the machine. Disraeli's remedy is to reunite the two nations, the rich and the poor, in a common loyalty to English traditions and institutions and in common opposition to the middle-class Liberal capitalists and Benthamites whose policy had brought things to such a pass. How this is to be achieved is not made very clear. Mrs. Gaskell's *Mary Barton* (1848) and *North and South* (1855) also deal with industrial conditions from no definite political point of view, and Charlotte Brontë's *Shirley* (1848) gives a vivid picture of anti-machine riots and the feeling that produced them.

There were novelists who were not concerned with the industrial scene, though critical of contemporary society. Thackeray (1811–1863), like Dickens, was both a sentimentalist and a satirist, but his attitude was very different from that of Dickens. He wrote of a higher stratum of society than that which Dickens was concerned with, and his satire was more specifically social satire in the narrower sense. As a rule, his social unit is the family and he is more concerned with relations within this small group than with wider questions of class and the stratification of society. He has affinities with Fielding, both in his method of treatment and in the kind of life of which he treats. In *Barry Lyndon* he gives the history of a rogue in the same satirical vein as Fielding's *Jonathan Wild*. But his greatest works, such as *Vanity Fair* and *The Newcomes*, deal mostly with life in the drawing-room—both with those who belong there and those who, like Becky Sharp, get there by hook or by crook—and the title *Vanity Fair* is an indication of Thackeray's scope and aim as a novelist. He is critical of upper-class society as he sees it, and paints it from the point of view of the ethical sentimentalist, who finds the hardness and cruelty and hypocrisy of society highly disagreeable and constantly intervenes with moral comment, yet who knows so well what he is describing that sometimes he is led into a half-sympathy with it. Becky Sharp, the hard and unscrupulous adventuress of *Vanity Fair*, can only exist because society has the kind of weakness and viciousness of which she can take advantage, yet Becky is not a wholly unsympathetic figure. Thackeray is showing up "society," and his moral indignation, his satiric comments and almost rhetorical digressions show where his sympathies lie and what his own views are. He is not concerned, however, to probe below the surface of the life he sees to seek causes and underlying factors: he looks at a small section of life and comments on what he observes.

A quieter and more objective novelist is Anthony Trollope (1815–1882), who portrays middle-class country society in its more domestic aspects. In his "Barsetshire" novels he averts his gaze completely from industrial life, and shows the old order at its most favourable. Trollope is troubled by all the new forces that are beginning to make themselves felt: in *The Warden* he satirises Church reform by showing its effect on the benevolent and unsuspecting individual to whom the abuses of the system are not obvious and whose whole life is grounded in the old order. The ever growing power of the Press is satirised; the all-powerful *Times*, as *Juppiter*, is shown as a ruthless exploiter of half-understood facts for purely political reasons. Stress is laid on the helplessness of the individual, typified by the Warden himself, in the grip of new impersonal forces; the only type of character that can be successful in such a world is the hard, unscrupulous careerist, who has no room for sentiment or irrational benevolence. Trollope is to be numbered among the backward-looking novelists: he sees country society as a pleasant and stable background against which is played the tragi-comedy of domestic life, and he resents any change or interference that may come to complicate the issue. Without Jane Austen's delicate satire and clarity of vision, he has given us in the "Barsetshire" novels a picture of Jane Austen's society some fifty years later.

Throughout the nineteenth century there is the constant contrast between literature of criticism and revolt and literature of acquiescence. At the beginning of the century the former is predominant, and right on to the present day it has constituted a large part of literature. After the French Revolution came the Godwinite writers, the Rousseauists and the rebel idealists. Then the new age took shape, and a literature of acquiescence grew up, but not before social and industrial problems had claimed the attention of writers so that from now on the " condition of England question " finds continual expression in literary work. So the chronological order is, (1) idealist revolt (for example Shelley); (2) acquiescence (for example Macaulay and later Tennyson) which partly overlaps with (3) revolt against social and general conditions (for example many of the novelists, Carlyle, Ruskin, Morris, etc.). Macaulay (1800–1859) is the first great prophet of the age of progress. Nowhere is the nineteenth-century Whig point of view put more clearly than in the concluding paragraphs of the essay on Southey's *Colloquies* (1850):

> " If we were to prophesy that in the year 1930 a population of fifty millions, better fed, clad, and lodged than the English of our time, will cover these islands, that Sussex and Huntingdonshire will be wealthier than the wealthiest parts of the West Riding of Yorkshire now are, that cultivation rich as that of a flower-garden will be carried up to the very tops of Ben Nevis and Helvellyn, that machines constructed on principles yet undiscovered will be in every house, that there will be no highways but railroads, no travelling but by steam, that our debt, vast as it seems to us, will appear to our great grandchildren a trifling encumbrance, which might easily be paid off in a year or two, many people would think us insane. We prophesy nothing; but this we say: if any person had told the Parliament which met in perplexity and terror after the crash of 1720[1] that in 1830 the wealth of England would surpass

[1] The South Sea Bubble crash.

all their wildest dreams—that London would be twice as large and twice as populous, and that nevertheless the rate of mortality would have diminished to one half of what it then was . . . that stage-coaches would run from York to London in twenty-four hours, that men would be in the habit of sailing without wind, and would be beginning to ride without horses, our ancestors would have given as much credit to the prediction as they gave to Gulliver's Travels. Yet the prediction would have been true. . . . On what principle is it, then, that when we see nothing but improvement behind us, we are to expect nothing but deterioration before us ? . . .

" It is not by the intermeddling of Mr. Southey's idol, the omniscient and omnipotent State, but by the prudence and energy of the people, that England has been carried forward in civilisation; and it is to the same prudence and the same energy that we now look with comfort and good hope. Our rulers will best promote the improvement of the nation by strictly confining themselves to their own legitimate duties, by leaving capital to find its most lucrative course, commodities their fair price, industry and intelligence their natural reward, idleness and folly their natural punishment, by maintaining peace, by defending property, by diminishing the price of law, and by observing strict economy in every department of the State. Let the Government do this: the People will assuredly do the rest."[1]

[1] *Critical and Historical Essays contributed to the " Edinburgh Review" by Lord Macaulay*, edited by F. C. Montague (London, 1903), Vol. I, pp. 245-7.

Here we have, as early as 1830, the two principles of nineteenth-century Liberalism—progress and *laissez faire*—enunciated with forcefulness and clarity. That Macaulay was not a Radical and that the Liberal point of view remained quite free from any " levelling " doctrines, can be seen from the speeches of Macaulay and Lord John Russell (both Whigs) against the second national petition of the Chartists (1842). " I am opposed," said Macaulay, " to universal suffrage. I believe universal suffrage would be fatal to all purposes for which government exists, and that it is utterly incompatible with the very existence of civilisation. I conceive that civilisation rests on the security of property. While property is insecure, it is not in the power of the finest soil, or of the moral and intellectual constitution of any country, to prevent the country sinking into barbarism, while, on the other hand, so long as property is secure it is not possible to prevent a country advancing in prosperity."[1] Therefore the extension of the franchise to the working class—to any class " which would, to a moral certainty, be induced to commit great and systematic inroads against the security of property "—would be fatal. Macaulay would, and did, support the middle-class franchise, but the demands of the Chartists for universal adult suffrage were more than he could stomach. (The suffrage was not extended to the working class until 1867, by which time the solidarity of the working-class movement was greatly increased, not only within the country but even internationally, and at the same time—a more potent factor—the capitalist system was working

[1] Quoted in M. Beer, *History of British Socialism*, Vol. II, p. 135.

so smoothly that everyone tended to assume that the workers had as much stake in preserving conditions as they were as any other class: the revolutionary atmosphere of 1815 to 1820 and of 1848 was gone.) Lord John Russell, in opposing the Chartist petition, used the other Liberal argument—the utilitarian. " ... The consideration of public good should prevail and no inalienable right can be quoted against that which the good of the whole demands. And as our society is very complicated and property very unequally divided, it might come that a parliament issued from universal suffrage might destroy or shake those institutions which are of the utmost value in holding society together."[1]

Macaulay, historian, essayist, and critic, is thus the first literary man who puts forward clearly and cogently the point of view on political and social questions which becomes dominant in the middle part of the nineteenth century. His work represents more than acquiescence in the new industrial civilisation: he is actively concerned to promote and encourage it in an optimistic and enthusiastic manner. The optimism of Macaulay might be compared with that of Pope. Both writers look with complacency on their own age and appreciate the great progress which has immediately preceded it and made it possible. Both believe in the automatic working out of everything for the best, in partial evil being universal good, in the complete pattern excusing the ugliness of particular parts. Macaulay is perhaps the more sincere, for behind the optimism of Pope and his age lay a cynicism and low

[1] M. Beer, op. cit., Vol. II, p. 137.

Ps

estimate of human nature of the kind found in the letters of Lord Chesterfield, which is quite foreign to the nineteenth-century Liberal. But the main difference between the two lies in the fact that the nineteenth century believed in continual progress and the early eighteenth believed that it had reached the summit of civilisation where everything was henceforth to rest. Macaulay's view of civilisation was dynamic, while Pope's was static, and to this extent Macaulay was the greater realist. Pope's mistake was to overlook the fact of change; Macaulay's was to identify change with progress and to judge progress by very superficial criteria.

Tennyson (1809–1892) is popularly regarded as the complete Victorian poet, and the popular view is to a large extent justified. Like Macaulay, he represents the literature of acquiescence, or at least of adjustment. He makes a genuine effort to assimilate all the new facts which the scientists and others keep bringing to the notice of the public throughout the century, and to interpret Victorian civilisation in its own terms. His optimism does not come easily, like that of Macaulay: he has an intellectual struggle and does try to face the implications of the scientific materialism which is becoming ever more popular in his time. But he is not a profound thinker, and whenever he finds that an honest attempt to grapple with the problems of contemporary thought is leading him into dangerous paths he hastily retreats into trite, conventional aphorisms. He accepts society as he finds it, and tries to persuade himself that its ideals are genuine ideals by identifying them, quite arbitrarily, with the conceptions of a watered-down and sentimentalised chivalry. His treatment of the Arthurian legends in the *Idylls of the King* is illuminating: the humbug of Victorian middle-class morality is transferred to Arthur's court, where, instead of appearing nobler and finer as Tennyson doubtless intended that it should, its weaknesses are shown up all the more clearly. Tennyson is in many ways a great poet: he had an extraordinary command over language and was able to interpret many aspects of experience in an effective and moving manner. Had he been content to describe, to paint the life he saw against the Victorian background, he would never have been led into that pseudo-prophetic manner which vitiates so much of his later work. But he was not content merely to keep his eye on the object and use his incomparable gift of language in clear-eyed observation and description; he came to regard himself as a philosopher and a teacher whose duty was to reconcile the discordant elements in Victorian civilisation and so evolve a new synthesis, a new unified conception of life which would at once explain and justify the society of his day. This is not necessarily a task unfit for a poet, but it was no fit task for Tennyson, who was too much of his age to see into his age clearly and too much prejudiced in favour of a preconceived solution to be able to approach his problem with real intellectual honesty. The questionings and fumblings of *In Memoriam* (1850), where he endeavours to reconcile religious conceptions such as the belief in immortality with the facts disclosed by science, however sincerely they may have been expressed, are vitiated by the determination, which was with him from the beginning, to work out an answer on definite lines, compatible with a certain definite attitude to life and society. He accepted Queen Victoria and the " respectability " she stood for, he accepted the Victorian middle class and its ideals, he accepted that great façade of religion and morality which hid so much cruelty and vice. He argued about the cruelty of " Nature, red in tooth and claw," but not about the cruelty of the Victorian father who kept his family " respectable " at the expense of repression, prudery, and dangerous ignorance about the most vital matters in human relationships; nor did he concern himself with the cruelties of industrial life. He took no cognisance of social problems, saw no need for any action to clear up the muggy atmosphere which was stifling so much that was healthy and spontaneous in Victorian family life. He idealised instead of examining, prophesied instead of humbly probing into the lives of those around him. These are great faults in a poet who sets out to be at the same time a thinker and an interpreter of his age to itself. In some of his work, where he is poet rather than preacher, dealing with the simpler and more " universal " experiences and emotions, he produces great poetry (" Break, break, break " is one of the finest poems in the language), but his more ambitious products are often vitiated by this lack of truth in his conception of Victorian society and his problems. He did not know enough about what was happening around him, was not able to see sufficiently clearly into the forces at work and the results they produced, to be able to estimate his age justly. He speaks *for* his age when he thinks he is talking *to* his age, and his thought is conditioned by his social environment to an extent he never realises. It was for this reason that the generation immediately succeeding him turned against him so fiercely: in discovering that Tennyson accepted and idealised where he pretended to be analysing and evaluating, later readers became so disillusioned and angry that they forgot his real qualities as a poet and those of his works which display those qualities unspoiled by the prejudices of his age. A poet, like any other man, cannot be entirely free from the prejudices of his time: the greatest poets, however, will choose those aspects of experience in the portrayal of which those prejudices have least chance of obscuring the truth about life and human nature. Shakespeare did that, and Keats at his best, but Tennyson very often failed.

Robert Browning (1812-1889), Tennyson's contemporary with whom it has long been the fashion to compare and contrast him, did not endeavour to define a broad and general attitude to the forces at work in the Victorian age in the way Tennyson did in *In Memoriam*, and to this extent he avoided Tennyson's superficiality of thought. He was more interested in men than in ideas, but men as individuals, not men in society. Social and political problems as such did not concern him; he made no attempt at systematic thought because he was too conscious of the richness and diversity of life to see any use in trying to reduce it to a system. He had his own " philosophy," if we can use that term, but it was not clearly thought out and was largely instinctive in its basis. He believed in life, insisting on its being worth while however frequently it might end in apparent failure; he believed, like Carlyle, in work and " carrying on "; he was of an energetic and optimistic nature, his optimism being neither the Whig optimism of Macaulay nor the painfully rationalised optimism of Tennyson, but a fundamental part of his character; and he had a genuine curiosity about men and the workings of the human mind. Browning has not Tennyson's tendency to use language as decoration, but he is intensely interested in language in his own way, always searching for new and even startling rhymes and rhythms in an endeavour to make the expression suit the directness of the thought. Browning is not a profound thinker, but we cannot bring that as a charge against him, because he never pretended to be: he is concerned primarily with the individual and the individual's reactions to specific circumstances, and the dramatic monologue is his most characteristic poetic form. His interest in human character is less the interest of the ordinary psychologist looking at everyday human activity and endeavouring to understand the motivating forces at work than that of the dramatist whose interest in the strange and the dramatic leads him to contemplate the exception rather than the rule—human nature at its most exotic or decadent or complex or otherwise exceptional. Thus many of his characters are set in late Renaissance Italy, when the exuberance and sensuality of the previous age had gone bad and produced types of character of extraordinary interest to one curious to probe into the dark places of the human mind. Browning was no more a great psychologist than he was a profound thinker, but he had a certain dramatic insight into character and a gift for rendering plausible his own interpretation of action in terms of character: given the facts, that is to say, he could supply inner motivation in a vigorous and convincing manner. He never really worked out a philosophic or religious position for himself. He had no regard for the dogmas of theology or for formal religion, but he was religious in the vague, general sense that so many of the " broad Church " thinkers of the time, in reaction against the narrow evangelicalism that had stifled so much in middle-class life, were religious. His work can hardly be said to constitute part of the literature of acquiescence in the Victorian age and all it stood for, as that of Macaulay and Tennyson does, because he does not really concern himself with his age as an age at all. His optimism is a personal matter and has no reference to any belief in economic progress or the glory of the British Empire. He was out of touch with a great deal in contemporary life, and his curiosity about the workings of the human mind did not lead him to inquire into the effect of industrial conditions on the minds of the victims or the effect of middle-class ignorance and prejudice in breeding inhibitions and repressions that poisoned so much in personal relationships and reduced to such an extent the possibility of human happiness. He was interested in the exceptions of his own day and in the curiosities of a bygone age, in Mr. Sludge the medium and in the Renaissance grammarian rather than in Tom, Dick, and Harry. But he did not make the mistake of dealing with the former and imagining that what he saw and said held good also for the latter.

Tennyson, in *In Memoriam*, had shown that he was conscious of the clash between science and religion which was developing in his time, and had endeavoured to work his way back to religion without ignoring the challenge of the scientist. The conflict developed a considerable time before the publication of Darwin's *Origin of Species* in 1859, though Darwin's popularisation of the theory of evolution (developed further in *The Descent of Man*, 1871) brought it more to the attention of the general public. A discussion of the conflict is no part of this study, but we must mention its importance in helping to broaden the basis of religion. Its immediate effect was in the very opposite direction—theologians became more dogmatic and scientists more arrogant. But it was not long before it was generally realised that a place had to be found for science and its discoveries in the general scheme of things. Agnosticism became more popular among thinking men who respected religion for its ethical teaching but had no use for its dogmas or institutions. The great T. H. Huxley, who did so much to popularise the scientific outlook, himself endeavoured to remove extreme elements from the conflict by formulating a tolerant agnosticism which allowed much more to religion than religion was inclined to allow to science. The disintegration of religious orthodoxy went on apace, and though there were still large numbers of extremists on both sides—those who denied the truth of every scientific discovery that was not compatible with the letter of the Bible, and rigid mechanists who believed that everything was reducible to mechanical cause and effect and it was only a matter of time before the whole universe would be observed and explained—an ever increasing number of intelligent persons found a solution in a broad, undogmatic religion where ethics completely overshadowed theology.

The liberal position in religion had already been suggested by F. D. Maurice and the Christian socialists, and the necessity for compromise between science and religion only encouraged a tendency which had been evident for some time. If on the dogmatic side the compromise-religion was altogether unsatisfactory and even, if investigated sufficiently deeply, self-contradictory, on the side of practical ethics it had much to commend it. This is the chief difference between the liberal movement in religion in the latter half of the nineteenth century and the deist movement in the eighteenth. The deist held that God had wound up the world in the distant past and that it would therefore go on automatically and everything work out for the best: this view thus denied all social responsibility and bred complacency, conservatism, and inaction in many of the most important spheres of human life. The liberal religious thinkers at the end of the nineteenth century, on the other hand—perhaps due to their inheritance from the Christian socialists—stressed social responsibility and the necessity for action in the sphere of practical ethics, and though their ideas of God were about as vague as those of the deists they would never have asserted that God had permanently retired immediately after the act of creation. Judged by its fruits, the nineteenth-century compromise was a far better thing than that of the eighteenth century. Even to-day it is a significant fact that both in this country and in America liberal religious thought, however self-contradictory its theology and dogma, tends to be on the side of the " left " in political and social matters.

Matthew Arnold (1822–1888) is perhaps the one literary man of the time who really faced up to the religious question, as he did to many other pressing contemporary problems. He did not argue up to a certain point and then take a jump back to where he started from, as Tennyson did. For Arnold there was no going back. In *Literature and Dogma* (1873) he makes it clear that an " inevitable revolution " has occurred in the sphere of religion, and he tries to define what the attitude of the thoughtful man of his day ought to be towards the Bible. He attacks theologians and clerics for their consistent misinterpretation of the Bible, and he despises the narrow outlook of the ordinary " religious " men of his day—their crude fundamentalism, their lack of imagination, their ridiculous stressing of the letter and cruel ignoring of the spirit, their unconscious hypocrisy. He is in revolt against the whole bourgeois attitude to religion and morality. The old theology, he maintains, must go, and if we are to retain the Bible we are to find a thoroughly humanist reason for doing so. He insists that the Bible is a " Book of *conduct* " and that to attribute to it any philosophical or metaphysical implications is preposterous. Yet conduct is but three-fourths of human life, and it is fatal to neglect the side concerned with " art and science, or, in other words, with beauty and exact knowledge." The good life, the adequate life, must include both " conduct " and " culture." The Bible has its place, but for its proper interpretation and appreciation culture is necessary. Otherwise the misinterpretations of theology, with all their practical implications, are inevitable.

Thus Arnold formulates his views on what is desirable in human life *before* he approaches the problem of religion; he does not first take his standards from its teachings, but takes from religion only what he requires to achieve the life he postulates as best. God becomes " a Power, not ourselves, making for righteousness," but a more personal and interfering God is not required. Arnold is not quite honest in retaining much of the old religious terminology, for he rarely uses it in the sense meant by the conventional religious thinkers. He is essentially a humanist, in the sense in which recent American critics have used that term—that is, he believes that the main end to be sought in life is the achievement of balance and sanity combined with a full and rich use of all the faculties with which man is endowed. His values are humanist values, empirically deduced from the experience of men. He attacks whatever frustrates and confines and narrows. One feels about Arnold that he never stated his humanist position frankly and directly because contemporary controversies were always confusing the issue. He recasts religion to serve his purpose, and treats every kind of criticism—Arnold as a prose writer is primarily and essentially a critic—as an opportunity for presenting what really amounts to a humanist philosophy, but he never has the courage to start with that philosophy, to set it up at the beginning as the criterion on which all products of the human mind are to be assessed.

Arnold's attack on the conventional religious ideas of the middle class of his day is but a small part of his general criticism of his age. He is the great antithesis of Macaulay. When Liberal politicians boast of progress and prosperity, like Mr. Roebuck in his speech to the Sheffield cutlers (" Is not property safe ? Is not every man able to say what he likes ? Can you not walk from one end of England to the other in perfect safety ? ... I pray that our unrivalled happiness may last...."), Arnold looks at his daily paper and quotes: " A shocking child murder has just been committed at Nottingham. A girl named Wragg left the workhouse there on Saturday morning with her young illegitimate child. The child was soon afterwards found dead on Mapperley Hills, having been strangled. Wragg is in custody." Arnold suggests that the only effective answer to Roebuck and his like is to reply to his songs of triumph by murmuring " Wragg is in custody." He could not tolerate the complacent humbug of the bourgeoisie of his day. He is a literary critic, but he defines criticism broadly as " a disinterested endeavour to learn and propagate the best that is known and thought in the world " and this can only be done by trying " to see the object in itself as it really is." Arnold was thus led to look closely into the middle-class life of his day and to lay his finger on its weakest spots.

Arnold was a man of letters, not a practical social worker, so his attack on his age is mainly directed against its lack of real culture and its warped attitude to life and literature rather than against specific social evils. But he did see clearly the connection between the evils he deplored and a more fundamental rottenness in society. The drab narrowness of lower middle-class life revolted him, and he realised that here was a threat to art and culture as well as to adequate living generally. In *Culture and Anarchy* (1869) he presents with force and clarity (even at the expense of almost wearisome reiteration) his case against the " Philistines," the selfish, unimaginative, complacent, ignorant members of the middle class in whose hands the destinies of the country so largely lay. He attacks their hollow optimism, their dull minds, their lack of culture. He opposes the Hellenistic ideal of " sweetness and light " to what he conceives to be the " Hebraism " of the Nonconformist attitude (by " Hebraism " he seems to have meant rather Pauline Christianity than prophetic Judaism). In trying to isolate a single factor responsible for the dreary insularity of the middle class, and to identify that factor with a one-sided " Hebraism " which was not balanced by a compensating " Hellenism," he not only imposes an arbitrary meaning on both those terms, especially the former, but allows himself to be side-tracked by contemporary controversies and thus never penetrates to a full understanding of the real social forces at work. But though his diagnosis of the disease was not quite adequate, he did see the symptoms very clearly and realised that they spelt danger.

Arnold's attack on the Philistines was timely; it came when the prosperity of the middle of the Victorian age was encouraging an optimistic materialism, a pious and complacent money-grubbing, a narrow and insular self-satisfaction, that threatened to destroy art and culture generally. What, after all, was the place of literature in a utilitarian age ? What would Samuel Smiles want with poetry ? The status of tolerated eccentric was being forced on the artist. The ordinary middle-class head of a family in the latter part of the nineteenth century looked on any form of art, if not as a vice which respectable people avoided, then at least as a waste of time, an activity indulged in only by unstable good-for-nothings and emotional foreigners. Occasionally the middle class would take an author to its bosom, if he were really old and had secured royal patronage, or if he wrote what was " edifying." The greatest writers were driven automatically into revolt against their age, whether in the way Arnold revolted, or Ruskin or Morris, or in the hysterical escapism of the naughty 'nineties. The matter has been put with some bitterness but with a great deal of truth by Richard Aldington in one of his outbursts in *Death of a Hero*: " There may be little differences in an English family, for the best of all friends fall out at times, but in all serious crises they may be depended on to show a united front. Thank God, there can still be no doubt about it—apart from pure literature of the sheik brand and refining pictures in the Millais tradition, an English family can still be relied upon to present a united front against any of its members indulging in the obscene pursuits of Literature or Art. Such things may be left to the obscene Continent and our own degenerates and decadents, though it would be well if stern methods were adopted by the police to cleanse our public life of the scandal brought upon Us by the latter. The great English middle-class mass, that dreadful squat pillar of the nation, will only tolerate art and literature that are fifty years out of date, eviscerated, de-testiculated, bowdlerised, humbuggered, slip-slopped. . . . They are still that unbroken rampart of Philistia against which Byron broke himself in vain, and which even the wings of Ariel were inadequate to surmount."[1] This is how a modern writer feels, looking back on conditions at the end of the last century. Arnold was engaged in a similar fight, though from a rather different point of view. He lived in an age befogged by prosperity and respectability, and his achievement in recognising the Philistines for what they were is greater than it may appear to us. Much of what Arnold strove for has become so completely taken for granted—at least in theory—that there is a tendency to forget his importance in the fight against bourgeois narrowness and complacency.

No adequate idea of the ordinary man's view of literature in the Victorian age is possible without taking into consideration the extensive magazine and periodical literature of the time. The " elegant extracts " type of compilation was already flourishing in the eighteenth century, and the view of art it represented became ever more popular. The insipid " moral " tales and ludicrous " edifying " verses that are to be found in such quantities in the magazines of the nineteenth century fairly represent the type of stuff middle-class families had for their general reading. Of course, many really good writers published in periodicals, but the general level of this literature was none the less appallingly low. It is not so much the badness of this stuff as literature which shocks the

[1] *Death of a Hero* (Penguin edition, 1936), p. 49.

modern critic as the view of the nature and function of literature which it implies—didactic in the very narrowest sense, essentially a class literature, intent on inculcating its shabby ideals and parading its cheap and sentimentalised emotions. Looking back on the nineteenth century to-day, we remember only the outstanding magazines, such as the *Cornhill*, and the outstanding writers who wrote for them, forgetting that these are rare exceptions.

Sentimentality is perhaps the greatest vice of this kind of literature. Ever since the days of Samuel Richardson sentimentality has been the shoddy tribute paid by the worldly bourgeoisie to feeling and suffering humanity. What their whole way of life denied they granted, in debased form, to moments of expansive emotion when they revelled in legitimate display of wholly proper feeling. We see the same thing in much popular literature of to-day: for most of the traits in Victorian literature which we have been discussing are still very much with us. It is easy to lay all the faults of popular literature at the door of universal education, and indeed the spread of literacy down to the lowest stratum of society has created a public that will be satisfied with the most appalling rubbish. When we consider the popular Press and the ordinary periodical literature read by the " man in the street " to-day, we can see how the existence of a vast uncultured reading public has made this sort of thing possible. But an extension of the reading public is as much an opportunity as an excuse, and the experience of, for example, Soviet Russia has shown that the " ordinary " reader is at least as responsive to good literature, if properly presented, as it is to bad. The growth of literacy might have been a grand opportunity for bringing an understanding and appreciation of real literature to those from whom hitherto it had been debarred. But the whole organisation of modern society has been against this result: the causes of the debasing of popular literature are primarily economic. So long as profit-making remains the main incentive to action among the great middle class a healthy popular art is inconceivable and every step forward in popular education means an increase in literary prostitution.

It is a mistake to regard the Victorian writers as oblivious to the faults of their age. Throughout the whole nineteenth century the literature of revolt (meaning by literature the work of the greatest writers) is much more abundant than that of acquiescence. Against Macaulay and Tennyson we can set Carlyle, Arnold, Ruskin, and William Morris, all strong critics of their generation. Carlyle (1795–1881) was the first of the nineteenth-century prophets. Beginning to write as early as the 1830's, he saw the rising tide of Benthamism, the growth of democracy, the emergence of a civilisation based on the individual commercial enterprise of a single class. All this disgusted him, and he looked around for a means of stopping what he regarded as the degeneration of society. But he was better at destructive than constructive criticism: while his exposure of the shams of his day can still be read with interest and admiration, time has shown how hollow were his remedies. Carlyle was not a systematic thinker, and could present no coherent scheme as an alternative to the contemporary order. He saw things in jerks, in flashes of emotion and indignation. In his anger at the mass-mind which democracy was developing, he turned to his doctrine of hero-worship, which he backed up by historical studies, such as his books on Cromwell and Frederick the Great, whose purpose was to show that it is the divinely appointed leader, and not the mob, who is best fitted to direct human affairs. We to-day, having had experience of the inherent viciousness of the *Führerprinzip*, cannot take Carlyle's doctrine of hero-worship seriously. We can sympathise with his antagonism to the soulless money-grubbing of his day, to conventional piety, to Benthamite political economy, but even the most superficial acquaintance with the historical forces at work during the last hundred years is sufficient to show that his social and economic ideas are based on complete fallacies. In *Past and Present* (1843) he contrasts the industrial civilisation of his day with mediæval monasticism, much to the advantage of the latter. But, apart from questions of the accuracy of his picture of the past, to present the Middle Ages as a practical ideal for social reformers of his day showed a lack of understanding fatal to anyone who wished to rank as a social thinker. Nineteenth-century civilisation was based on an economic foundation so utterly different from that which underlay the civilisation of the Middle Ages that no useful purpose whatever could be served by a comparison of the two; what was required was an understanding of the social and economic forces which had produced the evils that Carlyle so deplored, for only with such an understanding could a practical remedy be thought out. All Carlyle's social and economic writings suffer from this lack of realism, this ignorance of the real causes of contemporary conditions which made it impossible for him to work out any systematic remedy. Much of what he says is true, some of his utterances are wise and even profound, but our general impression of the man is of a thwarted Puritan looking with moral indignation at a society he can neither understand nor control, with no creed he can oppose to the creed of his enemies and therefore driven to botch up a doctrine out of the opposites of all the things he dislikes. He dislikes the factory, so he idealises the monastery; he dislikes the mass-mind and the " talking shop " that governs the country, so he preaches hero-worship; he dislikes Benthamism and *laissez faire*, so he directs the attention of his readers to the condition of the working class, the standard indictment of *laissez-faire* economics. There is little consistency in his ideas: his idealisation of work and his individualism are thoroughly Benthamite, his interest in the workers, shown in his *Chartism* (1839), has affinities with Socialism, his doctrine of the hero has something in common with modern German Fascism. He called himself "a radical and an absolute," meaning that he was concerned with changing things as they were, but that the best method of effecting the change was by some sort of absolutism. His generation got a certain amount of moral uplift from his fulminations, but did not attempt to examine the practical implications of his teaching—which was as well, for it would have been a profitless job.

John Ruskin (1819-1900) was to some extent a pupil of Carlyle, but though there was some similarity in their criticisms of nineteenth-century civilisation there was an essential difference between the remedies they proposed. The difference is due partly to the temperaments of the two men and more definitely to the fact that, by the time Ruskin was writing, socialist thought was becoming more influential in England. Early critics like Carlyle and even Matthew Arnold (born three years after Ruskin) were lone fighters, but Ruskin and, to a greater extent Morris, Shaw, Wells, and other writers at the very end of the nineteenth century and the beginning of the twentieth, had the advantage of association, however loose, with organised social movements. Ruskin began as an art critic, and from an examination of the nature and function of art came to an examination of the kind of society that was fitted to produce it. His identification of moral with æsthetic values is rather naïve, but he did see that " art " and " beauty " were not optional luxuries in a civilisation, but an integral part of any healthy communal life. He saw, as Carlyle saw and as Arnold saw, that the worship of Mammon with all its implications for social life was incompatible with honest thinking and adequate living and also—this was his own extension of the argument—with the production of a sound popular art. Carlyle attacked nineteenth-century commercial civilisation for its breeding of hypocrisy and shams, Arnold for its elimination of culture, Ruskin for its deadening effect on art. Ruskin could not resist the temptation to which Carlyle had succumbed in *Past and Present* of looking back to the Middle Ages for his ideal. Mediævalism side-tracks social thought again and again right through the nineteenth century: the obvious reaction to industrialism seems to have been the idealisation of a non-industrial society.

Ruskin, for all his mediævalism, did try to get down to the facts of contemporary life. He was interested in the condition of the working class: not only did he teach in the Working Men's College, lecture and write on social questions, and make suggestions for controlling some of the evils of unrestricted private enterprise, but he tried to put some of his theories into practice. At Oxford, where he was the first Slade Professor of Fine Art from 1869 to 1884, he organised road-digging for his undergraduates; he founded St. George's Guild, to which he contributed large sums of money, for the purpose of organising a model industrial and agricultural society; and he engaged in many small enterprises of the same kind. His experimental farms were hardly a success, but some of his co-operative undertakings in industry and handicrafts were more successful, though none were strikingly so.

Ruskin's thought was socialist in that he preached co-operation instead of competition and demanded (with reservations) that private enterprise should be submitted to some kind of organising social authority, but he did not accept any systematic socialist scheme of things. In *Unto this Last*, which appeared as articles in the *Cornhill Magazine* in 1860, until Thackeray, the editor, stopped the series in response to public clamour, Ruskin attacked the accepted economic theories of his day, pointing out that the abstract, mechanical view of economics ignored the moral factor and postulated an economic man devoid of all human qualities. The " one great fact " he wished to stress is that " there is no Wealth but Life." "Care in no wise," he says at the conclusion of the last section, "to make more of money, but care to make much of it; remembering always the great, palpable, inevitable fact—the rule and root of all economy—that which one person has, another cannot have: and that every atom of substance, of whatever kind, used or consumed, is so much human life spent; which, if it issue in the saving present life or gaining more, is well spent, but if not is either so much life prevented, or so much slain."[1] In his preface to the edition of 1862 (when the essays first appeared together in book form) Ruskin advocated "training schools for youth, established at government cost," where practical and moral education should be given; the establishment of "government manufactories and workshops for the sale of every necessary of life, and for the exercise of every useful art"; the employment, if necessary after special training, of those out of work, in the nearest government workshop; and the provision of "comfort and home" for the old and destitute. In *Munera Pulveris*, first published as articles in *Fraser's Magazine*, but also stopped by the editor (J. A. Froude) owing to public disapproval, he outlines a system of political economy as he would have it, developing a theory of value as "the strength or 'availing' of anything towards the sustaining of life," and applying his theories to branches of practical economic activity.

Ruskin continued to produce books, pamphlets, lectures, and articles in which he developed the details of his Utopia, addressing working men on social and

[1] *Works of John Ruskin*, ed. Cook and Wedderburn (London, 1905), Vol. XVII, p. 113.

moral problems. Even in his art criticism he had been essentially a moralist, and it is as a moralist that he approached social problems. Like the earlier Christian socialists, he applied the standards of morality and elementary justice to the activity of his age, together with his own additional argument from art—the health of a civilisation is to be judged by the quality of the art it produces. There is a lot of muddled thinking in Ruskin, and his approach to economics through art sometimes leads him into curious by-paths; but he had an inkling of the real nature of the problem he was facing, and did succeed in establishing some sort of contact with the working classes of his day.

William Morris (1834–1896) was another writer who approached economics through art, and he developed a more realistic attitude to social problems than Ruskin ever did. Architecture, painting, and poetry all occupied his attention as a young man, and in 1861 his interest in art led him, with some others, to join in the formation of a firm of manufacturers and decorators for the decoration of churches besides the production of artistic domestic furniture and fittings of every kind. Thus his bent for embodying his theories in practical activities was already manifest. Side by side with his activity as a decorative manufacturer, which went on throughout his life, Morris was engaged in writing poetry. He was influenced by Rossetti and the pre-Raphaelites, with their love of the Middle Ages and their insistence on fluent and simple beauty of description, though he had not their tendency to regard literature as an escape from the problems of contemporary life. (Rossetti had not this tendency to the extent that some of his minor followers had: his mature work has a reality and profundity not always recognised by modern critics: but in order to achieve this he had to concentrate on a very limited field of experience—there was no alternative for a poet at the end of the nineteenth century who refused to concern himself critically with the nature of contemporary society.) Morris never allowed his interest in the past to obscure completely his sense of present problems. He went to the Middle Ages because he admired Chaucer and mediæval art and was interested in the conditions that produced them: he went to old Icelandic literature because the simple, vigorous life of the Norsemen, as expressed in the Sagas, attracted him, and he thought it had a valuable message for his own age. His translation and imitation of Norse poetry, produced at a period when his love of Icelandic life and art had for the time being completely conquered his mediævalism, are some of the finest literary work he ever did. But his practical interest in art and craftsmanship never slackened, and he was constantly experimenting in decorative manufactures. In 1890 he founded the Kelmscott Press, designing his own founts of type and ornaments, with which he printed his own works and mediæval classics.

Morris's intense practical enthusiasm for art led him, as it had led Ruskin, to inquire into the function of art and the social conditions necessary for its healthy production. He thus came to see that the progress of civilisation from the industrial revolution onwards had involved an increasing standardisation and mechanisation of life and that a radical reorganisation of society was necessary if this debasement was not to continue.

Once his eyes were opened and he was able to see clearly the nature of the political and social forces of his day he was not content, as Ruskin was, with preaching his own remedies or even with trying out practical experiments in a new economy: he embarked on a study of politics and economics from which he emerged a convinced socialist, and, from 1882 till the end of his life in 1894, gave his ardent support first to the Social Democratic Federation, then, from 1884 to 1890, to the Socialist League, and even in his last years to the socialist cause by writing and lecturing.

By the eighties of the nineteenth century the Liberal tradition in England was becoming rather exhausted. The working classes, grown tremendously in influence and organisation, were becoming a political force to be reckoned with, and, with a trade depression, an Irish problem, danger in India and muddle in South Africa, and growing unemployment at home, the powerlessness of the Liberals to do anything to remedy matters became increasingly apparent. The prosperity of twenty years earlier had made it possible for Liberal Governments to pursue a policy of slow reform combined with self-congratulation on the state of things as it was, but when called on for a more active and immediate programme the Liberals, whose work, though few realised it, had by now been done, had little to offer. Attacks on free trade became common, and imperialist sentiment grew. But attacks on Liberalism from the right could find no support among the increasing number of discontented intellectuals any more than among the members of the working class. The socialist approach became increasingly popular.

Though the essence of socialist doctrine had been proclaimed in 1848 in the *Communist Manifesto* of Marx and Engels, Socialism gained little in popularity in England during the next thirty years. British leaders of working-class movements had supported radicalism in a general sense, even Liberalism of the Continental brand, especially when it was combined with nationalism—witness the sympathy expressed both by the Chartists and the London Trades Council with Italian and Polish nationalism and the popularity in England of men like Mazzini and Garibaldi—but they had little or no connection with socialist thought and socialist organisations. The influence of Marx, the first volume of whose *Capital* did not appear until 1867, was slow in making itself felt. But gradually Socialism separated itself out from other " ideologies " until by the early 'seventies there was a certain amount of clearly defined socialist activity on the Continent. In England, the International Working Men's Association, formed in London in 1864 largely under the influence of Marx, produced no immediate results in furthering Socialism, but though it split up into different sections in the beginning of 1872 its rather chequered career had not been in vain, as the manifesto of the British Section in March 1872 testifies. Trade-union leaders, who had long abandoned the revolutionary idealism of the Chartists, began to be attacked for their co-operation with the ruling classes. Different types of socialist thought became increasingly vocal. By 1880 the turning point had been reached and Socialism began to move forward rapidly. On the Continent, the socialist movement had reached a fair degree of consolidation after the reaction that had followed the failure of the Paris Commune of 1871 : in England, three Labour candidates were successful at the general election of 1880. In the following year, as the result of the efforts of H. M. Hyndman, a Marxist propagandist though not viewed with much favour by Marx, the Democratic (later Social Democratic) Federation was founded. The investigation of Marxism by English intellectuals went on apace. In the course of the next ten years there was drawn into sympathy with, if not whole-hearted support of, Socialism a number of important men of letters. The Democratic Federation was not originally formed as a socialist body, but it encouraged interest in socialist theory, and the growth of dissensions within the Federation was in some degree the measure of the intellectual vigour of its members.

Morris joined the Democratic Federation in 1882, the year when Henry George came from America to lecture on Socialism in Ireland and England, and he threw himself whole-heartedly into working for the movement. He took part in every kind of propagandist activity, from supplying funds to making speeches at street corners. He wrote poems in support of the cause, and his whole life seems to have been braced and intensified as a result of allying himself with a group who had a definite constructive programme. At the end of 1884, Morris, with Belfort Bax and others, left the Social Democratic Federation and founded the Socialist League. In his enthusiasm he was dissatisfied with mere talk and wished for " a socialist *party* which shall begin to act in our own time, instead of a mere theoretical association in a private room with no hope but that of gradually permeating cultivated people with our aspirations."[1]

The development of Morris's thought, from his early days at Oxford when he dreamt of a monastic life, shut off from the world and devoted entirely to art, to the time of the foundation of the Socialist League, shows the lengths to which a fearless examination of the place and function of art in society had led him. His conversion to Socialism was no sudden one; he came to it by relentlessly pursuing his ideas to their logical conclusion. The Social Democratic Federation fell asunder, the Socialist League after 1890 " became a romping ground of more than dubious characters who, being suspected of relations with the police, drove the better elements away in disgust, and finally broke up what was left of Morris's organisation,"[2] but Morris never lost his intellectual integrity and worked until the end for the ideals he had come to believe in. Some of his finest work was inspired by his Socialism. *A Dream of John Ball* (1888) is the most beautiful as well as the most profound of his romances, and *News from Nowhere* (1890), if a slighter and more superficial work, has always been one of his most popular. In addition to the more formal works inspired by his social ideas he produced numerous articles in *Justice*, the organ of the S.D.F. and the first socialist newspaper in Britain, and in the *Commonweal*, the organ of the Socialist League, which he edited from 1885 until 1889. He also collaborated with Belfort Bax in writing *Socialism:*

[1] Quoted from a letter of Morris (July 1884) by J. W. Mackail, *Life of William Morris* (London, 1899), Vol. II, p. 131.
[2] J. W. Mackail, op. cit., Vol. II, p. 230. The quotation is from a contemporary statement by a member of the League.

its Growth and Outcome, and wrote many articles and pamphlets, both alone and in collaboration with others, expounding his views. And all the while he kept up his practical interest in art.

Morris and the implications of his life and thought deserve fuller treatment than is possible here, and the reader is referred to J. W. Mackail's fully documented *Life* for a full-length picture of this fascinating personality. We may sum the matter up in the words of G. D. H. Cole: " Morris passed from art to Socialism, because he saw that under capitalism there could be no art and no happiness for the great majority. . . . He saw clearly that, so long as men are in thrall to the industrial system, there could be no good art and no good life for the mass of the people. Perhaps he did not see so clearly the way out—that was less his business. What he did see was to put clearly before the world the baseness and iniquity of industrialism, and its polluting effect on civilisation despite the increase of material wealth. He wanted passionately that the things men had to make should be worth making—a joy to the maker and to the user."[1]

What happened to those who refused to see the social implications of art is illustrated in the life and work of men like Oscar Wilde and Aubrey Beardsley and the school of " art for art's sake " poets that flourished at the end of the century. For an artist to glory in the functionlessness of art or to treat art as having value only in so far as it is self-expression is to admit complete defeat at the hands of society. We have already noted

[1] Quoted in Beer, *History of British Socialism*, Vol. II, p. 258, from G. D. H. Cole, *Self Government in Industry* (London, 1917), pp. 120-1.

the connection of these poets with romantic escapism. In a civilisation where the all-important factor is the " cash nexus " and society is organised on a purely profit-making basis, the artist finds sooner or later that he is not wanted. He can compromise only at the cost of losing his artistic integrity (a charge that can be brought against the later Wordsworth and the later Tennyson), and if he refuses to compromise he can become a rebel, either purely destructive or with a constructive programme, or alternatively make the best of a bad job and reply to society's lack of any sense of responsibility to him and his work by denying that he and his work have any responsibility to society. And that way lies decadence. The original fault lies with the bourgeoisie in refusing to take the artist seriously, but the artist too is to blame if he accepts the attitude of the bourgeoisie as the basis for a critical theory of art. And that is what the " art for art's sake " writers did, though they would have protested furiously if it had been pointed out to them.

The group of left-wing writers at the end of the century was in no way representative of the thought of the people. True, the Liberal party was showing signs of disintegration and " the great mass of electors were disgusted with middle-class Liberalism,"[1] but they had neither the inclination nor the education for Socialism. It was the Conservatives who profited by the exhaustion of Liberalism, and the great Conservative victory of 1895 was a clear indication of the way the wind was blowing. Imperialism and jingoism became increasingly

[1] É. Halévy, *A History of the English People, 1895–1905*, trans. E. I. Watkin (London, 1929), pp. 8–9.

popular. The traditional attitude of the Liberals had involved a certain amount of indifference to the problems of empire, if not a desire to be rid of the burden altogether. But imperialist sentiment had been growing ever since Disraeli's famous Crystal Palace speech in 1872, when he defined the Conservative point of view on imperial problems. Pride in the British Empire began to affect every branch of English thought. In literature, the movement coalesced with the tradition founded by men like Kingsley and J. A. Froude: both these writers had idealised the Elizabethan adventurer, the former in his *Westward Ho!* and the latter in his history of England and his little book on the Elizabethan seamen. The conception of the adventurous Englishmen going out to conquer new worlds was easily widened into an idealisation of the glories and responsibilities of empire. Seeley's *Expansion of England* (1883) first gave expression to the new feeling from the historian's point of view, and a little later Rudyard Kipling began to embody it in poems and stories. Kipling takes the ordinary Englishman, who actually does the job of holding the Empire together, and presents him as a loyal, careless, not over thoughtful fellow who makes history without realising it by merely " carrying on " in the position in which he finds himself. To Kipling and the imperialists empire-building is not a matter of self-interest or desire for personal aggrandisement (the Benthamite appeal to self-interest had resulted in discouragement of imperialist sentiment) but a responsibility to civilisation undertaken as a solemn duty and involving every kind of hardship and self-sacrifice. By shifting the centre of attention from the scheming politician in London who planned and directed colonial exploitation and expansion from political and economic motives to the British Tommy on the outposts who knew nothing of the ambitions of statesmen but saw only his immediate duty and his personal responsibility, Kipling was able to present the relation of Britain to her Empire in a way that made an immediate appeal to all classes. Politics and economics were left behind, and the great British public learned to turn its romantic gaze to the solitary soldier on the frontier, bearing his share of the White Man's Burden with fortitude and good humour. The doctrine of the White Man's Burden—the great civilising mission of the more fortunate races to the benighted folk across the seas—has effectively obscured the real factors underlying imperialist activity from Kipling's time to the present day. Kipling applies the same treatment to the public school as he does to the barracks, and his presentation of English public-school life in *Stalky and Co.* (1899) shows no consciousness of the class basis and the standardising purpose of this kind of education: the training of the man who will do or die without reasoning why is an important duty in a nation of empire-builders. We still hear talk of the " building of character " from those who do not appear to realise that what is really meant is the superimposing of a ready-made character-pattern on all alike. It would be interesting to speculate on the indirect influence of Dr. Arnold of Rugby on the imperialist ideal and the relation between *Tom Brown's Schooldays*, *Stalky and Co.*, and the film version of *Bengal Lancer*.

Kipling's *Jungle Books* contain some of his most

pleasant writing (and Kipling's writing nearly always has the quality of reading well): he gives us here, by implication, the nearest approach to an organised philosophy of life to which he attained. " He sets his hero, the little Mowgli, in the world of beasts, and the beasts taught Mowgli the law of the jungle which maintains the balance of species at the cost of a never-ending struggle, a truceless war. Must this struggle, this war, be condemned as evil ? Not when it is the law of the world. The spirit of conquest and aggrandisement must not be confused with the spirit of hatred, greed and delight in doing mischief for its own sake; it is the courage ready to hazard all risks which gives the victory to the better man. A species of Darwinian philosophy expressed in a mythical form was the basis of a moral code, chaste, brutal, heroic and childlike."[1] Kipling's view of life may have been crude and his question-begging blatant, his attitude to his country's institutions naïve and the lack of realism in his approach to social questions almost staggering; yet he was a great story-teller, and however much we disagree with the ideas implicit in most of his work we cannot but enjoy such books as *Puck of Pook's Hill*, containing a brilliant imaginative reconstruction of life in Roman Britain, and such short stories as *The Village that Voted the Earth was Flat*. He was a master of the technique of narration, and whenever he treats a subject to which his false conceptions are irrelevant and can get down to " the object in itself as it really is " he produces work of real value. It is the old question, At what point do the writer's prejudices become relevant ? Our estimate of writers so different

[1] É. Halévy, *A History of the English People, 1895–1905*, p. 21.

as Spenser and Kipling depends on the answer we give.

Meanwhile the novel had been exploited in innumerable ways and for innumerable purposes, until by the end of the century it was the jack-of-all-trades of literature. Any criticism that had to be made, any point that had to be got across, could always be done by embodying it in fiction. Sometimes the resultant novel was good, sometimes it was effective as propaganda but not as literature, sometimes it was neither. But, for good or evil, the novel, established as the main literary form by the middle of the century, continued to flood the bookshops and libraries of Europe until it seemed that there was no topic that remained to be treated, no story left unwritten. Yet as the cramping effects of bourgeois standards made themselves increasingly felt, novelists found more and more to criticise, more and more to describe and expose. All this gave impetus to the movement towards realism. In France Balzac (1799–1850) in his *Comédie Humaine*, a series of novels written over a period of twenty years, had attempted to penetrate into the essential nature of bourgeois society by giving a realistic description of society in evolution from 1815 to 1848. Balzac looked to the past, not to the future for his ideal; he was politically a legitimist and deplored the decline of an aristocratic régime and the rise of a purely commercial civilisation. But, though his solution was impracticable and even stupid, his antagonism to bourgeois society enabled him to describe its weaknesses with an almost savage realism. In one sense he is a caricaturist, for he concentrated his attention on the vices and shams of his day and omitted mention of any compensating factors, but the vices and shams that he exposed did exist, and he looked on them objectively, scientifically (or such at least was his intention), as the " natural historian " of society. The tendency towards " naturalism " went on rapidly in France, and parallel with it—often as part of it—went opposition to the bourgeoisie and all that they stood for. Flaubert (1821–1881) combined a painstaking perfection of style with a pitiless insight into the frustrations of bourgeois society. The two Goncourts wrote with laboured naturalism of the " seamy side " of life. Émile Zola (1840–1903) carried this tradition to its culmination and described aspects of contemporary life, both middle- and working-class, with the most detailed exactitude, flinching at nothing in his desire to show reality as it was. Realism of this kind tended to defeat itself, because it lost itself in description of details which were not organised under any directing scheme or centred on a single focal point. The result was a dissipated and therefore unreal view of life, and later developments of this tradition led to complete unreality and lack of balance.

The naturalist movement never became as popular in England as it was in France, but it did have a very great influence on the development of English fiction. As this influence became more marked the ordinary man's view of literature as the placid sentimentalising of middle-class life became ever less tenable. And criticism of society ceased to take the form of exposure of individual " abuses," as in Dickens, or satire of conventional vices, as in Thackeray, but turned to a closer examination of underlying causes. Samuel

Butler's *Way of All Flesh*, finished in 1884 though not published until 1903, after the author's death, contains no "naturalism" of the kind found in Zola or de Maupassant, but it is the most effective satire of nineteenth-century civilisation ever written in English. Butler has a focal point, a basis for criticism, which the morbid probers into "slices of life" rarely had. The French novelists had taught the English to be distrustful of the bourgeoisie and the bourgeois way of life —distrustful of them as a class, not as a group of erring mortals, as earlier writers had been inclined to regard them—and the English made use of the lesson in their own way.

There was another side to the revolt against the bourgeoisie, illustrated in the work of Flaubert, who combined detailed and effective realism with an overwhelming desire to escape from what he saw and described. Hatred of the middle classes might lead to exposure of the rottenness of their lives and ideals, but it might also lead to an unhealthy isolation of the artist. Flaubert's attitude to society was quite morbid in its desire for escape, and eventually it led him to seek his literary ideal in "a book about nothing, a book without any attachment to the external world, which would support itself by the inner strength of its style," as he himself expressed it. Realism becomes the very opposite, and assimilates to the "art for art's sake" type of literature. In England Walter Pater was a disciple of Flaubert, and Pater was concerned only with form and not at all with content, writing as an isolated intellectual, inbreeding to a fatal degree. George Moore's early work is written entirely under French influence, and we can see in it the combination of the " pure artist's " preoccupation with style and the realist's clear-eyed view of society. The atmosphere of social irresponsibility in which Moore's early days in Paris were spent can be judged from his *Confessions of a Young Man*, yet *A Mummer's Wife*, *Muslin*, and other of his earlier novels, show knowledge and observation of society to an extraordinary degree. It might not be fantastic to see a connection between *A Mummer's Wife* and Flaubert's *Madame Bovary*. Moore, however, had a healthier attitude than Flaubert, and in his case isolation resulted in his acquiring complete artistic objectivity without becoming in any way morbid.

Realism also assumed other forms. Thomas Hardy (1840–1928), describing the lives of country folk in " Wessex," presents a pessimistic view of life in its more elemental aspects. His is a disinterested pessimism; he is not concerned with the effect of institutions or the defects of a certain type of social organisation; he deliberately chooses the more primitive and unchanging aspects of life where evil is seen to be less the work of man than of God. He has no programme, no " abuses " to expose; the wrongs committed by individuals matter less than the essential lack of an order that makes for happiness and excludes waste in human affairs. This inverted romanticism is not valuable in itself, but the elemental quality in Hardy's writing, his marshalling of detail, and his sense of the unity of all life, give his work a power that places it in the front rank.

And so the novel flourished. Meredith (1828–1909) concerned himself with the individual and his reactions to his environment in a more or less psychological manner, though he made excursions into romantic adventure. He is essentially the intellectual, seeing the life of the mind as a problem to be explained and lingered over: he sees his problems too much in isolation from their background to be able to give real body to his work. He is unaffected by naturalism, and, though a feminist and a radical, does not launch any serious criticism against the contemporary organisation of society: his chief criticism of his age is that it has not his own high intelligence. R. L. Stevenson (1850–1894) wrote good adventure stories and went to live in Samoa. Joseph Conrad (1856–1924) produced a realistic, psychological treatment of adventure, describing the lives of ordinary men in strange places. George Gissing (1857–1903) developed the novel of social criticism, portraying working- and lower middle-class life with insight and clarity: he had neither the sentimentalism nor the geniality of Dickens whom he admired, and the deficiency probably enabled him to get nearer the truth.

None of the writers just mentioned had any clearly defined political affiliations. But the association of men of letters with left-wing politics did not cease with the death of William Morris. The Fabian Society, formed in 1884 with the object of promoting a slow but sure progress towards Socialism by evolution rather than revolution, began to attract intelligent young writers soon after its formation. George Bernard Shaw and Sidney Webb joined about the same time, and after that the intellectual vigour of the Fabian movement was assured. Later, H. G. Wells also joined, so that two of the most promising writers of their day were now associated with Socialism. Shaw and Wells are both critics of the society in which they find themselves. Shaw is essentially the satirist exposing the humbug in conventional standards, Wells the scientist seeking a method of organising human affairs on a more equitable and more efficient basis. Shaw was greatly influenced by Ibsen, who made drama a medium for the presentation of contemporary problems. Drama in England had long been decadent when Shaw arrived on the scene; it had consisted largely of crude melodrama and facile romantic stuff which possessed no literary merit whatsoever. In bringing his bold criticisms of English social life on to the stage, Shaw attracted immediate attention, though few thought of taking his criticisms seriously. His exposures and attacks were witty and amusing, and the British public soon came to adopt him as a sort of licensed iconoclast, which is a sure way of rendering a reformer ineffective. Shaw tended to play into the public's hands by frequently letting his wit get the better of his judgment, so that to-day he is commonly regarded more as a Funny Man than as the revolutionary which, at bottom, he is.

Wells did not make Shaw's mistake. He wrote many books in which he sketched his own idea of Utopia, and many novels in which characters argued things out. But Wells steadily retreated from the socialist position, and for most people his most effective criticism of society is contained implicitly in his group of short novels, *Mr. Polly*, *Love and Mr. Lewisham*, and others. The lower middle-class man is shown in his environment, and the facts are allowed to speak for themselves.

The situation reached by the beginning of the present century was that increased consciousness of the nature of the society in which they dwelt was preventing authors, and artists generally, from functioning as normal units in society. On the side of the public, there was the bourgeois conspiracy not to take the artist seriously; on the side of the artist, there was contempt for society, which expressed itself either in criticism from the side of the left or in retreat from reality. But psychology was opening up a new way of escape from the dilemma. Interest in the workings of the individual mind had already been shown by Meredith and others, but with the progress of psychological research a more scientific treatment of psychological questions by novelists became possible. Proust in France had begun a fashion of delicate probing behind the scenes of mental life, and the tendency increased as the new century advanced. The method was to take the individual as a psychological unit, not as a rounded personality that was part of a group life, and so it was really a way of escape from treating of men in society, of life in its fullness and reality. The psychological technique resulted in a freer use of the monologue and the reverie in literature, and in its extreme form employed the "stream of consciousness" method, where everything is depicted in terms of the consciousness of one or other of the characters. We must distinguish between the psychological approach as a technique and psychological analysis viewed as the be-all and end-all of the novel. The technique can be helpful and effective in presenting any kind of story, and its employment does not necessarily imply desire to escape from the facts of life in contemporary society, but the novel whose sole purpose is the analysis of the individual mind in isolation is fundamentally as escapist as the most romantic dreaming: for literature is not concerned with mental reflexes as such but with men and women as they think and feel in the life they lead, and the abstraction of the psychological element is cowardice in the novelist, though it may be bravery in the scientist.

The exposure of the hollowness of Victorian standards left the twentieth century with no common terms of reference to give meaning to its art. For artistic communication to be possible some degree of community of belief is necessary, and, as this broke down, artists began to find themselves stranded, cut off from contact with society and with each other. Thus there arose all kinds of extravagant movements in art and literature which attempted to base artistic activity on the personal reactions of individuals without reference to their intelligibility or universality. In poetry and painting, the use of a purely private symbolism became increasingly common. As time went on it became more and more clear to those who could see facts as they were that two things were necessary to make a regeneration of healthy art possible—a reorganisation of society in such a way as to allow the artist to assume his true function, and the acceptance of a minimum common ideology which would provide the requisite amount of community of thought necessary for artistic communication.

But the old traditions did not die suddenly. The old kind of poetry continued to be written, though becoming ever more out of touch with the spirit of the age—

and in art what is out of touch with contemporary reality, in the broadest sense, is out of touch with all reality, for all our data about life must derive ultimately from our own experience, however enriched by knowledge of that of others. The novel continued as the dominant literary form, and the new tendencies did not immediately swamp the old. Arnold Bennett directed a dry and clear light on to the surface of society. Galsworthy presented a picture of upper middle-class life from the latter part of the Victorian age to the nineteen-twenties, and displayed a social consciousness but no real knowledge of what had called that consciousness into being. His picture of the old Forsytes is convincing, and his portrait of Soames, the " man of property," sums up a whole aspect of middle-class life. But when Galsworthy comes to deal with the generation that was young when he was old, he shows less understanding. He realises that the young people are uneasy about the state of society and are unable to accept their parents' standards, but he does not really understand their problem. And he is always looking at social questions from above, patronising the victims of society rather than attempting to understand their point of view and the forces that produced them. Galsworthy is the last important writer to criticise middle-class society in its own terms: in many ways he is the last of the great Victorian novelists.

The revolt went on. D. H. Lawrence turned from the society of his day to nature and an idealisation of instinct and emotion at the expense of reason as expressed in modern civilisation. Virginia Woolf found refuge in subtle description of the minds of her characters, and James Joyce explored the nature of human consciousness. The more sensitive and genuine the writer the less able he was to adjust himself to society. And all the while thousands of shoddy, worthless novels, written to dead formulas to please a public who had no opportunity of learning what literature was, were turned out every year. The " yellow " Press laid its ugly hand on the nation, and popular standards were steadily mechanised, standardised, debased. Younger writers became more and more disillusioned and sought for some constructive programme to help to remedy a state of affairs which offered them no hope. Increasing numbers turned to Socialism and Communism: others remained disillusioned. The economic system which had been growing up since the beginning of the industrial revolution and earlier had finally succeeded in destroying all healthy relation between literature and society; the function of literature had become debased, and those who persisted in maintaining the integrity of their art were driven—sometimes metaphorically and sometimes literally—into exile.

Is this a melodramatic view of the situation ? Is it ridiculous to blame the economic system for the sickness of the arts ? And is it really so important that artistic activity is not a normal part of the activity of our generation ? Let us endeavour to answer these questions by answering one further question, What is the real function of literature in society and why does not literature fulfil that function to-day ? And this brings us to our brief concluding chapter.

CHAPTER V

Looking at the matter quite empirically, we can see that one object which literature generally recognised as great has achieved throughout history is the presentation of aspects of human experience in such a way as to produce a pattern out of the apparent chaos of human life and so help to a better organisation and understanding of the facts of our existence. The whole concern of literature is with life as it is lived by human beings. The poet presents emotions as men have felt them, the novelist and the dramatist show us characters acting and reacting in an endeavour to give us a sense of reality, a concentrated essence of physical and psychological facts as they occur in the lives of men. The facts recorded may not be true in the sense that they have actually occurred at some given time, but, if the work is to rank as literature, they must be true to type, true to our sense of probability, and, further, they must be organised so as to conform to our sense of what is permanent and significant in experience. If we examine the difference between a work of literature that has been considered great by critics of different tastes and times and one that has not been so considered, we will find that ultimately this consists in an ability on the part of the author of the former work to penetrate through the individual fact to its implications for general human feeling and action. The question is one of selection, organisation, and presentation—the kind of facts the writer deals with, the way he welds them together, and the language in which he records them.

Consider first the matter of selection. There is at the writer's disposal an infinite number of possible and actual facts about human life. Even when he has decided on his story, when he has limited his scope to a definite series of events within a certain framework, the question arises, How much of what happens, or what is supposed to happen, is he to include? Even in describing the events of a single day's activity it is impossible for the author to record *everything* that happened to his characters, everything they did, every thought they had, from rising in the morning until going to bed at night. On such a principle to write a novel in which the course of action lasted over six weeks would take as many years, if indeed it would be possible at all. It is obvious that selection is a main part of the author's task. The great writer will choose those facts which in combination will give the most living picture of reality—not of an abstract reality, nor the whole of reality, but a part of reality as it exists for men in this world. There is a true realism and a false realism in fiction. To present indiscriminately all the insignificant details of a man's life, noting each time he blows his nose, coughs, ties his shoe-lace, scratches the back of his head, or looks at his watch, is no more to give a "real" picture of life than to show your character only in his soulful moods of rapture or reverie. Selection should be such that it presents life as human experience recognises it; yet the finished work should claim more than mere recognition from the reader—it should enable him to feel that here are aspects of life more clearly seen into, more profoundly evaluated, more truly apprehended, than is possible for the ordinary man. The aim of the imaginative writer—and it is with him that we are mainly concerned—is the presentation, through the recording and description of particular fictitious incidents (though the incidents need not be fictitious), of significant aspects of human experience. And the test of what is significant is that it should arouse in the reader both recognition and deepened apprehension.

Right selection, then, is all-important in a work of imaginative literature. Next comes organisation, the arrangement and binding together of the facts selected in such a way as to give a sense of truth and completeness. The " plot " of a novel is not a mechanical matter of arranging more or less convincing causation, nor is it the purely mathematical arrangement of the detective story. It is something more organic than that: it is the linking of incidents in such a manner as to give the reader the impression that this is the way in which life really works with us. Aristotle put the plot first in his list of the requirements of a good drama or epic, and if we see literature as primarily concerned with the presentation of the " universal " through the " particular," with the illustration of the philosophic probable rather than the fortuitous actual in human life, we can understand the importance Aristotle attached to what we to-day are rather too inclined to regard as a mere matter of mechanical contrivance.

The third element in imaginative literature is the

presentation, the language in which the work is written. The problem of style is not one we can pause to discuss here, but the reader will appreciate, from his own experience in reading, the importance of having the language fit the matter, so that the meaning is conveyed in the most forceful and convincing manner. The most obvious sign of decadence in literature is preciosity of style; for when a writer comes to be concerned with making an impression more by the manner of his writing than by what he has to say, he is losing sight of his true function. Equally the thin, emasculated style that prefers generalisation and circumlocution to concrete expression is a sign of lack of adequate contact with real life, which alone can give permanent value to literature. The extent to which, in the most healthy periods of our literature, literary style has been ultimately grounded on popular speech (even in the loftiest and most poetic writers) is often forgotten.

If the nature of literature is anything like what we have outlined it becomes obvious that the only outlook that affords a genuine justification for literary activity is an outlook which, in one way or another, is fundamentally humanist. If human experience is valuable as such, if what men have thought and felt and done and continue to think and feel and do is important, then literature, which is concerned solely and entirely with human experience, is valuable. If the purpose of literature is regarded as being purely didactic, so that literary works become mere " gildings of the pill," then we must jettison the work of many of our greatest writers (including Shakespeare) and regard poetry, fiction, and drama as types of children's sermons, where morality is inculcated in such a way as not to bore those who are not serious-minded. If literature is regarded as an escape from life, then again we must throw overboard much of our greatest writing and retain only the fantasy and the adventure story—or at least regard these as the highest peaks of literary art. And if literature is purely the expression of the individual "soul," without regard to its more general implications, then the test of its worth is the extent to which it has relieved the writer, and the reactions of readers are irrelevant. The true individualist sees the individual in relation to other individuals, and aims at a sanity and balance in his treatment of human life which is impossible to one who isolates his own experience from the environment which has to a large extent conditioned it. In literature, as in society, a man fulfils his own personality more by mingling with and considering his fellows than by retiring alone to the ivory tower.

It is only on a humanist philosophy that literature can be seen as a human activity with a function and a value of its own in society. The literary critic is therefore *in his capacity as critic* interested in social questions to this extent: he is bound to be opposed to a civilisation in which the economic organisation is such that the lust for private wealth on the part of a large number of those who control affairs (and, therefore, set the standards and establish the criteria which others apply) brings about an inevitable distortion of human values. The honest critic cannot help seeing that there are certain types of social and economic organisation under which experience itself becomes increasingly standardised and superficial. A village craftsman who spends his days carving tables and chairs or making pots and pans, however limited his outlook and his income, has nevertheless the possibility of a personal existence, of a free experience of life which a worker in certain types of industrial organisation is denied. Modern inventions like the cinema and the wireless may do much to bring great art within the reach of the working classes, but they cannot stop the standardisation and consequent degradation of the lives of the majority of men which a certain type of social and economic organisation may make inevitable. Popular education may be a means to several ends: its purpose may be to provide the minimum of literacy necessary to workers in industries requiring a certain degree of technical and mechanical knowledge, and in this case increase in " education " will merely mean increase in the sales of the yellow Press and widespread reading of trashy novels; or its purpose may be to give the working classes an opportunity to enjoy types of art which would otherwise be outside their reach, in which case it will turn out, not semi-literates easily seduced by the vilest trash, not workers with enough knowledge to provide useful working material in industry but otherwise uneducated if not mis-educated, not people educated to be of use to others and to be of no use to themselves, but men and women of judgment and understanding, trained to appreciate literature and the other arts. It must be remembered, too, that there is no use in bringing art within the reach of a man the conditions of whose life and work ensure that he will never be able to make adequate use of it.

The machine is not necessarily the enemy of art, and the future of civilisation is not necessarily that depicted in Aldous Huxley's *Brave New World*. The machine can be used to make one half of society work for the other half, or three quarters work for the other quarter; or it may be used to kill all spontaneity and creativeness in life; or it may be used for the benefit of society as a whole, as a means to the right end. The right end is surely the making possible of a full and rich life to all men, and this can only be attained by ensuring that production for use and enjoyment prevails in every branch of human activity. The literary critic has a right to protest if he finds himself in the midst of a system whose contradictions are resulting in increasing dislocation and anomaly, where reality is obscured by a fog of catch-words and moral platitudes, and the experience of different classes is so diverse in every way that the artist has to decide which kind of life is " truer " and is prevented from seeing life whole. We know what chance the artist has in countries where those interested in maintaining a certain type of social and economic order in the state to which it had developed have established a reign of terror that forcibly removes any element which might help to show what is really happening and what human values really are. We know what has happened to Ernst Toller and innumerable others in Germany and Italy. It is the duty of the literary critic to consider the causes and effects of such movements, to consider why they have occurred in some places and not in others, whether it is true that " it can't happen here " and, if so, why. He must determine why a healthy relation between author and public is becoming more and more impossible even in this country. He must seek for the causes of the commercialisation of art, the influence of the yellow Press, and the degeneration of literary criticism, and examine the factors which are making for an obscuring of the function of art and bringing a creeping paralysis over literature. He must consider the nature of the Waste Land and ask himself why T. S. Eliot wrote his famous poem of despair in 1922 and then escaped to Anglo-Catholicism and a barren traditionalism. These are questions that are of vital concern to the literary critic, as they are to society as a whole.

What has been happening to literature in the last fifty years? It is a question the reader can try to answer for himself. But we suggest that he might begin by comparing the tone of Samuel Butler's *Way of All Flesh* with that of Richard Aldington's savage attack on the civilisation of his day, *Death of a Hero*, published in 1929. And, if he is concerned with what writers think about the world, he can compare the more recent attitude of writers like Stephen Spender, Ralph Bates and Ralph Fox. He can study the present state of the West-End theatre, and peruse carefully any given issue of *The Times Literary Supplement*. If he wishes to make a thorough examination of the nature and causes of literary decadence let him consider why Charles Morgan's *Sparkenbroke* has a smell of decaying corpses.

Those who seek for ideal conditions under which literature might fulfil its true function in society will be told that much great literature has been produced in the past even though these ideal conditions have not prevailed. It is true that, as long as conditions have allowed men of genius to get into touch with life and with the people, the literary instinct has sought and achieved satisfaction. But to-day we are living in an age when conditions are thwarting much literary activity and making it impossible for the mass of the people to realise what literature really is. Standards are being debased, tastes are being corrupted, the false and the decadent are gaining a widespread hold. To say that the majority of the people have always had debased standards and that there have been periods in the past when the worst has been generally accepted as the best, is to beg the question. What concerns us is not so much a comparison of the good and evil of the past with the good and evil of our own day as the investigation and fulfilment of the potentialities which the future holds. We are in many ways more fortunate than our ancestors. They accepted things as they were, being unable to see clearly the historical forces that produced them and therefore having neither the knowledge nor the physical means to be able to change them; but we have both the knowledge and the means; the progress of knowledge, scientific, psychological, and historical, has provided us with a method of analysing the defects of our civilisation and of consciously remedying them. With all our tremendous resources we *ought* to be more fortunate than our ancestors; our lives ought to be happier, our activity more rich and vital, our culture higher and more widespread. But instead we have allowed those very resources which might be utilised in the enrichment of life to impose, as it were, their will upon us and gradually to obtain a stranglehold upon our civilisation. Our chemists are busy studying poison gases and our factories are working overtime in the production of armaments. Those who gain materially from this growth of evil will try to convince us that this is the only way. This is not the only way. There is another and a better way in which we may employ the forces we have learned to exploit. We can use them to increase the happiness of the people, not the wealth of a section. Only then will we be able to bring new riches to our cultural heritage and enable all to share it.

The English cultural tradition is a fine thing, but most people, when they talk of it, forget that the masses of the people are allowed no share in that tradition, whose heritage does not extend to them. The unemployed who lounge without hope at street corners are in no fit state to appreciate Shakespeare or Milton, nor is the worker who spends his days hewing at the coal-face in a mine in order to keep his wife and children on a scanty diet in an unhealthy home. If we are seriously concerned with the great things that have been done in the past, and do not merely use the word tradition as a cloak to cover every kind of evil from loose thinking to exploitation, then we will appreciate the importance of the literary critic concerning himself with contemporary social problems. There are two wrongs to be remedied: we want to prevent the mass of the population from reading only trash and to stimulate the production of first-rate literature, and we want to ensure that everybody has the opportunity and the training to be able to share in our cultural heritage. Literary activity is one activity among many carried on by men in society, and the critic's duty is as much to point the way to social conditions under which literature can more adequately fulfil its function (once he has decided what that function is) as to pass judgment on works which have already been produced. These two tasks are not so dissimilar as may appear at first sight, any more than the two wrongs to be remedied are really separate and distinguishable. At any rate, the critic to-day has a special responsibility as the guardian of culture in a changing—some would say a disintegrating—world, and if there is available for him more knowledge than his predecessors had about the process of literary creation and about the social and other conditions which affect literary production, his responsibility is all the greater.

INDEX

INDEX

ADDISON, JOSEPH, 122–6, 130, 137, 143, 145, 146, 157–8, 169, 170
Aldington, Richard, 238, 275
Allegory of Love, The, 41, 42, 43, 44, 82
Alton Locke, 217
American War of Independence, 169, 174
Ancient Mariner, The, 194
Anne, Queen, 112, 136, 137
Antigone, 14
Anti-Jacobin, The, 185
Apologia pro Vita Sua, 214
Apologie for Poetrie, An, 94, 144
Arcadia, 93, 101
Ariosto, 86, 89
Aristotle, 94, 270
Arnold, Matthew, 129, 213, 234–9
Arnold, Thomas, 256
Arthur and the Knights of the Round Table, 23, 45, 89
Aube, 37
"Augustan Age," 126 ff.
Austen, Jane, 206–7, 221
Avowals, 121

BACON, FRANCIS, 115
Ball, John, 61, 95
Balzac, 258–9
Barclay, Alexander, 72
Barry Lyndon, 220
"Barsetshire" novels, 220–1
Bartholomew Fair, 99
Bates, Ralph, 275
Battle of the Books, 127

Bax, Belfort, 251, 252
Beardsley, Aubrey, 253
Beaumont and Fletcher, 102
Beer, Max, 214, 216, 225, 253
Beggar's Opera, The, 134, 210
Behn, Mrs. Aphra, 167
Bengal Lancer, 256
Bennett, Arnold, 266
Bentham, Jeremy, 183, 201
Bentley, Richard, 127
Beowulf, 20
Berkeley, Bishop, 124
Black Death, 60
Black Prince, 61
Blake, William, 180–2, 183
Bleak House, 209
Bodel, Jean, 22
Boiardo, 86
Bolingbroke, Viscount, 131
Book of the Duchess, The, 54
Borough, The, 175–6
Brave New World, 274
Brontë, Charlotte, 219
Brook Kerith, The, 14
Brown, John, 166
Browning, Robert, 229–31
Bryan, Sir Thomas, 78
Bunyan, John, 125, 143
Burke, Edmund, 169, 177
Burney, Fanny, 206
Burns, Robert, 177–80
Butler, Samuel, 115
Butler, Samuel, 136, 259–60, 275
Byron, Lord, 197–8, 205

Canonisation, The, 104
Canterbury Tales, The, 54, 55, 56–8, 59, 61, 68, 101
Carey, Henry, 130
Carlyle, Thomas, 222, 230, 241–3, 244
Caroline, Queen, 178
Cartwright, Thomas, 82
Castiglione, 124
Castle of Otranto, The, 53, 192
Cavalier poets, 105
Cazamian, Prof. Louis, 149
Chambers, E. K., 36
Chanson de Roland, 22
Chansons d'aventure, 37
Chansons de carole, 37
Chansons de geste, 22, 24, 26
Chapelain, 126
Charles II, 100, 114
Chartism, 217, 219, 224, 243, 250
Chaucer, Geoffrey, 53–64, 65, 66, 67, 68, 69, 70, 101, 248
Chesterfield, Lord, 138, 141, 226
Christian Socialism, 215–17, 233, 247
Christianity not Mysterious, 117
Civil War, 106, 115, 157
Clare, John, 177, 178
Clarendon, Earl of, 111
Clarissa, 147, 148, 150
Cobbett, William, 193, 199
Cole, G. D. H., 253
Coleridge, S. T., 185, 194, 196, 208
Collier, Jeremy, 114
Colloquies, 222
Combination Acts, 186
Comédie Humaine, La, 258–9
Commonweal, The, 252
Communist Manifesto, 250
" Condition of England question," 151, 236 ff., *et passim*
Confessio Amantis, 68
Confessions of a Young Man, 261

Congreve, William, 113
Conrad, Joseph, 262
Cornhill Magazine, 240, 245
Corn Laws, 201
Courtier, The, 124
Courtly love, 39–49, 80–5
Crabbe, George, 175–7, 178
Crusades, 22, 25
Culture and Anarchy, 237

DANIEL, SAMUEL, 93
Dante, 80, 82
Darwin, Charles, 232, 257
Deanesly, Margaret, 68
Death of a Hero, 238–9, 275
Decline and Fall of the Romantic Ideal, The, 189
Defoe, Daniel, 53, 120–1, 125, 134, 143, 206
Denham, John, 114–15
Descent of Man, The, 232
Deserted Village, The, 139, 140
Dickens, Charles, 208–10, 212, 219, 259, 262
Disraeli, Benjamin, 219, 255
Dombey and Son, 209
Donne, John, 72, 81, 93, 103–4, 105, 107, 108
Dowson, Ernest, 196
Dream of John Ball, A, 252
Dryden, John, 115, 125, 129
Duck, Stephen, 178
Dunbar, William, 69

EDWARD III, 60
Edward IV, 59, 163
Eliot, T. S., 275
Elizabeth, Queen, 93
Encyclopædists, 187
Engels, Friedrich, 250
Essay on Criticism, 128, 131
Essay on Man, 128, 131–3, 140, 166

INDEX

Essay on Population, 202–3
Estimate of the Manners and Principles of the Times, 166
Etherege, Sir George, 112–13
Euphues, 101
Evangelical religion, 210–15
Evelina, 206
Expansion of England, The, 255

FABIAN SOCIETY, 262
Fabliau, 52, 53, 54, 59, 66, 68, 69, 108
Factory Acts, 202
Faerie Queene, The, 14, 86–92, 150
Father and Son, 212
Ficino, 82
Fielding, Henry, 134, 152–7, 163, 206, 220
Flaubert, 259, 260, 261
Fox, Ralph, 121, 275
Fraser's Magazine, 246
French Revolution, 169, 174, 182, 185, 186, 221
Froude, J. A., 218, 246, 255

GALSWORTHY, JOHN, 266
Garibaldi, 250
Gaskell, Mrs., 219
Gay, John, 129, 130, 134, 158, 210
George III, 162, 185
George, Henry, 251
Gissing, George, 53, 262
Godwin, William, 183, 184, 186, 187, 198, 221
Goldsmith, Oliver, 138, 139, 145, 165
Goncourt brothers, 259
Gosse, Sir Edmund, 121, 212
Gower, John, 68
Greene, Robert, 100, 108
Grey of Wilton, Lord, 90–1
Grierson, Sir H. J. C., 83, 87, 97, 102

Groat's-worth of Wit, A, 100
Grosseteste, Robert, 67
" Grub Street," 137–8, 139, 140, 160
Gulliver's Travels, 158

HALÉVY, ÉLIE, 254, 257
Hamlet, 13, 14
Hammond, J. L. and B., 162, 186
Hardy, Thomas, 261
Hawes, Stephen, 71, 82
Helen Fleetwood, 218
Héloïse and Abelard, 26
Henry VII, 72
Henry VIII, 78, 85
Henryson, Robert, 69
Heroic play, 112
Heroic poetry, 20–1
Hind and the Panther, The, 115
History of British Socialism, 214, 216, 225, 253
History of the Royal Society, 115
Hobbes, Thomas, 115, 117
Homer, 89, 126, 127
Horace, 77, 79, 194
Hudibras, 115
Hundred Years' War, 32
Hutchinson, Mrs., 83
Huxley, Aldous, 274
Huxley, T. H., 232
Hyndman, H. M., 251

IBSEN, 263
Idylls of the King, 227
Immortality Ode, 188
Imperialism, 254–6
In Memoriam, 227, 229, 232
International Working Men's Association, 250

JAMES I OF SCOTLAND, 69, 81–2
John of Gaunt, 59

INDEX

Johnson, Samuel, 14, 138–40, 161, 166
Jonathan Wild, 220
Jonson, Ben, 93, 99, 103, 104–5, 107, 108, 115
Joyce, James, 267
Jungle Books, 256–7
Junius, 185
Justice, 252

KANT, 208
Keats, John, 193, 205–6, 229
Keble, John, 214
Ker, W. P., 29, 52
Kingis Quair, The, 69, 81–2
Kingsley, Charles, 215, 217–18, 255
Kipling, Rudyard, 255–8

LANGLAND, WILLIAM, 63–9, 95
Langue d'oc, 20
Langue d'oil, 21
Laski, H. J., 183
Lawrence, D. H., 266
Lee, Joseph, 133
Lewis, C. S., 41, 42, 82
Lewis, M. G. ("Monk"), 53, 193
Lillo, George, 165
Literature and Dogma, 234
Locke, John, 117, 124, 167, 188
Lodge, Thomas, 101
Lollard Bible, The, 68
London Corresponding Society, 175
Lorris, Guillaume de, 47–8
Love and Mr. Lewisham, 263
Lucas, F. L., 189
Lydgate, John, 54, 59, 82
Lyly, John, 101, 143
Lyons, Richard, 59
Lyric poetry, mediæval, 34–9

MACAULAY, LORD, 208, 222–6
Mackail, J. W., 252, 253
Mackenzie, Henry, 151, 156, 179
Madame Bovary, 261
Malory, Sir Thomas, 143
Malthus, Robert, 202–3
Man of Feeling, The, 151, 179
Marlowe, Christopher, 96
Marvell, Andrew, 115
Marx, Karl, 250, 251
Mary Barton, 219
"Matter of Britain," 22–3, 45
"Matter of France," 22
"Matter of Rome," 22–3
de Maupassant, 260
Maurice, F. D., 215–17, 218, 233
Mazzini, 250
Mencken, H. L., 197
"Metaphysical" school of poetry, 105, 107, 114
Michael Armstrong, 218
Middleton, Thomas, 99–100
Mill, James, 183, 201
Mill, John Stuart, 204–5
Milton, John, 83, 107, 277
Minot, Lawrence, 34
Molly Mog, 130
Monk, The, 193
Moore, Edward, 165
Moore, George, 13, 26, 121, 260–1
Morgan, Charles, 275
Morris, William, 193, 205, 222, 238, 241, 244, 247–53, 262
Mr. Polly, 263
Mummer's Wife, A, 261
Munera Pulveris, 246

NAPOLEONIC WARS, 183, 199, 200
Nashe, Thomas, 53, 100, 108, 143
Newcomes, The, 220
Newman, John Henry, 212, 214–15, 218

INDEX

News from Nowhere, 252
Newton, Isaac, 124
Nicholas Nickleby, 209
Norman Conquest, 17–19
North and South, 219
Novel and the People, The, 121

Odysseus, 121
Old Curiosity Shop, The, 209
Oliver Twist, 209
Origin of Species, The, 232
Oroonoko, 167
Owen, Robert, 200
Oxford Movement, 214

Paine, Thomas, 183, 186, 198, 199
Pamela, or Virtue Rewarded, 147–9, 150, 166
Paris Commune, 251
Paris, Gaston, 37
Parish Register, The, 176
Past and Present, 242, 244
Pastime of Pleasure, The, 71, 82
Pater, Walter, 260
Peacock, T. L., 208
Peasants' Revolt, 60
Peel, Sir Robert, 201
Pembroke, Countess of, 93
Petrarch, 80, 82
Pickwick Papers, The, 209, 210
Pierce Penilesse, 101
Piers Plowman, 63–7
Pilgrim's Progress, The, 143
Poe, Edgar Allan, 195
Poetics, 94
" Political Arithmetic," 116
Political Justice, 183, 187, 198
Poor Law Amendment Act, 203
Pope, Alexander, 130–4, 139, 140, 142, 145, 166, 169, 225
Pre-Raphaelites, 247
Prior, Matthew, 130, 137

Prometheus Unbound, 14
Proust, Marcel, 264
Provençal poetry, 21–2, 33, *et passim*
Public Health Acts, 202
Puck of Pook's Hill, 257

Radcliffe, Mrs., 53, 193
Reformation, the, 78, *et passim*
Reform Bill (1832), 200, 214
Religion and the Rise of Capitalism, 109, 133
Renaissance, the, 73, 76 ff.
Restoration, the, 110–15, 121, 125
Rêveries, 191
Reynolds, Joshua, 140
Richard II, 60
Richardson, Samuel, 84, 143, 144, 145, 146–50, 152, 153, 154, 155, 156, 206, 240
Rights of Man, The, 183, 186–7
Rise of European Liberalism, The, 183
Robert of Gloucester, 17
Robinson Crusoe, 120–1, 144
Rochford, Lord, 78
Roman de la Rose, Le, 47–9, 81, 82
Roman de Renart, 52
Romance, English mediæval, 28–33, 45
Romance, French mediæval, 22–8, 45
Romantic Movement, 53, 142, 157, 168, 170, 184, 188–99, *et passim*
Rosalynde, 101
Rossetti, D. G., 247–8
Rousseau, 167–8, 188–92, 221
Royal Society, 115
Ruskin, John, 205, 222, 238, 241, 243–7, 248
Russell, Lord John, 224, 225

Sally in Our Alley, 130
Scott, Sir Walter, 161, 180, 193
Scottish Chaucerians, 69

286 INDEX

Second Treatise on Civil Government, 167, 188
Seeley, J. R., 255
Self-Help, 213
Seneca, 96
Sentimental Journey, A, 151
Shaftesbury, Earl of, 131
Shakespeare, 14, 54, 55, 92, 93, 95, 96–9, 205, 229, 271, 277
Shaw, G. B., 134, 244, 262–3
Shelley, P. B., 14, 196, 197, 198–9, 205, 222
Sheridan, R. B., 122, 165–6
"Ship of fools," 72
Shirley, 219
Short View of the Profaneness and Immorality of the English Stage, 114
Sidney, Sir Philip, 81, 93, 94, 101, 144
Simon de Montfort, 34
Sir Charles Grandison, 147–8
Sir Thopas, 54
Skelton, John, 72
Smiles, Samuel, 213
Smith, Adam, 182, 183, 201
Smollett, Tobias, 134, 138, 156, 206
Social Contract, The, 167
Social Democratic Federation, 249, 251, 252
Socialism: its Growth and Outcome, 252–3
Socialist League, 249, 251, 252
Society for the Promotion of Christian Knowledge, 160
Southey, Robert, 185, 196, 222, 223
Sparkenbroke, 275
Spectator, The, 124, 158
Spender, Stephen, 275
Spenser, Edmund, 14, 41, 53, 72, 81, 82, 86–92, 94–5, 101, 150, 258
Spinoza, 124

Spratt, Bishop, 115, 125
Stalky and Co., 256
Statutes of Labourers, 60
Steele, Richard, 122, 123–6, 130, 143, 145, 146, 157–8
Surrey, Earl of, 78, 79, 103
Swift, Jonathan, 127, 135–6, 143, 176
Sybil, 219

Tales of Mystery and Imagination, 195
Tasso, 86, 89
Tawney, R. H., 109, 133
Tennyson, Alfred Lord, 222, 226–229, 230, 231, 232, 254
Thackeray, W. M., 219–20, 245, 259
Tillotson, John, 125
Toland, John, 117
Toller, Ernst, 274
Tom Brown's Schooldays, 256
Tom Jones, 152–4, 163
Tonna, Charlotte, 218
Tottel's Miscellany, 80
Tour Through England and Wales, 120
Town Labourer, The, 186
Troilus and Criseyde, 54
Trollope, Anthony, 220–1
Trollope, Mrs., 218
Troubadour literature, 21 ff.
Trouvère literature, 21 ff.
Two Years Ago, 218

Vanity Fair, 220
Vanity of Human Wishes, The, 140
Vaux, Lord, 78
Vicar of Wakefield, The, 144–5
Victoria, Queen, 228
View of the Present State of Ireland, 91
Village, The, 175–6

INDEX

Village Labourer, The, 1760–1832, 162
Vindication of a Regulated Enclosure, A, 133
Virgil, 89, 126

WALLACE, SIR WILLIAM, 34
Waller, Edmund, 114–15
Walpole, Horace, 53, 141, 192
Walpole, Robert, 119, 136
Warden, The, 221
Water Babies, The, 217
Watts-Dunton, Theodore, 194
Waverley, 180
Way of All Flesh, The, 260, 275
Wealth of Nations, The, 182, 201

Webb, Sidney, 262
Wells, H. G., 244, 262, 263
Westward Ho! 218, 255
Wilberforce, William, 186
Wilde, Oscar, 196, 253
Wilkes, John, 185
Wither, George, 83
Woolf, Virginia, 266–7
Wordsworth, William, 80, 185, 188, 189, 192, 195, 196, 254
Wyatt, Sir Thomas, 78, 79, 103
Wycherley, William, 113
Wycliffe, John, 61

Yeast, 217